MESSIAH

MESSIAH
The Life and Times of Francis Schlatter

Conger Beasley, Jr.

SANTA FE

© 2008 by Conger Beasley Jr.. All Rights Reserved.

No part of this book may be reproduced in any form or by any electronic or mechanical means including information storage and retrieval systems without permission in writing from the publisher, except by a reviewer
who may quote brief passages in a review.

Sunstone books may be purchased for educational, business, or sales promotional use. For information please write: Special Markets Department, Sunstone Press, P.O. Box 2321, Santa Fe, New Mexico 87504-2321.

Book and cover design ■ Vicki Ahl
body typeface ■ Franklin Gothic Book
Printed on acid free paper

Library of Congress Cataloging-in-Publication Data

Beasley, Conger.
 Messiah : the life and times of Francis Schlatter / by Conger Beasley Jr.
   p. ; cm.
 Includes bibliographical references.
 ISBN 978-0-86534-666-6 (softcover : alk. paper)
 1. Schlatter, Francis, 1856-1896? 2. Healers--United States--Southwestern States--Biography. I. Title.
 [DNLM: 1. Schlatter, Francis, 1856-1896? 2. Mental Healing--Southwestern United States--Biography. WZ 100 S3385b 2008]
 RZ408.S35C66 2008
 615.8'52092--dc22
 [B]
                    2008022499

WWW.SUNSTONEPRESS.COM
SUNSTONE PRESS / POST OFFICE BOX 2321 / SANTA FE, NM 87504-2321 /USA
(505) 988-4418 / ORDERS ONLY (800) 243-5644 / FAX (505) 988-1025

In memory of Darrell DeVore
(1939-2005)

Contents

Acknowledgments _____ 10

Prologue _____ 13

One   The Wanderer: From Denver, Colorado,
to Hot Springs, Arkansas _____ 19

Two   The Wanderer: From Hot springs to
the Isleta Pueblo _____ 54

Three The Healer in New Mexico _____ 86

Interlude _____ 123

Four   The Healer in Denver _____ 132

Five   Flight _____ 195

Epilogue _____ 228

A Note on Sources _____ 243

Bibliography _____ 245

Francis Schlatter "Healing the sick".
Courtesy by W. A. White, Raton, New Mexico

"The main-travelled road in the West . . . is hot and dusty in summer, and desolate and drear with mud in fall and spring, and in winter the winds sweep the snow across it; but it does sometimes cross a rich meadow where the songs of the larks and bobolinks and blackbirds are tangled . . . . Mainly it is long and wearyful and has a dull little town at one end, and a home of toil at the other. Like the main-travelled road of life, it is traversed by many classes of people, but the poor and the weary predominate."

—Hamlin Garland, *Main Travelled Roads* (1891)

"My walk was the fire I went through for the world."
Francis Schlatter (1895)

Acknowledgments

The author would like to thank the following individuals and institutions for their assistance during the research of this book:

David Wetzel, Cheryl Carnahan, Tom Doerk, Janet Sourk,
Soodie Beasley, Lisa Madsen, Rod Keating, John Henry,
Jim Glendinning, Susan Taylor, Robert Thatch,
Bryan Tolhurst, Betsy Beasley, Megan Wyeth, Frank Hamilton

Wallace Broege, director, Suffolk County, (New York) Historical Society
David Kerkhof, Suffolk County, (New York) Historical Society, Librarian
Kathy Then, Suffolk County, (New York) Historical Society, Librarian

Karen Schmiege, Serials Librarian, Main Library, Albuquerque, New Mexico
Mike Chadburn, Needles (California) Regional Museum
Tillie Fauntleroy, Betty Daws, Deanie Roberts, Throckmorton, Texas
Priscilla McAnally, Paris, Texas, Public Library

Gary Carruthers, New Mexico State Library
Louise Stiver, Museum of New Mexico
Debra King, Museum of New Mexico
Tomas Jaehn, Museum of New Mexico

* * *

It was a wintry afternoon in Santa Fe. I was standing in the courtyard of a house on the outskirts of town, basking in the bleak warmth of the February sun. A young man stepped out to join me. He introduced himself. His name was Diego Rose.

"I understand you are a writer," he said.

"I am."

"Would you like to hear a story?"

"Of course."

For the next two hours he regaled me with a detailed account of the life of Francis Schlatter, a man whom I had never heard of. Diego knew about him from having worked as the stage manager of a play about the healer's life. The play was written by Frank X. Hogan. It was produced in 1989 in a limited run at the Engine House Theater in Madrid, New Mexico, by The Turquoise Trail Theater Company.

Diego could hardly contain himself as he recited the events of Schlatter's life. Story after story spun off his lips, each more absorbing than the other. I was transfixed by the narrative and vowed that, if I ever got the opportunity, I would write my own account of Schlatter's life.

Diego, I can't thank you enough for meeting up with me that wintry afternoon and sharing the story. Here is your book.

—Conger Beasley, Jr.

**Francis Schlatter "Treating in the rain".
Courtesy by W. A. White, Raton, New Mexico**

Prologue

A Union Pacific train speeds west across the drab, khaki-colored plains, toward the distant smudge of a dark, smoky city nestled at the foot of a range of towering, snow-tipped mountains. Inside a chair car near the middle of the long, swaying train sits a quiet, reserved, solidly built man in his mid-thirties. He sports a bushy mustache and sleek brown hair closely trimmed along the contours of his finely molded skull. Although his background is humble, he looks prosperous and well-heeled. He wears a dark-blue suit, spangled across the vest with a shiny gold chain, a derby hat cradled in his lap. The year is 1892, and although a severe monetary crunch is about to wreak havoc on the U.S. economy, there's little indication of it at this moment in the man's dress and deportment.

The man's name is Francis Schlatter. A native of Alsace-Lorraine, where he was born in 1856, he has resided in the United States for nearly a decade. His English isn't fluent; he speaks the language with a definite accent. When flustered or agitated, he stumbles over certain words. In addition to English, he speaks German and French.

Alsace-Lorraine, sandwiched between Germany and France, has endured a long and fractious history; for hundreds of years it has been the target of contention by various kings, queens, duchies, and religious zealots. Under a cloud of chronic warfare it has been taken and retaken by conquerer after conquerer. The area is rich in natural resources, wooded, well-watered, rife with potash, coal, and iron ore, populated by sturdy, hardworking peasants.

In A.D. 843, King Charlemagne's holdings, once part of the Holy Roman Empire, were divided between French and German nobles. Battle followed battle, war followed war, as the combatants—Catholic and Protestant—fought to secure the region for their side. The hilly landscape created a perfect arena for bloody combat at close quarters.

The Peace of Westphalia (1648), marking the close of the Thirty Years War, returned most of Alsace-Lorraine to France. The gallicization of the provinces accelerated on the heady philosophical swell of the French Revolution in 1789. By the mid-nineteenth century the region had become thoroughly frenchified. France's shattering defeat in the Franco-Prussian War (1871) returned control of the provinces to Germany.

Growing up in Alsace-Lorraine, Francis had been a dreamy boy, introverted and shy. He liked being off by himself, deep in the woods and grassy fields outside his native village of Ebersheim. His older sister said she often dreamed about him; in her dreams he was always alone, a solitary figure, an outcast.

He was born blind, a condition that lasted about a year. His sight was restored, so he later learned, by the purity of his mother's faith, fueled by her fervent prayers.

Francis was a teenager when the Franco-Prussian War broke out; whether he was involved as a combatant or a witness we do not know. We do know that his family was divided between French and German loyalties. His formal education was spotty. Both parents were dead by the early 1870s. Trained as a shoemaker at his father's behest, he immigrated first to London, England, then to America, arriving in New York most likely in 1884.

Virtually nothing is known of his émigré life in London, a period lasting nearly a decade, from the early 1870s to the early 1880s. Presumably, he supported himself during this time by working as a cobbler.

How long he spent in the port city of New York after immigrating to the United States and what he did to support himself remain obscure. Sometime in the mid-1880s he moved out to Long Island, first to the town of Greenport on the North Fork, where he became friends with William Ryan, the son of Irish immigrants. Ryan worked as a bayman on a fishing steamer that plied the waters of Long Island Sound and the inner bays of the North and South Forks. Eventually, Francis moved with Ryan to the village of Jamesport, where Ryan's family lived. There, he established himself as a first-rate shoemaker. "Everybody agrees that Schlatter was the finest shoemaker they ever saw, and that he made good wages." (*The Brooklyn Daily Eagle*, November 19, 1895).

Around this time, Francis became interested in spiritual matters. He began to hear a powerful voice inside his head, a voice he later identified simply as the "Father." That voice was to determine his fate.

"Frank," as he was known, "was an innocent sort of a fellow," considered by those who knew him "to be a little off." (*The Brooklyn Daily Eagle*, December 2, 1895). He boarded with the Ryan family in Jamesport for awhile, then with a Mrs. Bartlett and later with a Mrs. Corwin, widow of a local sea captain.

His life in Jamesport, a village of 500 people located on the north shore of Peconic Bay, appears to have been idyllic. The place was sleepy and genteel; the two main industries were fishing and small-crop farming. Clam, scallop, and oyster beds abounded on the bottoms of the nearby bays and sounds. The shady old-growth forests that once covered the island were mostly gone by the time Francis arrived, cut down to supply firewood to the growing influx of foreigners crowding into tenements in nearby New York City.

Shore whaling on Long Island was mostly a thing of the past when Francis arrived in the 1880s. An occasional dead leviathan still washed up on the beaches, attracting clouds of gulls and terns. Villagers flensed the blubber off the carcass with hooks and knives. The strips of oily fat were then boiled over a fire and rendered into a viscous fluid that had many practical uses.

With the native Indians muzzled early on, with few predacious animals stalking the woods, with little in the way of an outlaw or gun-toting frontier tradition, life on Long Island circa 1890 was peaceful and serene. The fragrant air, the flowering shrubs, the lush grass, the tidy villages with their shingled saltbox houses and graceful white churches laid out in balanced configurations, provided a comfortable habitat.

At Bill Ryan's insistence, Francis flirted briefly with being a bayman, but his heart wasn't in it. He was a landlubber, eager to get back to shoe making. He had a knack for the craft, a feel for the leather and stitching, an eye for details. He worked long hours, earning a decent wage—about fifteen dollars a week. He dressed respectably, befitting his station. He wore his hair short and parted in a whitish line on the left side of his skull. His upper lip was smudged with a curly black mustache. His chin and jaw were pink and hairless. When he smiled, he displayed a full set of teeth.

Maybe not so much in his own mind, because he was shy about such things, but to others it was obvious that he was one of the most eligible bachelors in the Jamesport region. Unfortunately, he wasn't very outgoing; something reclusive at the core of his personality seemed to hold him apart. According to the few who really knew him, he rarely went out in the evening, preferring to remain indoors, reading a book or practicing his English. Despite all the things there were to do—brass band concerts in the town gazebo, recitals, picknicking on Long Island Sound, moonlight sails on Peconic Bay, baseball, bicycling, tennis, croquet—his only social outlet seemed to be the Ryan family. The family consisted of Bill, to whom he was very close; Bill's parents, Thomas and Eliza Ryan; Bill's five sisters—Louisa, Hattie, Eliza, Lelia, and Effa; and Bill's three brothers—John, Thomas, and Albert.

Francis's principal amusement was playing croquet with Bill and his sisters. At times he would get so excited he would shout out in three languages, much to the delight of his companions. His marital potential seemed fulfilled when he became engaged to a girl named Kate from nearby Staten Island. Kate eventually threw him over for another man; no one knew exactly why.

In the early 1890s Jamesport was abuzz with religious activities. Since 1835, the town had played host to an annual Pentecostal summer camp meeting, held inside a grove of ancient oaks near the track bed of the Long Island Railroad, which came through Jamesport in 1844 on its way out to Greenport. The camp meetings were a special draw for Francis and the Ryan family; they enjoyed listening to the flamboyant preachers and singing the old-time hymns. Something in the fervor of the Pentacostal faith—God-fevered, spirit-fraught—struck a sympathetic chord in Francis.

The only distressing note in all this happy activity was Bill Ryan's failing health, which seemed to slip away from the vital parts of his big, strong seaman's body. As the months passed his expression became vacant, he had trouble walking, his voice dwindled to a husky rasp.

In addition to worrying about Bill, Francis was disturbed by the voice inside his head, which repeatedly indicated to him that his time on Long Island might be drawing to a close. Francis was confused. Each day the voice grew clearer and more insistent.

When Bill was diagnosed with cancer, Francis became even more confused. He had a notion that, if he only knew how, he could help his friend recover. Further, he believed he could help other people he didn't even know recover from their afflictions.

He did what he could to comfort his friend. He even purchased a magnetic belt for Bill, in hopes that the belt would replenish the cosmic force known as "fluidum," the proper balance of which could ensure good health and longevity.

In the meantime, life on Long Island rippled along at a delectable pace. The people were congenial, there was plenty of work, the climate was temperate, in the spring the wetlands bordering the narrow beaches were alive with singing birds.

The town of Riverhead (population 1,000), a few miles east of Jamesport, straddled the mouth of the Peconic River at the point where the current slipped into Flanders Bay. On Sunday mornings Francis, frequently accompanied by Bill Ryan before he took sick, walked the six miles from Jamesport to attend different churches in Riverhead—Methodist, Catholic, Congregationalist, Presbyterian.

As Bill's condition worsened, Francis prayed even harder for him to recover. Although raised a Roman Catholic, he seemed to be searching for a more reliable faith, one that would really work, a deeply personal belief in the tangible proximity of God—God as a viable presence with Francis as his humble avatar, the instrument through which He might reveal Himself in a more helpful way to those who needed Him most.

Bill Ryan died on June 29, 1889. Francis was devastated. Friends said he became interested in spiritualism after Bill's death. Dreams haunted his sleep, visions of ethereal young women in white robes and gowns who floated in and out of gothic-style windows, accompanied by clouds of butterflies.

He continued to mend shoes and socialize with the Ryan family, but his heart wasn't in it. The voice inside his head told him it was time to leave. Where would he go?

He finally decided on Denver, Colorado. Bearing a letter of introduction from New York entrepreneur M. M. "Brick" Pomeroy to his western manager, A. S. Whitaker, asking that Whitaker help Francis find work as a shoemaker, Francis rode the train from New York to Denver sometime in the late summer or early autumn of 1892. It is not clear why he journeyed two-thirds of the way across the American continent to a part of the world so different from the leafy folds of his native Alsace-Lorraine or the rolling farmlands of eastern Long Island. There are two possible explanations: (1) Francis had invested his savings in a tunnel-building operation somewhere in the Rocky Mountains, and the investment was languishing as a result of the shaky U.S. economy, and he came to Denver to see what he could do to salvage it; or (2) the city of Denver in 1892—a booming metropolis of more than 100,000 people—was one of the capitals of the alternative spiritual world, and with the intensification of the voice inside his head, Francis rode out West to learn more about what that voice might mean to him personally.

Whatever the reason, his life was about to change in ways he couldn't possibly imagine.

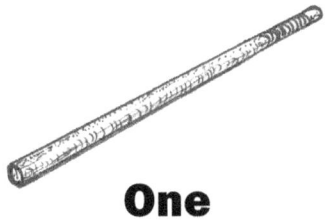

One

The Wanderer
From Denver, Colorado,
to Hot Springs, Arkansas

It must have been lonely for Francis Schlatter during his early days in Denver. The town wasn't friendly to outsiders. Maybe it was the icy winters, the blazing summers, the hard, dry soil in which shady green things had difficulty growing, the mile-high altitude, which made people dizzy and short of breath until they got used to it, the grimy air from the factories and smelters clustered on the outskirts of the city. Despite the shaky economic situation that plagued Denver in 1893, long trains pulled into the downtown station every day to disgorge fresh loads of immigrant families from back East. They were clannish people, outlandishly dressed, speaking a variety of impenetrable tongues, looking bewildered and hopelessly lost, carrying their belongings in pillowcases and cardboard boxes. The citizens Francis met in the streets or in his little shoe shop at 1848 Downing Street weren't all that friendly either. Their lack of warmth made him miss the kindness and cordiality of the people he'd known back on Long Island.

Francis Schlatter was thirty-seven years old in 1893. By the standards of the day he was impressively built, standing around five feet ten inches in his stocking feet, with muscular arms and a brawny chest. His shoulders were broad, his eyes transparently blue, his face free of unsightly marks or blemishes. The mustache he had worn when he came to Denver the year before had flowered into a full beard that obscured his jaw and fleshy lips. His glossy brown hair fell to his shoulders. When he smiled, which wasn't often, a gap showed on the left side of his upper jaw where a couple of teeth were missing.

It took awhile, but eventually he began meeting people. By nature, he was awkward and shy; it was difficult for him to make small talk. His sense of humor was limited; he seemed to come alive only when the subject of religion came up. Then his face became animated, his cheeks flushed with color; the expression in his deep blue eyes became more focused and intent.

John W. Roucher, a friend who lived at the same boardinghouse as Francis at 1812 Lafayette Street, said that upon first glance, little in Francis's appearance made him stand out among others. "It was only when you spoke with him," Roucher said, "that he showed a greater grasp and deeper command of religious matters than anyone else. At one point he said to me that when the time came he knew he would develop into a great healer and teacher. He believed devotedly in this." (*The Albuquerque Morning Democrat*, July 21, 1895).

In the meantime, he kept busy making and repairing shoes. He attended spiritual meetings where the works of popular author Helen Wilmans were discussed. He attended political rallies where fiery speakers harangued the crowd regarding the plight of the poor and dispossessed. He took long walks by himself into the Rocky Mountain foothills, listening to the voice inside his head. He stayed out all night, wandering the rowdy streets of Denver's rougher districts. He was preparing. He was readying himself.

***

At three p.m. on March 25, 1893—about six months after arriving in Denver—Francis experienced an event he later referred to as his "conversion." He was sitting at his workbench in his little shop on Downing Street. He was about to drive a nail into the heel of a boot when the Father, Son, and Holy Spirit materialized before his eyes—not as an apparition but a flesh-and-blood evocation, as if they were literally in the same room with him. As he later wrote in his memoir, *The Life of the Harp in the Hand of the Harper* (1896), "At the moment I beheld the Father seated, holding a Book in the left hand—The Book of Life. Jesus was upon His right, holding a lily in His hand. On the left the Spirit, the similitude of Jesus. Whereupon Jesus stood up and walked to me and handed me the Lily." (*Harp*, 15).

The lily. Emblem of chastity, purity, and simplicity; emblem of sweetness, holiness, and tenacity.

"From that hour," said his friend and confidante Ada Morley Jarrett, "he heard audibly the Father's Voice."

But he couldn't take action immediately. "He hesitated," Jarrett said, "shrinking in contemplation of the pain, fully conscious of the significance [of what he was about to undertake]; he lingered, realizing the method and meaning, questioning the fathomless depths of spirituality as no one else could." (*Harp*, 16).

The message was clear. He'd been chosen to do what he'd been yearning to do for longer than he could remember. He'd been singled out to heal people of their afflictions.

But before he could do that, he must be tested.

***

For the next few months the Father played a cat-and-mouse game with Francis, telling him what to do, then saying nothing. Francis remained patient. His time would come. What the Father had in mind he didn't know; he only knew it would be demanding, taking all his strength to endure.

***

At about this time, knowing his days in Denver were numbered, Francis realized that his shoe business was no longer profitable and that he had to shut it down. In the company of Willis Lamping, son of the landlady who owned the boardinghouse where he lived on Lafayette Street, Francis tried to collect eight dollars in outstanding debts his customers owed him but failed to do so. Without that eight dollars he was unable to pay his bills.

Before leaving Denver, Francis gave Lamping the contents of his shoemaker's kit (except for a few tools, which he took with him). He kept his books on the spiritual life, especially copies of Helen Wilmans's *The Blossom of the Century* (1893). He filled a good-sized valise with these items, including a diary in which he had written several sketches and stories. Regrettably, at some point while Francis was on the road, Lamping mislaid the valise, and it has never been found.

***

One day in late July 1893, he was working in his shop when the Father told him it was time to leave. He wasn't alarmed or upset. By now he knew the voice—a deep voice, bold and commanding.

This time when he heard it he listened intently. Something important was about to occur. The burning urge he felt in his heart to cure people of their afflictions was about to be challenged.

Out in the busy streets of the state capital the sky was streaked with sleek gray clouds. A light wind stirred the dust of the unpaved streets. The voice inside his head was forceful and calm. "Lay down your tools," it said, "and put on your coat, and walk east, and keep walking till I tell you to stop."

Francis did as he was bid.

***

From that hour presumably until the day he died, he heard distinctly, in varying strengths and tones, the sound of the Father's voice—steady and compelling, the source point of all his subsequent behavior, the trigger. To understand Francis Schlatter, we have to understand the nature of the voice that for the next three years was to guide and direct him over a vast expanse of terrain, from the Pacific Coast to the Ozark Mountains, from Denver, Colorado, to northern Mexico.

Was it the voice of God? Or was it psychosomatic, a mental aberration, the product of a schizophrenic disorder? Likely, it included elements of both. Writing about Joan of Arc, another visionary from Alsace-Lorraine, biographer Mary Gordon said the "experience of [the voices she heard in her head] happens to her on the deepest level of a creature of flesh, blood, mind, and spirit; the whole of herself is absorbed in the vision that emanates from what she knows to be the source of love and truth and salvation . . . it is this source that provided her remarkable sureness, her superhuman courage, her faith in her own authority." (Gordon,26).

The same thing could be said about Francis Schlatter.

***

The morning of that first day of his new adventure, on the outskirts of Denver, Francis encountered a group of vagrants, thrown out of work by the economic depression of 1893. They looked ragged and scruffy; their beards were tangled and wild, their clothes tattered and filthy. They had blankets looped around their shoulders and carried canvas bags stuffed with stale bread and shriveled apples. They mingled around a water tank next to the railroad tracks, cooking pots of shelled corn over skimpy fires. The wooden legs of the tall, wobbly tank were plastered with notes, messages, and queries:

> Anybody seen chas. Laughlin? tell him his brother needs to find him. there mother died in june. send word p.o. Longmount colo.

***

The Panic of 1893—the worst economic depression to that point in U.S. history—dealt Colorado a staggering blow. By midsummer the local economy was reeling under the impact. Politicians and businessmen predicted it would take a long time for the state to recover. Overgrazing, a series of devastating winters, and stricter federal land laws had led to a severe contraction of the cattle industry. Settlers from back East, lured by false information regarding the fertility of the soil in eastern Colorado, plowed the crust of the semiarid plains in a futile effort to raise corn and wheat.

The 1890s started out promisingly, with Colorado mines producing 60 percent of the nation's silver. The Sherman Silver Purchase Act of 1890 required the federal government to buy up to 4.5 million ounces of silver each month from Colorado mines. When Grover Cleveland, an opponent of the Sherman Act (he called it a "dangerous and reckless experiment in free, unlimited, and independent coinage"), was elected president for the second time on the Democratic ticket in 1892 (he had served earlier, in 1885-1889), the federal government's generous silver purchases slowed to a trickle. When the act was repealed in 1893, the spigot went dry.

Shortly after the Panic began in the spring of 1893, the price of silver fell from $1.05 to 62 cents an ounce. All along the Front Range of the Rocky Mountains, disgruntled mine owners shut down their operations. Hundreds of laborers crowded into shanties and makeshift tents along the banks of the South Platte River, which flowed through Denver. Local employers took advantage of the swelling labor pool to replace workers who refused to work for rock-bottom wages.

As the depression worsened, affluent Denverites withdrew their savings from local banks. On July 18, 1893, six banks shut their doors. The next day, three more suspended payments. By late July, a dozen banks had collapsed. Local charities were stretched to the limit. On August 11, 1893, the People's Tabernacle, directed by the Reverend Thomas Uzzell, "the Fighting Parson"—a figure much beloved in Denver for the help he gave to the dispossessed and poor—announced that it could no longer feed single men, only women and children.

***

That first day, toting a bag full of tools and leather half soles, Francis traipsed from Downing Avenue to Colfax Avenue, dressed in the garb of an ordinary workman—coveralls, blue denim shirt, blue bandana, leather sandals, straw hat with a floppy brim. He followed the trolley line through the suburb of Fairview, where he crossed the South Platte River and headed east over the open plains. As the sun dipped behind the jagged rim of the Rocky Mountains miles to the west, he slipped into a fenced lot and laid down in a patch of tall grass. A half hour later it began to rain. At the Father's command, he hurried to a sod house a quarter-mile to the north. He reached the house just as a terrible storm broke overhead; water seeped through a dozen cracks in the roof, soaking him to the bone.

The next morning the Father told him to abandon his soggy pack of leather pieces and the tools of his trade—hammers, nails, pincers, iron last.

"But how will I live?" Francis protested. "I have only three dollars in my pocket."

"I will take care of you."

Francis left the tool bag in the sod hut, thinking it might be useful to somebody else, and began walking east, mindful of the prickly pear cactus and spiny tips of the Spanish bayonet that tufted the sparse grasslands of eastern Colorado. That night it rained again. Francis awoke on the open prairie around two a.m. A sharp pain stabbed his left breast. Pleurisy. "Well, I'm in a nice fix now!" he muttered.

"You will not have it long," the Father said.

True to His word, the pain was gone in five minutes. (*The Life of the Harp in the Hand of the Harper,* 20).

***

The following day another storm soaked the wide, empty land. The dreary blackness of the moonless night was cut by crackling bolts of lightning. Tired and hungry, Francis sat down on a rock and watched an express train for Kansas City howl by, belching a stream of fiery cinders from its fluted stack. Inside the dining cars, sitting at tables covered with crisp white cloths and decorated with tiny vases of colorful flowers, passengers dug into plates heaped high with food.

Francis soldiered on until the eastern horizon was flushed with an aurora of soft gold light. Later that morning, following the steady line of the Rock Island tracks, he trudged through the crossroads town of Limon.

***

By 1893 the American West was girded with a tight, interlocking network of private railway companies. In addition to the main trunk lines that ran between the major cities, feeder spurs linked smaller communities to the bigger markets. Consolidation was the byword of the day; the feverish construction of new roads in the 1870s and 1880s had been replaced by more efficient operation of those already in existence.

The image of the major railway companies devouring one another like flocks of hungry locusts had softened, but only somewhat. The expansionist fervor of the 1880s slowed as credit dried up; European investors, wary of the U.S. economy they had helped undermine, took their money elsewhere.

The gap between the haves and have-nots worsened as the 1890s progressed. Those who could afford it, like the passengers

Francis saw on the Kansas City express, sped across the plains in pampered comfort. Those on the skids, like himself, either walked or swung onto freight cars, where they sat out the long, grueling ride clinging to the tops of boxcars or hunkered down on the rods between the wheels.

＊＊＊

Francis spent the next night in a ditch alongside the tracks near the hamlet of Aden (no longer on the map). The next morning he went to a section house east of Aden and asked to buy a loaf of bread. The woman who ran the house offered to give him butter, coffee, and meat. "I can't eat those things," he said. "I can only have bread and water."
He offered to pay for the bread, but she said no.

＊＊＊

The next day went by like all the other days. Steady wind, glaring sun, puffy clouds, drenching rainsqualls. At one point the Father ordered Francis to wait for hours at a spot along the Rock Island tracks.
There's no more telling image of Francis's steadfast devotion to the Father's directives than the spectacle of him sitting passively for a long period of time by the tracks in the middle of a vast, rumpled sweep of shortgrass prairie. Unless the Father sanctioned it, Francis was virtually incapable of doing anything on his own.

＊＊＊

The next morning he started east again. Later that day he crossed the Colorado line into Kansas. A few miles later he met up with two boys dressed in ragged clothes and wearing straw hats. He talked to them for awhile. Their mother was dead. The father had gone to Wyoming to find work, leaving the boys, ages nine and eleven, to fend for themselves.

"What a horrible world!" Francis lamented in the memoir he later wrote about those difficult days. "Here is a family. They want to do it right, but everything is against them. Those boys said they would be thankful if they only had bread to eat. In them the spirit was right. I wish I could do something for them!" (*Harp*, 22).

***

Day after day Francis toiled his way across the wide, brooding sweep of western Kansas—walking, fasting, sleeping out in the rain or under a sky full of crinkling stars, watching with awe and apprehension the occasional grass fire glimmering along the horizon.

Despite a daily rash of blisters that erupted between the toes of his aching feet, along with sharp pains that stabbed at his ankles and knees, his body was slowly becoming conditioned to the demanding effort of the trek.

***

One day, strolling along the dusty streets of Goodland, Kansas—a new railroad town, with brick and limestone buildings taking root on every corner—he paused at a baker's shop to buy a loaf of bread.

"Did you come from the depot?" the baker asked.

"Yes."

"Are you riding in the cars?"

"No, I have to walk."

The baker gave him five cents back.

"What's this?"

"We sell to traveling people at one price and to the poor at another." (*Harp*, 23).

***

Francis walked from Goodland to Colby, Kansas, a distance of thirty miles, through stifling heat; the trek took two days. The evening

of the second day, as the sun melted like a liquid wafer along the line of the western horizon, he noticed the ghostly vestige of a buffalo trace where a big herd, gone from these parts for over a decade, had once passed.

On the outskirts of Colby the Father told him to stop walking, to tie one end of his muslin cover to a telegraph pole, and, with a broomstick, to tie off the other end to make a tent. There, huddled under the fabric, he fasted for two days. At the end of the second day the section boss of that portion of the Rock Island track crunched up to the flimsy tent in his heavy boots.

"Hello," he called. "Are you alive under there?"

"I am here."

"Aren't you afraid of rattlesnakes? The country is full of them."

"Me? No. I have no need to be afraid of either man or beast."

***

August 10, 1893. *The Colby* (Kansas) *Free Press*, a populist paper that carried as its banner "Equal Rights to All and Special Privileges to None," featured an article on its front page that possibly contained a reference to Francis Schlatter. "One day this week," the article said, "we talked with a man tramping from Colorado eastward. He said if [Benjamin] Harrison [a Republican] had been reelected president [in 1892] instead of [Democrat Grover] Cleveland times would have been all right. We asked him to tell us why, and he forthwith said he 'didn't know what any of the political parties advocated. This is the way you will always find them—ignorance and republicanism together.'"

***

By the mid-1890s an estimated 60,000 tramps were drifting around the United States. The majority had been thrown out of work by the Panic of 1893. That number of people freewheeling across the landscape presented a serious problem for local authorities. A snippet in *The Phillipsburg* (Kansas) *Weekly Dispatch* for Thursday August 17, 1893—about the time Francis passed through—emphasized the danger itinerants posed:

> While reading a book the other night, J.M. Fishback, station agent of the Atchison, Topeka & Santa Fe railroad, was suddenly confronted by a tramp who fired a pistol and seriously wounded Fishback in the neck. The tramp escaped.

***

Something in the sedentary, settled, middle-class culture developing in the United States at the end of the nineteenth century was deeply suspicious of the specter of the itinerant, the tramp, the westward-going wanderer—as if this strange, irascible, nomadic figure represented a kind of living, breathing refutation of the material rewards and benefits that could only be reaped in the new industrialized America by putting down roots in one place.

***

August 21, 1893. Francis passed through Pendleton, Kansas (no longer on the map). With his last ten cents he bought a loaf of bread. The day was cold and rainy. He tramped alongside the Rock Island tracks eating the bread and taking bites from a wizened apple he had picked up in an abandoned orchard.

The next day was sunny and warm. Toward evening he fell ill. That night and for the next two days his condition worsened. By the third day he could barely walk.

Around noon, a mean-spirited section boss threatened to have him committed to the county poorhouse if he didn't move on. Francis limped off, but he was too weak to walk more than seven miles. At sundown he came to a gully deep enough to conceal himself. The Father told him to camp there for three days and nights without food or water. This was sometime around the first week of September. The heat was punishing. At night, prairie fires crackled around the horizon.

The afternoon of the third day—hot, hungry, ravaged with pain—Francis rose in rebellion against the Father's dictates.

"You want me to fast when I can't even stand on my feet. Here I am, out on the prairie, without money, and even if I had money, you wouldn't let me get anything."

"Don't worry," the Father replied. "When I want you to have water, you will have water."

"But how shall I get it?"

"Someone will bring it to you. When I want you to eat, you will have food. You must be patient." (*Harp*, 25).

Francis calmed down and enjoyed a good night's sleep. The next day was blazing hot, and he suffered terribly. That afternoon a young man he did not know brought him a plate of food and a bucket of water. "I thought you could maybe use this," he said.

Salty tears trickled down Francis's sweaty cheeks as he shoveled the food into his mouth.

***

The next day a fellow named Charley Gumm took Francis to the farm he rented from a wealthy landowner. Gumm's niece had a hip disease. Charley had heard a rumor that Francis was a healer. He let Francis camp out in his backyard. That Sunday a wagonload of people came to see "the crazy man." Only halfway across Kansas, and Francis already was something of a celebrity.

When the owner of the farm heard about the visitors, he told Francis to pack up and leave or he'd throw Gumm off his land. Francis didn't want that to happen to Charley. The next morning at seven o'clock sharp he pulled his bindle and rucksack around his shoulders and headed east.

***

After walking all night under a twinkling canopy of stars, Francis came to a cornfield where, at the Father's direction, he stayed for three days, eating two ears of raw corn a day and nothing else.

After leaving the cornfield, he spent the next three days in a peach orchard. The smell of the ripe fruit made his mouth water. Fat bees droned between the branches. He ate so many peaches his stomach cramped.

***

Five miles east of the town of Beloit, Kansas, on the Father's orders, Francis spent three days and nights in a hole in the middle of a haystack. The straw was pleasant and warm. Three ears of corn a day was all he was permitted to eat. He took no water. The skin around his mouth grew sore from eating the hard, dry, uncooked kernels.

The next day Francis was invited into a house located at the back of an apple orchard a half-mile from the road. There, he was able to dry his clothes in front of a stove for the first time since leaving Denver. The owner let him sleep in the barn. The next morning he invited Francis to have pancakes. The Father said no.

Back out on the road, his resentment boiled over. It was the first Saturday of October 1893.

"You promised to take care of me!" Francis wailed. "My mouth is raw and swollen! The pancakes would have been perfect! I'm starving! How shall I get something to eat!"

"Go over to that farmhouse there and ask them for something to eat, and they will give it to you."

"Is that the way you're going to take care of me? Ordering me around like that?"

"Yes."

"It isn't fair!"

"It's not suppose to be," the voice declared. (*Harp*, 27).

At the house he experienced a pleasant surprise. He was fed the most satisfying meal he had enjoyed in months—beans, mashed potatoes and gravy, all the milk he could drink, and dessert.

***

At a farm owned by a fellow named Dan Driscoll, twenty miles from Courtland, Kansas, the Father told him not to talk about healing but instead to discuss politics and the world situation. Driscoll, as it turned out, "was a good Populist," Francis wrote in his memoir, "and I was of the same opinion while I was yet on Long Island, and also when I left Denver." (*Harp*, 28).

***

The Populist Party was a prominent factor in national politics in the 1890s. Beginning in the late 1880s, efforts were made to unite farm and labor organizations in a common front to counteract the greed of the Republicans and the indifference of the Democrats to the plight of the ordinary farmer and factory worker. The Populist Party stood for social and economic reform. To relieve unemployment and raise farm prices, the party wanted the federal government to increase the amount of money in circulation by printing more paper notes and coining unlimited silver. The Populists also supported the eight-hour workday, direct election of U.S. senators, and government ownership and operation of all transportation and communication lines. Many people considered the Populists wild-eyed radicals. The new party made a surprisingly good showing in the 1892 national and local elections, polling over a million votes for the presidential candidate, James B. Weaver of Iowa, as well as winning many state offices throughout the Midwest and the West.

***

Two days after leaving Driscoll's farm, Francis was sitting on a blanket next to the road when a carriage pulled by a pair of bay-colored horses with matching black manes and tails came along, driven by the county sheriff. The sheriff pulled the horses to a stop and looked down at the shabby figure huddled in the grass.

"What are you doing?" he asked.

"I'm tired and I'm taking a rest."

"Where have you come from?"

"Denver."

"I know you boys from Denver have it very hard out there," the sheriff commiserated. "Where are you going?"

"Hot Springs, Arkansas."

"You have a terrible walk ahead of you. Have you any hope?"

"More than ever." (*Harp*, 28).

***

The next day the Father let him accept a ride in a carriage. Francis and the driver discussed politics. Like many of the people he encountered in Kansas, which in the 1890s teemed with Populist fervor, he and the driver were of like mind regarding the avarice of the big-money moguls back East.

When they pulled into the town of Clay Center, the driver gave Francis twenty-five cents. "Go to a restaurant and buy yourself a decent meal," he said. The Father told Francis to keep the quarter in case he needed it later. He told Francis to walk through Clay Center to a house about five miles outside town, concealed in a stand of trees. Francis did as he was bid. He found the house and climbed the ramshackle steps and tapped on the front door, which hung from a single hinge. The door creaked open. A small man with a friendly smile invited him in. "You see," the Father whispered, "they have the faith. They not only pray but they execute their prayers in their daily life by their works. This household does My will." (*Harp*, 29).

Francis ate a hearty meal with the man and his family. The man of the house, his wife, and another adult who seemed to be a relative, did not ask who he was or why he was traveling through the country.

They urged him to eat and drink as much as he wanted.

***

Novelist William Burroughs claims the term "the Johnson family" gained credence as a code of conduct among tramps and hoboes who were forced to hit the road in the 1890s when the economy went belly-up. "To say someone is a Johnson," Burroughs wrote, "means he keeps his word and honors his obligations. He is a good man to do business with and a good man to have on your team. He is not a malicious, snooping, interfering self-righteous trouble-making person."

With a Johnson, Burroughs adds, "you eat first and talk business later." (*The Adding Machine: Selected Essays,* 73).

***

And so it went, with Francis walking, endlessly walking, through the towns of Manhattan and St. Marys and Topeka—sometimes encountering people who were Johnsons, sometimes not. In Topeka the twenty-five cents the Father had told him to hold back came in handy. Trudging through the downtown streets, he bought ten cents worth of bread and ten cents worth of cheese, which he eagerly devoured.

Topeka was the capital of Kansas. According to the 1890 census, it boasted a population of more than 30,000. It was the biggest town Francis had encountered since leaving Denver. Kansas had been settled in 1854 by abolitionists from New England dedicated to making sure its soil was never darkened by the shadow of human slavery. That evening in Topeka, Francis might have walked past the scaffolding that jacketed the dome of the unfinished state capitol; begun in 1866, a year after the Civil War ended, the capitol wasn't completed until 1903.

***

That night the Father directed him to slide down an embankment and sleep under a railroad trestle. Francis unfolded his blankets in a little clearing and fell into a comfortable sleep. The next morning he woke up refreshed and finished the rest of the bread and cheese. "Oh look, there's another bum," he heard a worker say to a companion as they crossed the bridge above the spot where Francis had spent the night.

The remark nettled him. Other than the fact that they had jobs and he didn't, there was no difference between them. They were all workers. They were all experiencing hard times in the aftermath of the terrible economic rupture, brought on, he believed, by money-mad robber barons who cared nothing for ordinary people or the well-being of the country.

Francis was glad to get out of Topeka. He seemed to have a phobia about big towns. The countryside gave him the most pleasure. "Oh! I was happy when I was through [Topeka]" he said in his memoir. "Out again among the flowers, and birds gave me their sweet melody. Then again was I among my friends." (*Harp*, 30).

***

Lawrence . . . Olathe. Wary of entering the booming metropolis of Kansas City across the Missouri state line, which in the early 1890s boasted a population of around 130,000—bigger than Denver—Francis turned south to follow the tracks of the Fort Scott & Kansas Railroad.

***

South of Paola, Kansas, on a Sunday morning, Francis came to a sturdy country house with red-brick walls and a rambling front porch furnished with rocking chairs. The front door was open. "You go in there," the Father instructed. Francis stepped inside. His sandals scuffed the smooth, puncheon floor. In a sitting room he found a little old lady dressed in the fashion of a southern belle of Civil War vintage. A thin, sallow-cheeked boy with dirty blond hair stood next to her. Whitish eyes like tufts of cotton plugged the sockets of his narrow face. It took Francis a moment to realize both were blind. The boy held onto the old lady's arm, while she squeezed his fingers. When Francis asked if he might have something to eat, the boy relinquished his grip on the old lady's arm, tottered toward him, and with trembling fingers touched his weathered face. "He's here," the boy called over his shoulder. "It's him."

Just then another woman, clad in a shapeless frock, charged out from a back room. She was short and dumpy with greasy brown hair. In a ranting voice, she told Francis to leave the house. "No, you can't have any food!" she cried. "You must leave right now!"

Francis was bewildered. The old lady and the boy looked dazed and confused. The ugly woman's lipless mouth was grim and unrelenting. Francis backed out the entryway. Outside, standing in the road, alone with the birds and trees—a playful breeze rippling the locks of his shoulder-length hair—he was so distressed he couldn't keep from crying.

"I know that family," the Father said. "I sent you in there to give them another chance to really help someone in need. Not the boy and the old woman, but in the past that other woman—the boy's mother—has mistreated true and faithful people. I lay a fresh curse upon her life, and the lives of those just like her. Despite the cloak of piety they carry, they serve Me only with their lips." (*Harp*, 31).

***

The next day Francis trudged past the boggy wetlands of the Marais de Cygnes ("Marsh of the Swans"), near the confluence of several silty prairie streams a few miles from the Kansas Missouri border. Wild turkeys glided across the old military road linking Fort Leavenworth with Fort Scott. Great blue herons with their stick-like profiles flapped awkwardly from pond to pond. In the amber glow of the prairie autumn, ducks and geese milled about before taking flight in migratory flocks.

"On and on I went," Francis said, "and the Father provided for me."

***

Near the line between Kansas and the Indian Territory, the land lost its horizontal thrust and commenced to buckle and fold. Trees, which in Kansas were usually clustered in leafy galleries along waterways, began to bristle on every hillside.

***

One pleasant Sunday afternoon a wild sow with sharp, gleaming tusks tried to attack Francis but pulled up short about five yards away. The sow retreated and came for him again, then stopped abruptly as if restrained by an invisible wire. The beast then charged a third time but shuddered to a halt with a piercing squeal in the same spot.

***

One dark, moonless night Francis crept past the town of Tahlequah, capital of the Cherokee Nation, in the northeastern corner of the Indian Territory. The weather had turned cold. The ground was sprinkled with frost. He spent the night out on the prairie, pummeled by high winds. The next day he was sick and could barely move. His right foot puffed up as if bitten by a snake.

"You had better throw those shoes away," the Father said. "You won't be able to put them on again."

"But it is so cold," Francis said.

"Remember that Jesus walked barefoot and bareheaded."

"Jesus lived in a warm climate," Francis protested. "I live in a cold one."

"That makes no difference. I want you to walk barefoot and bareheaded."

Francis threw the shoes and hat away and walked on in the cold. (*Harp*, 32).

***

The next day the condition of his right foot worsened. That afternoon it was so swollen he couldn't see the ankle joint. He wandered off the road and laid down on a pile of leaves under the twisted branches of an oak tree. For the rest of the day he huddled under the tree, crying and moaning. The next day he tried to get to his feet, but he fell down. The following night, still unable to stand, he covered himself as best he could with his blankets. A cold rain drizzled down. His ankle throbbed with pain.

The morning sky was lit with pallid sunbeams. Francis managed to crawl back to the road. Presently, a mixed-blood Cherokee came along in a wagon and offered him a ride. The Father said yes. When the Cherokee heard how long Francis had been in the cold and wet with nothing to eat or drink, he remarked that he had never known a man to remain so cheerful in the throes of such suffering. He took Francis to his house and fed him cornbread and bacon.

***

The next day, feeling better—the swelling in his ankle greatly reduced—he managed to hobble several miles to the Illinois River. At a small Indian settlement he was treated to a bowl of rabbit stew. He had entered the "flint district," as he called it—the Ozark Mountains, a sparsely populated region occupying parts of Missouri, Arkansas, and Oklahoma. The soil was thin and stony. Hardwoods, interspersed with pines, covered the steep hills. Hogs rooted freely. The grassy valleys between the long, curving ridges offered limited cattle forage. To the west and north lay the broad, fertile prairies of the Midwest.

***

One lovely moonlit evening Francis came to the banks of the Arkansas River—the widest, most formidable river he had encountered. Across the gleaming surface lay Fort Smith, Arkansas, a town of about 11,000 people. In the 1890s Fort Smith was an important industrial and railroad center, the second-largest city in the state after Little Rock. It stood on a point of land at the spot where the Poteau River flows into the Arkansas.

Francis found himself at the foot of a long, narrow bridge. It was a toll bridge, but he didn't know this. A wooden shack sat at the end of the bridge on the Indian Territory side. The man who operated the bridge had just hung out a lantern, which cast a warm glow down the bramble-covered bank.

"Good evening, sir," Francis said to the man, who sat outside the little house, smoking a pipe.

"Good evening," the man replied. He got a clear view of Francis as he stood in the light—shoeless, hatless, dressed in stained coveralls, a blue denim shirt, and tattered jacket, rucksack and blanket hanging from his shoulder. A wandering man, like so many others.

"This way, friend," the man said, pointing at the entrance to the bridge with his pipe.

Francis was halfway across the moon-spangled river when he realized that the bridge was a toll bridge, and the man had not charged him. "Father managed to get me over the bridge without having to pay," he said later. "He put the pity in that good man's heart so a poor, barefooted vagrant could cross the river without a price." (*Harp*, 34).

***

Francis ducked and darted through downtown Fort Smith, walking this way and that, sometimes on the high wooden sidewalks bordering Garrison Street, as if disoriented by the wide avenues and horse-drawn traffic. In an open space on the outskirts, out of view of any houses, he piled up a stack of leaves and stretched out. Despite periods of pelting rain, he slept fairly well.

The next day he obtained a lift from a man in a wagon. The man was bothered by the sight of Francis's bare feet—calloused toes, skin contusions, open sores, discolored nails. He was curious: Where had Francis come from, and where was he going? When Francis told him that everything he said or did was guided by the Father, the man muttered "I think you're crazy" and ordered him out of the wagon.

***

It rained steadily every day as Francis meandered through the slick, wet woods of western Arkansas. Sometimes when he asked for food he got it, sometimes not. When he couldn't find a proper roof to sleep under, he rolled himself into his wet blankets and leaned against a tree. "But oh, my poor feet," he complained at one point. "They were so sore I could hardly walk!" (*Harp,* 36).

***

Near the town of Danville he was told to scale a "terrible mountain." He had done little uphill climbing. He had just crossed Kansas with its steady grades and rises. The Ozark portion of the trip must have been daunting. Grassy valleys alternated with woody ridges. While the views from the summits were glorious, down in the valleys there wasn't much to see. Isolated houses sat bunched together with other houses, corrals, and outbuildings. Then, as now, Ozark farms, unlike the tidiness of their Kansas counterparts, gave the sense of having been pieced together from bits of this and that—implements, materials, people, animals, whatever could be found and appropriated. Wood-frame houses with shingled roofs, spindly wide front porches, rooftops slanting down to lean-to-like annexes, coils of kitchen smoke twirling out of stovepipe flues, formed the basic design of these country habitations.

That night Francis wanted to camp on top of the mountain, but the Father told him to forge on. On a rocky shelf partway down the other side, he lit a fire with one of the precious matches he carried wrapped in an oilskin and fell asleep with his head pillowed on a rock.

***

The terrain, the gloomy weather, the bitter hardship plunged Francis into a fit of despair. The trails through the slick forest were few and confusing. The woods were dark and unrelievedly dull. Dreary clouds shut out the sun, making it difficult to gauge the correct route to Hot Springs. Sharp rocks cut his naked feet. He had socks and a few rags to cover them, but he continued to go barefoot. Surely the irony wasn't lost on him; a cobbler by trade, he could easily have whipped together adequate footgear from a few scraps of leather. But the Father wouldn't let him.

A few people along the way welcomed him into their homes, fed him, and did what they could to make him comfortable. Others ordered him to move on. Again and again, in a brutal cycle, he found himself at the limit of his endurance, unable to take one more step; yet somehow, by a tenacious effort of will, he managed to take that step and forge on.

One night, with yet another dark mass draining down through the trees, he slumped at the foot of a tall pine. The wind made a raspy sound through the green-needle branches. He fell into a fitful half-sleep.

The next morning when he awoke, he couldn't feel his feet. The sun glimmered through the canopy, lighting the trees. A feeble ray touched his chest, warming his shivering flesh. He rolled onto his side and shoved himself into a sitting position. From there, grunting and heaving, he struggled to his feet. The bark of the loblolly pine he clung to with both hands tore free of the trunk. Steadily, painfully, his eyes burning with tears, he dragged himself up to a standing position; perched on one foot, he collected his things and limped to the road.

Which direction, he wondered. Left or right?

He started in the direction the Father told him to go. "Faith," he

thought. "I must have faith. Faith is all I know. It is all I can ever know. It is what I am. It is who I am. It is all I have. It is all I will ever have."

Again and again that day he stumbled uphill and down, as if fated to follow a certain path, like a Hindu fakir forced to walk across a bed of burning coals. All paths led to the same place, he decided—the fixed point of implacable faith that pierced his body to the quick like a quivering bird to the trunk of a tree. Later that day, with pain flaming up and down his legs, he found himself at the same place he'd started from that morning. His heart sank like a stone. He had had bad moments, and he would have many more, but this was the worst so far—a withering blast of rock-bottom anguish, as awful as anything he was to suffer in his two-year trek across the Southwest. A terrible cry retched forth from his throat. He fell to the ground and broke down in a fit of weeping.

"Will this never end?" he cried out to the Father. "I am getting as stiff as an old stage horse! You heal others, but you don't heal me!" (*Harp*, 37).

The voice was silent. The forest pressed upon him like a shroud. The wind creaked and groaned through the leafless trees.

***

The next day he forded the Ouachita River. The current was swollen from the recent rains, and he had to struggle to cross the rocky bottom. Twice he lost his footing and was nearly swept away. He emerged on the other side, cold, wet, and shivering. His precious stash of matches was soaked; despite his trembling fingers, he got one to work. Fortunately, he found plenty of wood. The blaze leaped higher and higher. It took all night to dry his clothes.

The next day, two farmers in a creaky wagon took him into Hot Springs. His feet hurt so much that he could hardly walk. He sat shivering in the back of the wagon. They reached Hot Springs at dusk. Francis went to the post office to see if he had received any mail. The post office was closed.

Who was he expecting mail from? Who in Denver had he told that he would be passing through Hot Springs and could be reached there?

Later that evening he came upon a house with a bonfire burning in the yard and a pack of children clad in filthy rags dancing around it. As soon as they saw Francis, they ran into the house. A short time later a man and a woman came out.

"What do you want?" they demanded.

Francis said he was looking for someone. He couldn't remember the name. He seemed dazed and confused.

He turned and went back along Central Avenue, the main drag through town. He seemed to have lost his bearings. So many mixed signals. He didn't understand what the Father was doing to him.

The Father told him he wanted him to go straight up the canyon to the top of Hot Springs Mountain, on the northeast edge of the city. Francis did as directed. It was cold at the top; fortunately, in the pitch blackness he found a gully filled with leaves. He burrowed into the pile and slept through the night. The sun of a new day touched his face. He stirred around in the leaves, smiling. He combed his long hair. He was mending his clothes with a needle and white twine when a young man appeared.

"Did you sleep here last night?" he asked.

"I did."

"Have you had anything to eat?"

"No."

"I'll get something for you."

The man returned a few minutes later with a cup of coffee and a plate heaped with biscuits and bacon. The nice young man went away again and came back with a pair of shoes and overalls.

"If you intend to go into town dressed as you are, you're sure to get arrested. They don't like strangers in this town. It's too bad the shoes are so small."

"That's all right. I've gotten used to not wearing any." (*Harp*, 39).

***

Francis made his way down the mountain to the post office where he found some letters and Denver newspapers waiting for him. In his memoir he says he was discouraged with what he received, but he doesn't say why. Bad news from somebody back home? Bad news about the continuing economic hardship in Denver?

"Get out of here," the Father suddenly whispered.

"What?"

"You heard me."

Francis was happy to oblige. Big towns afforded him little comfort. They troubled and confused him. He was always losing his way.

He described himself as "greatly troubled" as he went back down Central Avenue, where the majority of bathhouses and posh hotels were located. He muttered to himself as he gimped along, a tattered figure sporting an unruly beard and a mane of touseled hair sprinkled with dried weeds and pine needles.

He was minding his own business when he was stopped by a black policeman in an impressive uniform—derby hat, black knee-length boots, blue serge tunic with brass buttons, shiny brass badge pinned to his chest.

"Where are your shoes?" the officer asked

"My feet are so swollen I can't wear them," Francis explained.

"Where is your hat?"

"I don't wear one."

The man looked him up and down. "You better come with me." (*Harp*, 39).

A white policeman fell in behind them. The trio attracted a crowd as they proceeded to the station. In his memoir Francis claims it was "hundreds of people." Possibly so. He was a compelling figure. He was beginning to be noticed.

***

In the fall of 1893 Hot Springs, Arkansas, boasted a population of between 12,000 to 13,000 people. In the decades since the Civil War it had developed into a major health spa. For hundreds of years people had been attracted to the spot. First were the native people, ancestors of the Quapaw, Caddo, and Osage, who came to soak themselves in the warm thermal waters that seeped from cracks in the rocky outcroppings in clouds of salubrious steam. Then came the Europeans, beginning with Hernando de Soto, who in the 1540s traipsed through the wilds of the American Southeast looking for gold. They were followed by traders and settlers starting around 1820, who saw the potential of the waters as a healing potion for all kinds of physical complaints. In the 1890s the rich and famous, the beau monde of America, rolled into town in private railroad cars.

When Francis Schlatter appeared in 1893, the mule-drawn trolley cars had been replaced by new electric cars. At the top of Hot Springs Mountain, overlooking downtown, there was an observation tower. Horse racing was growing in popularity, and a new track had just been built at the southern edge of town.

The people who came to Hot Springs were mostly doctors, lawyers, politicians, and businessmen—bigshots in their hometowns. Many were legitimately ill, although just as many, if not more, came to enjoy the rest and leisure and to partake of the social life that swirled around such splendid hotels as the Arlington and the Majestic. These high rollers transformed Hot Springs into something more than an ordinary watering hole. By the 1890s, from January to June—the height of the social season—the little Ozark town was a place to strut and promenade, to see and be seen, to indulge in extracurricular romance. It was also a place to take the waters, internally and externally, in hopes of curing the gout and dyspepsia and arteriosclerosis that accompanied the opulent lifestyle of the fin de siècle.

***

The Garland County jail was located on the same lot as the county courthouse. The light inside the damp interior was dim and murky like a glass pitcher full of stagnant weeds and water. There, the sheriff and his deputy asked more questions, which Francis answered as best he could. It was the first time in his wanderings that he had been inside a jail. The more they questioned him, the more suspicious they became. Who was he? Where was he from? Why had he come to Hot Springs?

He told them that he was guided by the Father.

"Can we not see this Father," the sheriff asked.

"You may see Him before you know it," Francis replied.

The sheriff reprimanded Francis for his uppity manner. "Take him to the cage," he said to the deputy. "He is as crazy as a bedbug." (*Harp*, 39).

That epithet would bedevil Francis for the rest of his life. Garland County court records indicate that he was incarcerated on December 1, 1893. Next to his last name in the docket ledger—misspelled "Slatter"—someone wrote "Crazy."

The tag stuck back then and continues to stick today.

***

Inside the cage, a spacious, high-ceiling cell furnished with double- and triple-decker bunks, the prisoners watched him carefully. Some were curious. Others, sensing he was different, were wary.

Francis went calmly about his business, washing his handkerchiefs in a pail of water. An inmate approached.

"They want you to go over there and stand trial in their court," he said.

"What sort of court is that?" Francis asked.

"They call it a kangaroo court. All new prisoners are required to attend." (*Harp*, 40).

At that moment a curious thing occurred—the sheriff and his deputy walked out of the jail, presumably so they wouldn't witness what was about to happen.

The prisoners, ready to begin the mock trial, took their places at the far end of the common cell. Francis refused to participate. The inmate came to him a second time and told him the court was ready.

Francis ignored him and continued to rinse his handkerchiefs.

A prisoner named Eugene Donahue had been chosen judge. "That fellow has got to come over here," he said in a loud voice. "If he don't, we'll have to knock some sense into him."

Francis went on washing his handkerchiefs. The jail floor was reinforced with solid steel plates that fit together like the pieces of a mosaic. Although his feet were tough and thorny after so many weeks of walking the Ozark hills, he could still feel the chill hardness of the plates.

Donahue whispered something to a young black boy. The boy came over to Francis, crying and shaking.

"They told me to tell you that you had to go over there," he said. "If you don't go over there, they'll give me a licking."

Francis looked at the little boy. "Don't worry. I'll go." (*Harp*, 40).

The boy led Francis to the other end of the cell. Donahue told him to sit down. Francis accepted the chair that was offered.

"You are charged with jail-breaking—with breaking into jail—and are fined one dollar and a half," Donahue declared.

"I have no money," Francis replied.

"You have a watch," Donahue said.

He did indeed, a gold-plated watch that he held in great esteem. He had bought it when he lived on Long Island, with money he had earned as a cobbler.

Francis asked the Father what he should do.

The Father told him to hold on to the watch.

"You cannot have it," Francis said.

"This court then declares that you must suffer fifty lashes with a rubber hose," Donahue said.

Two strong men threw him down over a table. A fourteen-year-old boy named Dee, big and strapping for his age, brought the hose down on Francis's bare back. The spirit came over Francis, and with a surge of strength he tore himself free of their grasp. The inmates, including Dee, scattered to the far corners of the cell.

Francis stood up, pulled his shirt down, and went back to his washing. The inmates gathered again, and the court reconvened. Francis was called over, and this time he went. A man named Charley Williams, a good man, Francis decided, by the sensitive cast of his features, stepped forward. "I will pay this man's fine," he volunteered.

Francis asked the Father if that would be all right, but the Father said no.

"This man does not have to pay my fine," Francis said. "You have asked for my watch. Well, you cannot have it."

"Then there was a dead silence," Francis wrote in his memoir. "No one spoke. You could have heard a pin drop." (*Harp*, 40-41).

Rough hands seized Francis and laid him out on the table. Someone jerked his overalls down to his knees. Singleton, a tall, muscular black fellow—peeved because Francis had broken away the first time—beat him savagely. Williams, who was keeping count of the blows, said as the hose struck Francis the fiftieth time, "Stop! That's it! That's fifty!"

Francis's back and buttocks were a sheet of flame. Red welts bubbled off his ruptured flesh. Blood trickled down the backs of his legs.

He nearly fainted when he stood up. Charley Williams helped him button up his overalls. He guided Francis to a chair, but Francis hurt too much to sit. He turned his face to the brick wall and wept bitterly.

Charley looked at him pityingly. The others looked away, lost in their thoughts. A black dot no bigger than an ordinary house fly buzzed mindlessly inside Francis's head. He had known despair and what it was like to be totally bereft of hope, but this may have been the worst moment of his life. The fly continued to buzz.

"You will get out of jail when My time comes, not theirs," the Father whispered consolingly. "I will prepare things for you. Believe in me."

The prisoners watched Francis uneasily. Something about his demeanor touched them. He was so easy and natural, without artifice or pretension. His pale blue eyes were as clear as the morning air.

"The police are crazier than him," Singleton said in a gruff voice.

The others nodded.

***

Three weeks later the sheriff came to the common cell. He looked at Francis in silence for a minute or two. He was small for a sheriff, thin, clean-shaven, with hazel-green eyes—more church looking than sheriff looking. He was rumored to be a dead shot with a pistol.

"You got any more sense now than when you came in?"

"No more, no less," Francis replied with a shrug.

The sheriff shook his head and disappeared into his office. (*Harp*, 41).

***

The Father told Francis not to eat meat in jail but to restrict his diet to coffee, vegetables, and bread. Francis told this to the trusty who prepared the prisoners' food. "You'll have to get permission from the deputy sheriff," the trusty said.

The deputy sheriff wanted to know why Francis wouldn't eat meat.

"I am doing some healing among the prisoners, and when I do that I can't eat any meat."

The deputy was interested. "What sort of healing are you talking about?"

"Ailments, sicknesses. Nothing big. A few minor things."

"You can do that?"

"I can't do lots of it yet. But the time will come."

The deputy, who carried a Bible in a pouch slung around his

neck, which he read from now and then, gave Francis a curious look. "All right," he said. "I reckon that'll be all right." (*Harp*, 41).

***

Months passed. Francis continued to attend to the needs of his fellow prisoners. At first he thought, pridefully, that might be enough to secure his release. But it wasn't. The sheriff kept him in jail. He had never been formally arrested. He had not been arraigned before a judge. He had no idea why he'd been collared in the first place. He was not aware that he had broken any law.

In all, he would languish in the Garland County jail for over five months without a hearing or being told why he was there. Any other person would have thrown a fit. Francis accepted it—as he did everything—with stoic resignation.

***

One night he had a dream that reminded him that when the Father was ready, He would get him out. In the dream Francis stood in a big room with a high ceiling in a house full of many rooms. A bird flew in the open window. It flew into a second room and then a third. Then it turned and flew back. "Catch it," a voice cried. "Catch it!"

In the morning Francis remembered the dream and understood. The Invincible, Invisible Hand was at work, removing the last obstacles from his path.

***

One day the deputy sheriff asked Francis if he wanted to work. The Father told him he could, so Francis said yes.

The deputy unlocked the cell and Francis stepped out, a free man for the first time in months. The Father said, "Whatever he asks you to do, you do with all your strength and power."

Francis was so quick and prompt and diligent the deputy nicknamed him "Cyclone." He chopped and split wood and scrubbed the jailhouse floor. He swept out the courthouse when the court wasn't in session. He washed dishes and cleaned windows and emptied latrines and did just about anything that needed to be done.

He eventually went to work for the deputy's wife as a lowly scullion, cleaning her house, cutting her grass, pruning her hedges. He did the same for the sheriff and his family. From an ordinary jailbird, he became a virtual slave of the sheriff and his deputy.

The deputy's wife took a liking to Francis and tried to help him, as did the deputy. They both recommended that he be released. Other than vagrancy, Francis had never been formally charged with any wrongdoing; keeping him locked up this long was clearly against the law. It seemed Francis had been put behind bars solely because he looked strange and acted strange.

"Sheriff," the deputy said, "I think this Schlatter fellow is all right now. He's been behind bars long enough."

The sheriff disagreed. He liked having Francis around. Francis was too good a worker to let go.

"How would you like it if I set you up in business?" he asked him one warm day in March as they stood on the jailhouse steps watching a spring storm rumble over the valley.

"I had a business once," Francis replied, "but I had to give it all away to do my Father's work."

"And what is that work," the sheriff asked.

"I knew what it was last year, but I cannot tell you what it will be this year." (*Harp*, 42).

Cryptic answers such as this must have baffled and confused, if not downright irritated, the people who tried to befriend him.

***

The circumstances under which Francis finally broke free are a bit confused. It appears that one day he was taken to the deputy's

house to do chores, and while the deputy and his wife were talking in another room the Father said, "Go! Now!"

    Francis was taken by surprise. He wasn't ready. His personal articles were back in the jail. He had no money or blankets or warm clothes. It didn't matter. The call sounded in his head, and he spun on his heel and walked out of the deputy's house at a fast clip. Not a run but a vigorous walk, a quick shuffle that carried him down the street.

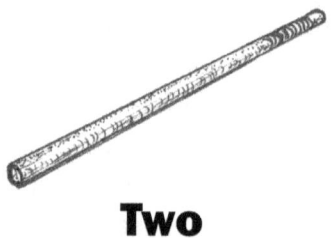

Two

The Wanderer
From Hot Springs to the Isleta Pueblo

That first night out of jail Francis slept on the other side of Hot Springs Mountain. The hills of west-central Arkansas had changed since he arrived five and a half months ago. Then it had been gloomy autumn, the forest floor littered with dead leaves and wet needles. Now it was spring. The dogwood and red bud were in full bloom. The limbs of the oak, hickory, and elm trees glistened with foliage.

The next morning the Father directed him to the home of a black family, who gave him something to eat. Francis felt a certain urgency; he didn't think the sheriff would send a posse after him, but he worried anyway.

"Now you have to walk," the Father said. "I will give you strength."

And walk he did, through the rugged mountains west of Hot Springs, up and over steep ridges and hills. Sometimes he found something to eat, sometimes not. Three days later he passed through the hamlet of Huntington, into the Indian Territory. Spring was in full stride: birds twittered, fresh grass sprouted in the glades and meadows, water tumbled through the rocky creeks.

One day the Father directed him to a section house on a stretch of the Missouri Pacific Railroad, east of the town of Folsom, in the Indian Territory. The people were kind and good. Seeing that he had no clothes other than what he was wearing, they gave him a couple of shirts, a hat with a generous brim, and an extra pair of pants. Francis was touched by their generosity. They were mostly roustabouts—Indian, Negro, white; they poked fun at him, but with a kind of humor that wasn't hurtful. They reminded Francis of the prisoners in the Garland County jail, once he got to know them. After supper, cooked by a Choctaw woman in a lean-to out back, they gathered on the front porch. The air was warm and moist, laced with the scent of blooming azaleas and honeysuckle. A mockingbird gurgled from a nearby shrub. The talk eventually turned to spiritual matters.

Francis was tempted to let down his guard. It had been a long time since he had discussed anything of this sort with a sympathetic audience.

"Did not Jesus say that if we have faith only as big as a grain of mustard seed, that we can move mountains," he asked.

"But Jesus is not alive any longer," the foreman said.

He was an Indian with an intelligent face, who had been to a government school and could read and write.

"Yes, He is living," Francis said. "And He is right here before you. And some day, when the Father is ready, He will move mountains."

"You believe that is your destiny?"

"Without question."

"How do you know?"

Francis tapped the side of his head with his finger. "I carry it all here. It is written as clearly as ink on a blank sheet of paper."

"And how will this power show itself?"

"As a healer," Francis said, his throat swelling with hope and pride. "I intend to make sick people well again." (*Harp*, 44).

***

On the prowl again, toward no specific destination, listening as always to the Father's commands: "Turn here. Turn there." Up and down the steep, scrubby hills of the Ozark plateau, fording clear, splashy creeks, a strange, lonely, forsaken figure with no one to speak to, no one to hear his pleas, no one to understand, the grim, bossy, unrelenting voice inside his head offering his only link to the world.

One afternoon he split logs for a family in return for a plate of food, which he ate out back, sitting on an upturned log. The man of the house came out and stood around, seemingly anxious to ask Francis something.

"You are a man of the Lord?"

"I am."

"I could tell that. You have a special look about you."

"And how is that?" Francis was curious to know.

"It is like a mark you carry. A brand."

"Have I been disfigured?"

"No. But it is clear you have been chosen to serve the Lord in a special way." (*Harp*, 44).

A rush of self-pity flooded Francis's veins. Yes, and who else could possibly bear up under the strain, he wondered to himself. Was it a question of being chosen, or was it a voluntary acceptance of a measure of suffering few people would ever agree to, freely or otherwise?

***

The next day he crossed the Red River, from the Indian Territory into Texas. He could have crossed at several places. The Red River in early May flowed wide and shallow between distant barriers of bright green hills. Ferries plied the frothy blood-red current, tethered to links of inch-thick wire that spanned the river from bank to bank. The portions of the bottomland that hadn't been cleared by settlers were tangled with canebrake, a tough, wiry, bamboo-like plant that offered sheltering places for panthers, black bears, and longhorn cattle. A well-known crossing point for cattle thieves was Slate Shoals, where the Red River ran like a liquid film over a ledge-like formation that connected the Indian Territory with the northeast corner of Lamar County, Texas. Paris, the bustling county seat with a population of 8,000—ninety miles northeast of Dallas—had been founded in 1824 by cotton farmers from Mississippi and Alabama. In 1894, when Francis passed through, it was the hub of a thriving agricultural area.

The town plaza was bounded by two- and three-story brick stores edged with glowing white cornices, the windows shaded by green canvas awnings. The stores displayed bold signs identifying their merchandise—furniture, millinery, hardware, clothing. On weekends the plaza was packed with farmers and their wagons in from the country to barter and trade. Lamar County was prosperous and growing; solid houses built of limerock slabs with wide front porches and glass windows fretted with lead frames sat in the center of spacious lawns in the shadows of shiny magnolias and stately live oaks.

The evening Francis came through, he was snubbed by a trio of young women dressed in hoop skirts and bustles and fancy hats decorated with gaudy feathers. They stared at the hatless, barefoot vagrant as if he were an alien from another planet. "What do you call that thing," one of the women remarked in a voice loud enough for Francis to hear.

He burned with anger and shame. At the same time, he knew he had to keep quiet. He couldn't snap back or take offense. He'd been in jail too long. He didn't want to repeat the experience.

"You will have your say soon enough," the Father whispered consolingly. "And there will be no backtalk then. But you must bear the burden first." (*Harp*, 45).

***

West of Paris, on the road to Fort Worth, Francis went thirty-six hours without food. When he complained to the Father, the Father showed him a house set well back from the road. Francis tapped on the door. The door swung wide with an audible creak. A tall fellow with a cadaverous face and flaring eyebrows cursed him in a shower of spit.

Francis crept from the house in humiliation. The wind kicked up and a furious rain crashed down. He prayed to the Father to stop the rain. "I am so hungry! I am so wet and cold!"

Within a few minutes, as if a tap had been turned, the rain ceased.

***

Fort Worth was a bawdy town of 10,000 people. It was founded in 1849 as a military post on an upper fork of the Trinity River. Proximity to the Chisolm Trail in the 1870s accelerated its growth. Cowboys driving longhorns from Texas ranches to the Kansas railheads bedded down their herds on the outskirts of town and rode in for supplies and a little fun. Merchants flocked to Fort Worth; the first railroad arrived in 1876. Within a few years, the town was shipping cattle all over the Southwest.

In Fort Worth the Father told Francis to hide out during the day. He looked so worn and threadbare He feared he might be thrown in jail.

"Let me work just long enough to buy some new clothes," Francis said.

The answer was always the same: "When I want you to have new clothes, you will have them. When I want you to have new shoes,

you will have them. When I want you to have food, you will have it. Follow me. Do exactly as I tell you." (*Harp*, 46).

***

That night the Father woke Francis from a restful sleep in an abandoned roundhouse in the Fort Worth rail yards. Francis loped across the tracks like a coyote, sticking to the shadows. No tramps, thieves, or railroad bulls; he eased through the freight yard past boxcars full of bawling cattle. He hopped across the tracks, over a bridge, then over another bridge. "Go down there," the Father said, indicating a path that rippled off the second bridge like an oily black ribbon.

The night was inky dark. No moon lit the sky. Francis fumbled and searched and backtracked but managed to stay on course. At the junction of two roads, the Father told him to take the one to the left, and he found himself walking alongside the tracks of the Texas Pacific Railroad. A few miles more and he came upon a copse of trees. "Lie down and rest," the Father said. The rain pattered from the sky in plump drops.

On he went the next day through a terrific downpour that soaked him to the bone; on through the town of Weatherford (population 4,000), where he spent the night in a watery ditch. "Out of doors every night," he wrote in his memoir. "No clothes, no food, no bed. It was just horrible, terrible! But I had to go. There was no going back, because then I could neither live nor die. My bridges were burned behind me. I tell you I am going to do this work, and it will be done right." (*Harp*, 46).

***

Barely three decades earlier the land west of Fort Worth had been Comanche Indian country, where fearsome warriors had raided Anglo and Hispanic settlements. All that was gone by the time Francis passed through—the Indians had been removed to the territory north of the Red River, to a reservation located around the Wichita Mountains. All across north Texas tiny towns were trying to take root where water was available and the railroad might someday pass through. A few big cattle spreads still held sway, despite the influx of settlers from back East who nibbled at the edges of these huge estates with their incessant claims. The horizon expanded, the trees thinned out, the live oaks gave way to wiry mesquite. Francis found himself in open-range country where the sky seemed to bow around the rim of the earth in a stupendous arc. The sun acquired a molten edge that pierced his eyes and lit up the back of his skull, as if someone with a pitch-pine torch had entered his brain cavity, looking for something to burn. Prickly pear cactus grew everywhere. Needle-tipped yucca swayed in the gusting wind. Scissor-tailed flycatchers sailed overhead. Acacia and post oak trees mingled their gnarly profiles with those of the mesquite. As if cowed by the spectacle of the expanding horizon, the stunted vegetation seemed to shrink into the crust of the red earth, looking for a place to hide.

Francis may have passed near Fort Belknap, part of the line of defense erected by the U.S. Army in the 1850s to keep the Comanches from attacking settlements in east Texas. A stiff wind tore at the seams and edges of his loose clothing. He passed family cemeteries, where people disposed of their dead; some of the cemeteries were tidy and clean, others slovenly and unkempt. Clumps of larkspur, gentian, and morning glory bloomed in colorful patches.

***

Francis seemed to have wandered around north-central Texas instead of proceeding in a direct line. West of Weatherford, per the Father's instructions, he approached a house in a little town to ask for food. He was greeted by two girls and a young man with a cowhorn sticking out of his ear. The girls wore matching pinafores and black ribbons in their strawberry-colored hair. They seemed sweet, although when Francis drew near they sicced the dog on him. Normally, dogs avoided him, but this dog tore at his sleeve and trouser legs. Francis was shocked.

Later, huddled under a bush outside of town, he mended the rents with a needle and thread. "There has not been a dog for all this time that could touch a thread of my body," he scolded the Father. "And I know this dog could not have torn my coveralls if You had not wanted him to. But I suppose you thought I didn't look ragged enough." (*Harp*, 46).

***

He passed through the towns of Cisco and Albany before reaching Throckmorton (population 1,000). Francis paused on the outskirts. Around noon the sheriff showed up with his deputy. The two men quickly established a rapport with the wanderer.

At his house in Throckmorton, the sheriff treated Francis to a heaping plate of bacon and pinto beans, topped off with cherry pie. He let him sleep in the new jailhouse built the year before out of slabs of tawny-colored limerock.

Francis says he spent one night in the Throckmorton jail. Harry Magill in his book *The Biography of Francis Schlatter, the Healer, with His Life, Works and Wanderings* (1896), claims he was arrested for vagrancy and brought before a court and sentenced to three days' imprisonment. After serving the term, he was told to leave town within three days or suffer a longer stint in jail.

The docket ledgers at the Throckmorton County courthouse for the year 1894 list no Francis Schlatter who was incarcerated. Most likely, Francis was detained for the night and given a dry cell to sleep in; because he wasn't charged with any wrongdoing, his name wasn't mentioned in the court records. According to local tradition, Throckmorton authorities treated vagrants in the aftermath of the Panic of 1893 with kindness and charity.

***

On his way out of town the next morning, a man called to Francis. "Hombre," he said. "Can you help me? Can you make me well again?"

The man was short, slim, in his mid-thirties, with a jaundiced complexion and fitful, light-gray eyes. The brutal club of his right foot was wrenched inward at a cruel angle, and he walked stiff-legged with a limp.

Francis sat with him on the front stoop of a hardware store. For about twenty minutes he held the man's hands and looked into his eyes and recited the Lord's Prayer. The two men attracted a crowd, which blocked the entrance to the store. The owner came out to protest, but when he saw what was going on he slipped back inside.

The bug-like murmur of Francis's voice unnerved some of the people in the crowd, and they began to fidget and laugh. Francis asked the man how he felt. "Better," he said.

Francis felt something let go in the center of his chest, a feeling of relief that had been piling up for a long time, a sweet rush of emotion that surged all the way to the tips of his fingers. He stood and turned to the crowd.

"In three days you will have more faith than you have now," he said to everyone present in a quiet voice laced with conviction. It was a warm spring day. A light wind ruffled the air. A young woman out in the street fell to her knees in the dust and clasped her hands in front of her face.

Francis strode off, renewed in purpose and strength.

***

Across the wastes of West Texas Francis plodded, past the fledgling towns of Abilene, Colorado, and Van Horn. The vegetation dwindled to clumps of twisted shrubs and stunted trees. The wind blew steadily. Buzzards circled overhead, their black wings glistening in the fiery sun. The land looked as if it had been scorched by withering

flames. Sticks of cholla and padded cactus poked from the blackened sand.

Terrain like this was totally unfamiliar to Francis. He was a greenwood European from the leafy groves of eastern France. Despite his long trek across the American Southwest, he was accustomed to deep woodlands—damp shade alternating with sunlit fields. West Texas was like a vision of Hell he had read about in the Scriptures—a bitter wilderness, parched and depleted, where nothing flowered or grew.

***

At a section house next to the Union Pacific tracks somewhere west of Van Horn, Francis asked for something to eat. The Irish boss of the crew, whose job was to maintain the tracks in perfect working order, looked him over carefully.

"Where ye come frum, me lad?" he asked.

"Denver," Francis said.

The smell of food inside the cramped, dingy section house was tantalizing. The wind gusted against the sturdy adobe walls. It took a while for Francis's eyes to adjust to the gloom. A lone window, papered over with a patch of opaque sheepskin, let in a bleak sliver of light. A half-dozen filthy, begrimed faces bobbed over a plank-wood table.

The section boss's name was Callahan. He was scrawny and thin. His neck was marked with a glistening rash.

"We already know about you," he said. "Rumor of your arrival has come to us on the waves of the wind."

Francis waited patiently. The man's Celtic charm caught him by surprise.

"Why didn't you come sooner?" Callahan asked.

"If I could have, I would have."

Francis was puzzled. Did word of his presence in western Texas precede his arrival?

"Keep talking and you'll get something to eat," the voice whispered.

"Do you need me for something?" Francis asked.

"We got a lad here . . . he's not been feelin' too good in the stomach."

"Fix me something to eat and I'll treat him," Francis said.

Callahan piled a plate with chunks of lamb, fried onions, and boiled potatoes. After finishing, Francis sat on a bench outside the adobe-walled section house. He invited the boy with the bad stomach to sit beside him. The boy's breath smelled sour. Francis knew that if any healing was going to happen, it had to take place outdoors. That's where the power was; that's where it came to him, unobstructed.

While Callahan and the others looked on, Francis talked to the boy in low tones. He took the boy's right hand in his left hand and pressed it between his calloused fingers. Then, with his right hand—his lips moving in murmurous prayer—he rubbed the boy's stomach.

Francis knew at that moment what he had suspected all along. Healing was a matter of transferring the Father's energy and power, which passed through his body, into someone else's. It was all about conduits—creating paths along which a positive influence could be transmitted to offset the presence of a negative one.

"You'll be feeling better soon."

"I already do," the boy replied. (*Harp*, 47).

***

Francis reached El Paso, Texas, sometime around July 1, 1894.

In 1598 conquistador Don Juan de Oñate, at the head of a motley legion, marched up from Mexico City to the spot where the Rio Grande turns east toward the Gulf of Mexico. In a ceremony solemnized by a handful of Jesuit friars draped in black robes, Oñate, in a high-pitched voice, claimed all the land he could see—all the land watered by the Rio Grande and its tributaries, all the land touched by the dry scent of the desert wind, all the land within the sound of his puny voice—for His Majesty, King Philip II of Spain.

For centuries little more than a sleepy oasis drowsing in the desert sun, by the mid-1890s three railroads had converged on El Paso, sparking a land boom that boosted the population to around 11,000.

We don't know how long Francis lingered in El Paso before heading west for California and the Pacific Coast. Not long certainly, a day or two at most. He had a habit of moving quickly through urban areas to the open country beyond. In a town as colorful as El Paso, it's hardly likely that his appearance caused the slightest stir. This wasn't the Deep South, with its Protestant rigidity and class stratifications. El Paso was more Hispanic than Anglo. The Catholic Church reigned supreme; behind the church lay the relics of an earlier, earth-based Indian faith.

***

Now he found himself in the middle of a terrible desert that stretched west from El Paso across New Mexico and Arizona to the dry sinks of southern California—a great sweep of sand and shrubs and savage cactus broken by steep mountain ranges, down from which cascaded the rocky chutes of alluvial fans that spread out across the desert floor in wide, chunky arcs. Rocky Mountain meltwater, carried south by the Colorado River, periodically flooded the sandy depressions between the solitary ranges, turning them into huge wetlands for migrating animals and birds. It was midsummer, and the sky and air were blisteringly hot. Francis walked at night, following the westerly line of the Southern Pacific tracks, his path illumined by the light of a steady moon that lit up the sky from dusk to dawn. His sandals made a soft crunching sound in the gritty sand. Curious animals—including the kangaroo rat, a creature with a special kidney adaptation that enables it to survive without water—ducked out of his way.

As soon as the sun nudged its fiery nose over the eastern horizon, he sought refuge in an arroyo or the shadow cast by the wall of a section house or the brittle shade of a mesquite tree. He passed unchallenged through the railroad towns of Deming and Lordsburg, in New Mexico Territory. Outside Lordsburg he stayed for three days with a Mexican family, healing a young woman who had developed complications after giving birth to her fourth child. Her husband with two of their children, black-eyed and half-naked, had stopped him on the trail and begged him to follow them. The woman lay on a pallet of palm leaves in an open-sided wikiup, tended to by a witchy hag whose only remedy was to daub the sweat from the young mother's face with a soiled cloth. Francis prayed earnestly for some kind of signal from the Father. "Please, Father," he whispered, "please make it work."

He took a deep breath and leaned over the woman. He felt the energy flow. The tips of his fingers tingled and pulsed. An hour later the woman sat up with a beaming smile and asked for something to eat. That night her husband fed Francis all the beans and rice and fresh tomatoes he could consume. He slept in a comfortable hammock under a cabana shaded by a canopy of dried palm fronds.

***

From the sketchy description Francis provides in his memoir, it appears that, whether aware of it or not, he practiced a technique that today we would call Theraputic Touch (TT). According to Dr. Richard Gerber in his book *A Practical Guide to Vibrational Healing* (2001), certain people are born with an innate ability to reorient blocked or misaligned energy patterns in the body's physical system. Research findings in the 100-plus years since Francis Schlatter's time suggest that something important happens to healers at a subtle vibrational and spiritual level when they lay hands on a patient. Recent experiments reported by Dr. Gerber indicate that hands-on therapy, such as that practiced by Francis, not only relieves pain and stress but can recharge an ailing person's bioenergy field.

By definition, anyone engaged in healing must be in tiptop mental and physical condition; one of the dangers, of which Francis was surely aware, is the possibility of a "bleed-through" of the patient's symptoms into the healer's energy field. More than 90 percent of the molecules that make up the human body are water molecules. Dr. Gerber suggests that the bioenergy emanating from a healer's hands is directly transferred to the water molecules of the patient's body; this biologically activated water, he believes, provides the catalyst for internal healing. Once the patient's bioenergy field has been realigned into a healthier pattern, improved changes in the cellular pattern of the entire body are likely to follow.

***

On into Arizona Territory Francis trudged, walking mostly by night through the murk of the missing moon, up and over swales of drifting sand that radiated a residual light left by the ferocious glare of the sun. Tucson was full of leather-chapped cowboys in town on a toot, shooting up the bars. Slugging back shots of mescal, they burst into the millinery stores and stole all the female clothing they could find. Wearing floppy hats and lacy shawls and bone-white corsets, they rampaged through the cathouses, tattooing the walls and floors with tobacco spit, dangling girls by the ankles from second-story balconies. The local police had their hands full trying to restore order, and Francis slipped undetected through the streets, sticking to the shadows cast by the portales.

At Yuma, eyes averted, full of disheartening memories of his days in Hot Springs, he passed the formidable rock-slabbed walls of the Arizona Territorial Prison, holding pen for some of the worst villains in the Southwest. At Yuma he was confronted by the sluggish width of the Colorado River. Although wide, the river was so shallow he thought he could wade across; but somebody warned him of the dangers of quicksand, so he crossed at night in a pirogue gouged out of the trunk of a cottonwood tree, guided by a Chemehuevi Indian who, in lieu of payment, had his congested chest and throat treated by the white shaman until he could breathe again without wheezing.

Francis continued to heal sporadically among the Indians and Mexicans as he crossed the Imperial and Coachella valleys in southern

California. Waking in the early evening after a restless sleep under the shade of a paloverde tree, he invariably found several families waiting patiently for him to open his eyes. They brought food and water. Francis didn't speak much Spanish; they didn't speak much English. It didn't matter. He knew why they were there. They sensed something about him, a power, a gift that not even he, at that moment, fully appreciated or understood. Word of his flourishing powers preceded his appearance in the tiniest desert community, as if whispered on the wind by a wandering raven. "The *curandero* is coming. The *curandero* is here."

***

Outside the town of Indio, California, Francis healed a wealthy white rancher of a urinary infection. He disappeared before the rancher could offer him money, slipping over Banning Pass and down into the Los Angeles Basin. In late September 1894 he walked into Los Angeles, a city of 75,000 souls. West Second Street was a greasy, clamorous, oil-soaked gulch. Crude derricks pegging the ground like spindly toothpicks roared and rattled with a hideous din. Francis could not help but wonder how such an edenic place with such a perfect climate—never too hot, never too cold—could have become so frightfully despoiled.

He spent one night in the heart of the city. Fearful of fire, the earth erupting in a rash of hellish explosions, he fled east along the base of the San Gabriel Mountains to the leafy, bucolic, citrus-growing town of San Gabriel, where he spent the next couple of months mulling over his fate. He liked San Gabriel. He liked the weather. Day after day of perfect wind and skies—the mornings patched with scrims of salty fog blown in from the sea; the evenings mild and soothing, with mockingbirds whistling in the grapefruit orchards. The people were friendly. They left him alone. The police didn't bother him.

He settled into a boardinghouse, where he took his meals. The house was run by a woman whose husband had been killed in China during one of the opium wars. The boarders were Johnsons. Nobody asked embarrassing questions. Francis told them he was from Denver and that he had worked there as a cobbler until the failing economy forced him to hit the road. The boarders understood. They had all felt the pangs of the Panic of 1893. They knew what hard times were about. California, they concluded, was the solution to their problems. Like them, Francis considered staying, putting down roots. But when a couple of months had slipped by, he felt he had no choice but to go on. His period of apprenticeship, the slow accumulation of strength to minister to the sick and infirm, had not ended. The fate the Father had in store for him was more complex and demanding than he had thought.

***

Was there a pattern to his peregrinations? If we were to draw on a map all the places he'd been so far, would it form a graphic figure, an ideogram of sorts, that might help explain what he was doing and why? Clearly, since walking west from El Paso, he had felt the power coalescing inside him. How much more wandering did he have to do before he could settle down?

At one point he told the Father that he did not feel he had enough willpower to do the "terrible" work He had in mind for him.

"Not now, maybe," the Father agreed. "But you will have that power soon enough." (*Harp*, 48).

***

Thanksgiving night, 1894, Francis walked from the town of Pomona to Colton. He'd spent several weeks hanging around the boardinghouse in San Gabriel and helping with the grapefruit harvest. The voice inside his head had been strangely quiet. The long spell of relaxation had put him at ease; the muscles in his legs and arms were slack and out of shape. During the twelve-mile walk from Pomona to Colton, a rash of blisters bubbled between his toes. The road between the country towns was pleasantly shaded by long lines of aromatic eucalyptus trees. He stopped to remove his shoes and air his toes. The evening was pleasant and cool; a light breeze, laced with the scent of wet salt from the sea, teased his nostrils. A new moon hung in the western sky like the ring of a lopsided tire.

A buggy passed, a farm wagon packed with produce, young men in knickers and bow ties wearing straw boaters and riding bicycles. It was Thanksgiving evening, and most people were indoors with family and friends, partaking of turkey and dressing and mashed potatoes and gravy. From the opposite direction came a fellow on foot, dressed, like Francis, in workingman's garb—denim shirt and overalls. He walked up to Francis as if he knew who he was and looked at him in a frank, open fashion.

"My name is Lou," he said. "Who are you?"

"My name is Francis."

Lou shook hands with a soft grip. A scar gashed his smooth white cheek. He had green eyes and curly, carrot-colored hair. He told Francis he was deaf in one ear. "If you want to talk to me, you'll have to speak directly into my other ear."

Francis told him he could fix his bad ear.

"How can you do that," Lou asked.

"By touching the ear with my fingers," Francis said.

"That's it? Nothing else?"

"Yes. It's easy." (*Harp*, 48).

He led Lou to a grassy embankment and told him to sit down. Then he came up behind Lou and put his right hand on the nape of his neck. With the fore and index fingers of his left hand, he touched Lou's bad ear. The tips of Francis's fingers tingled pleasantly.

They stayed together that night. Lou was a drifter, an itinerant farmhand; he'd been out of work for a while and had no money. Francis said he would feed him whenever he was hungry.

Lou couldn't remember where he was from. He thought he'd been born in Ohio—how many years ago or the name of the town he couldn't recollect. He also had no recollection of his parents. He'd lived so long in California he had forgotten. When he was still in his teens, he fell off a boxcar and injured his head. The wound affected his memory, also his hearing.

***

Francis and Lou decided to go to San Diego together. Lou wanted to see about getting hired to work in the citrus fields outside the city. He could scale a tree faster than a Mexican; he rarely dropped or bruised the fruit. Despite his fair complexion, the sun didn't bother him. As if coated with a kind of glaze, his skin resisted reddening or turning brown.

It took three days of steady walking to reach San Diego, south through the agricultural towns of Riverside, Temecula, and Escondido. Plaster and wood-frame houses, painted a delicate eggshell white, clung to the steep, pine-covered hills that pitched down through brush-choked arroyos to the sea. In 1894 San Diego (population 16,000) was a sleepy port of call for sailing schooners and broad-beamed freighters that plied the tricky offshore currents between Los Angeles and the Mexican harbor of Ensenada.

Awakened from its California lethargy, the voice told Francis to go to San Francisco by boat. He didn't say whether Lou was supposed to go. Francis wondered about that. He was infatuated with Lou. Lou was younger than Francis; despite not knowing who he was or where he came from, he was good company. He made Francis laugh.

Packet boats carrying passengers and cargo sailed between California's coastal cities several times a week. Francis checked the departure schedule for the boat to San Francisco; he then secured a room with two beds at the Hotel Forrester in downtown San Diego.

Before retiring, Francis asked the Father what he should do with his money—put it under the mattress or leave it in his pocket? The Father said to leave it in his pocket. Francis obliged and fell into a deep sleep. The next morning the twelve dollars he had on his person was missing. Lou was asleep in his bed. Francis suspected he had taken the money, but he couldn't prove it. Lou, still full of mirth, behaved as if he was innocent. Nonetheless, the missing money soured their relationship. They parted the following day at the foot of the gangplank to the boat for San Francisco. As the boat pulled away with a blast of steam and a shrill whistle, Francis waved to the crowd on the pier, but Lou was nowhere to be seen.

***

San Francisco, population 300,000, was the biggest city Francis encountered during his two-year trek around the American Southwest and California. He arrived two days after leaving San Diego. He debarked from the packet boat at the Embarcadero and trudged south through the busy streets to the outskirts of the city.

What was it about population centers that made him uneasy? Did the voice inside his head falter under the press of too many people? Did He become disoriented?

Francis found the road to San Jose (population 8,500), a picturesque little town of whitewashed bungalows with orange-tiled roofs basking under a canopy of palm trees, colorful bougainvillea draping the walls of the homes and downtown buildings. The streets were crowded with people on bicycles: men riding old-fashioned velocipedes; women mounted on newfangled matching safety wheels, laughing and giggling, enjoying a new sense of mobility and freedom. Francis followed the trolley tracks through town into the countryside. Passengers on the trolley looked at him curiously. His legs were still wobbly from the voyage up the coast, and he walked with a clownish roll. After sleeping on deck for two nights, buffeted by the ocean wind, his blue shirt and coveralls were encrusted with dried salt.

The voice told him to proceed through San Jose to the farm villages of Niles and Tracy. It was chilly in the Bay area; he asked the Father if he could buy a blanket and some cotton cloth to make a tent. The Father assented. In Tracy he bought a blanket and a strip of cotton, which he fashioned into a crude tent with a needle and thread. He also bought a hatchet and a fifty-pound sack of flour.

    In the town of Lathrop he fell in with a drifter named Harry. The first night they camped together, Harry robbed Francis of nearly all his clothes. Francis was asleep in the tent they shared when Harry crawled out with the clothes and ran off into the brush. Francis was distraught. First Lou, now Harry. What had he done to deserve this?

    The next morning he shouldered the fifty-pound bag of flour. On top of it he piled the tent, the tent pole and pins, hatchet, cloth bag, frying pan, coat, water pail, and the few clothes he had left. The weight was staggering. For the next few days he ate nothing but flour and water, flavored with a pinch of salt.

***

    He found himself in the San Joaquin Valley, the Great Central Valley of California, traditional home of the Yokut Indians, a gentle, amiable people. A Spanish expedition in 1806, under the command of Lieutenant Gabriel Moraga, had deemed the valley too swampy for farming and advised against establishing a mission or presidio there. American trappers led by Jedediah Smith spent the summer of 1807 snagging beaver from the marshes and rivers. In 1844 the beauty and potential of the place were rhapsodically described by the U.S. military explorer John C. Fremont: "One might travel the world over without finding a valley more fresh and verdant, more floral and sylvan, more alive with birds and animals, more bounteously watered."

    A mosaic of seasonal wetlands, fed by snowmelt from the nearby Sierras, threaded the soggy basin when Francis came through in the winter of 1895. The air shimmered with flocks of migrating waterfowl: ducks, geese, sandhill cranes. At the same time, the valley was undergoing a profound change. Agriculturalists had discovered the fertility of the soil, and on the higher stretches they were draining the creeks, marshes, and wetlands at a destructive pace.

    How much of this Francis witnessed is difficult to say; certainly, by the 1890s the so-called Fresno scrapers, a trenching tool consisting of a metal blade and buckets, were tearing through the tough native grasses, converting the ecosystem into wheat and barley fields. The coming of the miners in the 1850s, tapping for gold in nearby Sutter's Creek, followed by hordes of settlers after the Civil War, doomed the old hunting-and-gathering life that had sustained the Yokuts and their ancestors for hundreds of years.

Magnolia, live oak, and sycamores grew to towering heights in the forest galleries shading the rivers and creeks. Willows and cottonwoods rose from the marshes to form protective canopies where animals such as the badger, kit fox, and river otter took refuge during the hottest days. The tule elk, the smallest member of the North American elk family, still roamed the valley, although in drastically reduced herds. In the distance—a faint smudge on the horizon depending on the clarity of the air—rose the twin barriers of the coastal range to the west and the Sierra Nevadas to the east.

***

One night in February 1895, after several days of terrible privation and suffering, Francis sat down on a stack of railroad ties and cried and cried. Memories of the two men—Lou and Harry—who had betrayed him triggered an outpouring of anguish and grief. What had he done to deserve such treatment? He had only wanted to help them. His life was so lonely. He had to sacrifice so much to kindle the healing fire that would cure people of their ills. Someday he hoped to be able to reach out and touch any person, anywhere; until then, the presence of the Father's spirit, the vexing, bodiless, impersonal voice, remained his primary connection to reality.

***

The fifty-pound bag of flour soon gave out. Francis was penniless. A man he met on the road bought the coat he was wearing for two dollars. Francis bought a shock of wheat for twenty-five cents, plus a bag of salt. Feasting on boiled wheat, he walked over Tehachapi Pass, through the town of Mojave, to a point six miles east of the railroad junction at Barstow, where he pitched the tent.

The Father told him he could heal—but healing, as he was beginning to learn, was a two-way street; lack of faith on the part of the people who sought him out prevented him from healing as much as he wanted. Most of the people he met could not believe an ordinary tramp, a man dressed in rags with two upper teeth missing—despite his ministerial bearing and clairvoyant eyes—could heal anybody of anything.

At Barstow, Francis rested for a week, then continued his journey. The wheat was gone, but he managed to obtain some bacon and flour.

The only way he could have crossed a piece of terrain as daunting as the Mojave Desert was by following a well-worn trail, first blazed by Indians, that ran 140 miles from an old encampment outside Barstow east to the Colorado River town of Needles. Every 20 miles or so there was a freshwater spring, a cluster of willows, cottonwoods, and tall Washingtonian palms where he could slake his parched thirst and languish in the shade and fall asleep to the sound of palm fronds rustling in the wind.

***

He crossed the Colorado River at Needles, California (population 4,000), by way of the longest (back then) steel cantilever bridge in the world. The March wind charging downstream nearly blew him off the span. A whirling riot of swallows swirled around the bridge, dark flecks like buckshot, scattering and congealing. How much different it was crossing the great river this time, following the bridge, as opposed to a few months earlier when he'd been ferried across in a dugout canoe! Big coal-powered engines rumbled in the Southern Pacific rail yard in downtown Needles near the impressive wooden depot, built in 1883. The engines had to crank up a head of steam for the long uphill climb out of the wide, rocky river bottom to the higher elevations of the Mojave Plateau.

***

At Kingman, a cattle and mining town nestled in a wide valley in northwest Arizona, with the last of his money Francis bought five cents worth of crackers and five cents worth of cheese.

East of Kingman he climbed out of the mesquite and creosote habitat of the Lower Mojave Desert. As the road wound up the long incline of the Colorado Plateau, he entered the cooler, more comfortable heights of the piñon-juniper forest.

He dawdled in the village of Hackberry in northwest Arizona for several days. He arrived with enough water to last a single day. When that was gone he went three days without food or water, sleeping on and off in a dreamy, half-starved, comatose state between the roots of a twisty juniper tree. Two dogs scouted him out and bedded down with him, licking his fingers and warming him at night with their smelly fur. After four days he knew he had to push on. He got to his feet but could hardly walk in his weakened condition. With the pack on his back and the bedroll draped around his shoulder, he felt his strength return. He inched his way in an easterly direction between two huge mesas slabbed with talus slopes.

***

Months later Francis was asked by Harry Magill, author of *The Biography of Francis Schlatter, the Healer, with His Life, Works and Wanderings* (1896), which tortures were the worst, those of the body or those of the mind.

"Those of the body," Francis replied. "They were the worst. I rarely suffered mentally. The worse the pains to the body, the happier I grew. That was how I was supposed to suffer. I was supposed to be racked with pain. It was the Father's way of testing me. As long as I

suffered, I knew I was being singled out. But I will say that sometimes the physical suffering was accompanied by a terrible darkness. I know I fought Satan every step of the way." (*Biography*, 31).

Later that year, after he had returned to Denver, Francis told Magill, "Satan would tell me to throw down the things I carried and go back. And I would answer, 'No, you cannot make me do as you want as long as the Father does not wish it. You cannot lead me astray because the Father is with me.' (*Biography*, 31).

"And then," he added, "there were the visions . . ."

A special expression stole over Francis's face at moments like this, Magill said. His face, his whole being, glowed with an inner radiance.

"Oh, those beautiful, magnificent visions," Francis cried. "One night—it was full of moonlight and bright as daytime—I saw the grandest vision ever seen by mortal man. All the prophets passed before me in single file, nodding and waving. Behind them rose the ramparts of a fabled desert city.(*Biography*, 32).

"Another time I saw my mother. I remember this distinctly. She comforted me, at the same time she scolded me for not listening as carefully as I should to the dictates of the Father. Another time the Father Himself passed in front of me and said that I was ready to begin healing in the cities. 'It is in the cities where the hardest healing takes place,' He said. 'The people there are too full of themselves. They lack the patience and openness of country people, who are willing to believe anything. I saw so many visions during the time I was on the road. Every night there was a different one, bursting with fire and color. Satan had no choice but to flee and tempt me no longer." (*Biography*, 32).

***

East of Peach Springs, Francis crossed a stupendous plateau dotted with flocks of cattle and sheep. Bitter friction marked the relationship between rival herders. The majority of white settlers were cattle people; the Indians of the region—Navajo, Hualapai, and Hopi—

ran sheep. The grassy, elevated tablelands were speckled with prairie dog villages; their squeaky, high-pitched barks followed Francis as he wound his way between their mounded burrows. He had entered the immense altiplano of northern Arizona, a place where the earth seemed to thrust itself against the sky, and the sky fell back obligingly to give it room. Despite the fact that it was April, the leaves came late to the trees and shrubs of this high country. During the day the sun burned with a feverish light. At night the air rising out of the deep canyons furrowing the plateau clung to the ground with a lingering chill.

He passed through Ash Fork and Williams into the deep ponderosa forests of the Colorado Plateau, where the scaly orange trunks of the tall pines secreted a faint vanilla scent in the afternoon sun. He camped near Flagstaff (population less than a thousand) at the base of a snow-covered volcano—the San Francisco Peaks—sacred to the Hopi and Navajo.

On July 4, 1876, so the story goes, an immigrant group from Boston stripped the bark and branches from a solitary pine and raised the American flag, founding the city of Flagstaff. In 1882 the Santa Fe Railroad came through, giving lumber and cattle investors access to distant markets and enabling tourists to ride the train to the rim of the Grand Canyon.

***

The road north of Flagstaff was filled with ankle-deep snow and slush. Francis waded through several icy creeks. Snow piled thick on the slopes between the trees, slowing his pace. He sank to his knees in the deep drifts. With each step his sockless shoes filled with ice; by noon his feet were so cold he couldn't feel them.

One afternoon, in a clearing just below the tree line, he saw a plume of smoke. A few minutes later he came upon a log cabin tucked in a grove of stunted fir trees. He rapped on the door. A small man with squinty eyes, prominent nose, bushy eyebrows, and sleek black hair pulled it open with a creak. Francis asked if he could warm himself by the fire. The man said yes. It took a couple of hours, but his feet finally thawed. He slipped his shoes back on. He intended to go back outside, but it had turned cold and snow was falling. The cabin owner made a pot of coffee. He was from France, and he and Francis began talking in their native tongue. For Francis it had been so long. The sensation was delicious.

The man's name was Degrelle. He'd been in the United States for twenty years. He'd lived in Stockton, California, where he worked as a wheat harvester. Currently, he was a sheepherder. When the snow finally melted, he intended to go down to Flagstaff and bring a herd of twenty to thirty sheep up to feed for the summer in the high, grassy meadows near the tree line.

Degrelle asked Francis who he was and what he did for a living.

Francis said, "I am a healer. I was born to cure others of their afflictions."

"Well, you won't find many prospects in this forest," Degrelle cautioned. "Few people live here. It's too harsh. If you try and go over to the other side of the mountain, you won't make it. You'll starve to death. Nobody but me and another fellow live in this forest. He's French, too, from Amiens. Seems you have to be French to live on this mountain. No one else is that crazy."

"The Father is testing me," Francis said. "He's been testing me for a long time now. If he wants me to walk over the top of the mountain to the other side, I'll have to do it."

"I don't have many provisions," Degrelle confessed. "I came up the other day from my sister's house in Flagstaff. Unfortunately, I brought enough for myself only."

Francis told him not to worry. "I can go days without eating," he said. "The Father sustains me."

Degrelle smiled indulgently. "Well, if you don't eat, then neither will I. If you can fast, then so can I. Us Frenchies ought to stick together. We'll eat what I have in the morning for breakfast." (*Harp,* 53).

The dark slipped down through the trees like a pot of spilled ink. Degrelle showed Francis to a straw pallet covered with a fluffy, feather-packed quilt. That night it snowed. The wind rattled the walls and roof of the little cabin until it rocked on its corners like a tin box.

Degrelle and Francis entertained each other with stories about their native towns. Francis described the deep woods of Alsace-Lorraine, how he used to hide from his family in a hollow chesnut tree whose branches spiraled toward the sun like tongues of flame. Degrelle countered with tales of the Cotentin Peninsula, where he grew up in a seafaring family. In the mornings, before the sun scattered a carpet of sparkling jewels across the surface of the water, he helped his father and two older brothers fold the nets into accordion-like piles at the bottom of the bulky rowboats they then oared out into the bay off Cherbourg.

***

The next morning they ate the breakfast Degrelle had promised—hot oatmeal and homemade scones dripping with butter and elderberry jam. An hour later they ventured out into the fresh snowy whiteness, heaped between the trunks of the dwarf-like trees. The paths went together partway before diverging, one branch leading back in the direction of Flagstaff, the other around the side of the mountain. The nostalgic evening, the warm companionship, the hearty breakfast had put Francis in a pleasant mood. At a second fork in the trail Degrelle said, "This is my way, to the southeast. The snow is too deep. You had better come to Flagstaff with me. On the road you want to go on there is only one camp, and that is the last for twenty-five miles."

Francis thanked him for his hospitality. "I have to go my own way," he declared. (*Harp*, 53).

"I guess you do," Degrelle agreed. "Goodbye, my friend. May God be with you always."

They embraced on the snowy trail like a pair of clumsy bears. Francis's eyes were moist as he trudged between the trees.

***

Following Degrelle's advice he turned north again, drawing closer and closer to the great canyon that somewhere out there—although he never saw it with his own eyes—split the vast tableland into a stunning chasm. A couple of herders tending a modest flock told him he would likely starve to death if he kept going in that direction. "Nobody lives there," they warned. "Not even the Indians."

***

Francis found the sheep camp in the pine forest on the other side of the mountain at a place called Smoky Station. When he asked for work, the foreman told him he only had about forty head and couldn't pay him much.

"That's all right," Francis said. "It doesn't matter. Money means nothing to me." (*Harp*, 54)

The foreman was a mixed-blood Navajo named Alex Begay. He told Francis he could stay for the time being. He was impressed with the way Francis acted and looked. He sensed he was some kind of holy man. He listened when Francis told him stories about where he had been and what he had seen over the past two years. Francis was a clunky, hulking, slow-moving *Bilagaana* (white man), inwardly focused, diligent, and hardworking; Begay liked that. Not too many *Bilagaana* he knew were that way.

Around mid-April herders came in with their flocks from the outlying regions. Overnight, the camp teemed with sheep. Begay needed all the help he could get; he told Francis to get busy doing whatever he could. Francis was handy with an ax, and he built new corrals and pens. He also cooked, baked bread, and mended worn-out clothing and boots.

One day Begay received orders from his boss in Flagstaff to bring all the sheep into town, where they would be sheared and dipped and shipped back East to the packing plants. Begay and his crew

rounded up every stray they could find and drove them down off the plateau. They arrived in Flagstaff the first week in May. When Begay tried to pay him for his work, Francis shook his head.

"I knew right away that you were a different kind of white man," Begay said, "but now I think you're a bit touched in the head."

"It's all right," Francis said. "The Father provides."

"Well, maybe He does for you, but not for the rest of us."

"He can provide for us all, if we would just let Him."

Begay was impressed with Francis's humility. "My friend," he said, "I know you have come a long way and suffered many bad things."

Francis rubbed his face with balled-up fists like a child. Hot tears gushed from his eyes. "My walk was the fire I went through for the world," he said in a choking voice. "I was preparing." (*Harp*, 55).

Begay took his hand and pressed it affectionately. Like most Indians he was sympathetic to so-called crazy people, believing they offered a link between this world and the next.

"Good luck to you, my friend. Wherever you go."

***

Francis later claimed he was put in jail in Flagstaff for a few days, for what infraction he doesn't say. Maybe he was thinking of the time he served in Hot Springs, Arkansas. Whatever, there is no evidence in any court or newspaper record of his having been incarcerated in the Flagstaff jail.

***

There are many reasons people take to the road—adventure, inspiration, escape, the hope for a more fulfilling life. The least understood is a life of willful poverty, travel by people who have nothing and want nothing, who beg for food and shelter, who follow a path bereft of familiar comforts and relief.

America in the 1890s was full of people walking. The vast majority who journeyed on foot did so because all other means of conveyance—horses, carriages, wagons, trains, bicycles, boats—weren't available or were too expensive to obtain.

Writer Charles Lummis and naturalist John Muir walked to experience the shape and texture of the landscape as a means of exalting the body and mind. So did Henry David Thoreau and Ralph Waldo Emerson. The point of their ambulations was to open their senses to the beauties of the natural world.

By contrast, Francis Schlatter did not take to the road to rhapsodize about the wonders he encountered along the way. The trip for him was an ordeal, an act of penance. The more pain he suffered, the more qualified he became to exercise God's healing power.

In the Gospel of Mark, Jesus charged the Apostles to go forth into the world, taking nothing that might sustain them: "no scrip [bag], no bread, no money in their purse, nothing save a staff." Since that time, as Joseph Amato wrote in his book *On Foot: A History of Walking* (2004), "every sincere pilgrim was expected to travel in poverty, the more zealous and dedicated going barefoot, leaving their hair and beard uncut." (*On Foot*, 51).

Unlike Muir or Lummis, Francis took to the road to suffer unremitting pain, to rid himself of superfluous notions and desires, to narrow the focus of his sensibility until it became a laser-like projection of God's implacable will. The point of his tribulations was to draw himself up tighter and tighter, to purge his consciousness of personal desires, to meld with selfless intimacy into the demands of a higher purpose.

***

One afternoon on the Navajo Reservation in the northwestern corner of New Mexico Territory, a man staggered through a terrible sandstorm kicked up by a swirling wind. The wind blasted the figure, knocking him off balance, whipping his clothes into a rumpled froth, conking his hair and beard into a starchy cowl. For hours he plodded through a blizzard of choking sand that blotted out the sun. Blinded by stinging gusts, he stumbled against the side of a hogan. Fumbling for the entrance, he slipped through and fell to his knees on the hard-packed floor. Inside, a young mother—her face frantic with worry—sat by a small fire, holding an infant against her breast. A Navajo, presumably the father, brought a gourd dipper full of water. The man, a white man—his face and hands coated with gritty sand—drank deeply. "Thank you," he croaked.

A spasm racked the infant. For hours the mother had tried to coax it to drink from her breast, but the child refused.

"Sick?" the white man asked.

'Two-three day, she sick," the husband said. "We send for a doctor. He no come."

The man approached the mother. His gentle manner put her at ease. He was so coated with dirt and sand she couldn't tell if he was Navajo or *Bilagaana*. Then she saw his blue eyes.

"May I?"

He reached out and touched the infant's tiny head. The mother placed the bundle in the white man's hands. The flesh felt clammy and feverish. The expression in the dark-brown eyes was murky and dull. A grayish drool leaked between the child's bloodless lips.

The white man tucked the infant in the crook of his left arm. With the thumb of his right hand, his lips moving murmurously, he massaged the child's forehead and chin.

The father squatted on his heels next to the white man, his eyes riveted—like the woman's—on his calm, reposeful, bearded face. The white man's eyes rolled up toward the ceiling. He continued to mumble a heartfelt prayer.

The child fell asleep. The man handed her back to the mother. "She will be better in a little while."

He drank more water from the dipper. Then he slumped against one of the windowless walls of the eight-sided hogan, tipped his head back, and fell asleep. He rested, undisturbed, for several hours. When he awoke, the father and mother were sitting in front of him, gazing at his face. Outside, the wind had died down. The baby lay on its back on a blanket on the hard mud floor, gurgling contentedly.

***

Two days later the man left for Albuquerque under the blazing stars of a beautiful July morning. The next day he arrived at the Isleta Pueblo, south of Albuquerque. Rumor of his arrival preceded his appearance by several hours. The plaza was packed with Indians—small, slim, dark-complected people wearing sandals and straw hats, loose white linen shirts and trousers, with cloth blankets and rebozos draped around their shoulders and arms. The man strode into the center of the plaza, stopped, and looked around. He carried a bedroll and a canvas bag over his shoulder. His face and neck, the backs of his hands, and the gnarled toes of his exposed feet were plastered with dirt and grime. His long, stiff hair, parted in the middle, dipped below his shoulders. His blue eyes glowed with an incandescent fire.

The date was July 6, 1895.

The voice inside his head was terse and to the point: "Now you may heal them all."

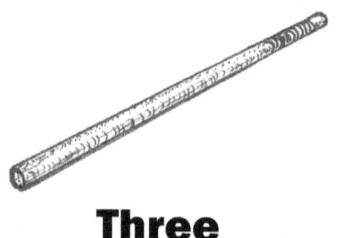

Three

The Healer in New Mexico

F rancis likely rested up for a few days after arriving at the Isleta Pueblo in early July 1895. The pueblo was located about fifteen miles south of Albuquerque. It was the largest Tiwa-speaking Indian pueblo in New Mexico Territory, with a population of over a thousand living quietly in the bosques and grasslands on both sides of the Rio Grande.

"The people of the Isleta pueblo," wrote Charles Lummis in his book *A Tramp across the Continent* (1892), "own over a hundred and fifteen thousand acres of land under United States patent, and their little kingdom along the Rio Grande is one of the prettiest places in New Mexico. They have well-tended farms, orchards and vineyards, herds of cattle, sheep, and horses, and are indeed very different in every way from the average eastern conception of an Indian." (*Tramp*, 141-142),

St. Anthony Mission, established in the early 1600s—one of the oldest mission churches in the United States—provided the focal point of the reservation. The Isletans accepted Christianity from the Spanish with little resistance. During the Great Pueblo Indian Revolt of 1680, missions across northern New Mexico rose in rebellion against their Spanish masters. Churches were ransacked and burned, houses and fields pillaged and torched. Refugees streamed south along the Rio Grande to the safety of Old Mexico. A few Spaniards took refuge in St. Anthony Mission, which was partially destroyed; in 1716 the mission was rebuilt and rechristened St. Augustine.

It was cool inside the church in early July when Francis arrived. Brass-hinged double doors gave entry to a flagstone vestibule. A long nave, flanked by rows of hand-carved pews, led to a simple altar. Tiny windows, notched high up in the walls, let in small amounts of light. Polished *viegas* bolstered the split-log ceiling.

In the mid-1890s the church walls rose high above the adjacent plaza. A pair of belfries, topped with spires, tolled the hours of the day. Adobe houses and primitive jacales and open-sided ramadas crowded the narrow streets that meandered through the mission town. The hot summer dust hung in the desert air like a dull yellow veil. Acequias bordered the fields that lay on the outskirts of the pueblo, laced with pools of scummy green water. Then, as now, the kivas, where the Indians celebrated the old earth gods away from the prying eyes of the Catholic priests, were tucked discretely out of sight.

Headline in *The Albuquerque Morning Democrat,* July 17, 1895:
IMITATOR OF THE CHRIST IN NEW MEXICO
Miracles Said to Have Been Performed by Him.
Blind Man Given His Sight.
Paralyzed Woman Regains the Use of Her Arms, Long Useless.

***

It took about ten days for the news to reach Albuquerque (population 5,000) announcing the appearance of the humble shoemaker from Denver. After this brief respite, Francis plunged into the taxing effort of treating the physical complaints of local pueblans.

Word of his curative power spread like wildfire up and down the Rio Grande Valley. Two Albuquerque papers, *The Morning Democrat* and *The Daily Citizen*, sent reporters to follow the man and talk to the people who claimed to have been healed by him. (The names of these reporters are unknown; it did not become the practice of U.S. newspapers to identify the writers of articles they published until well into the twentieth century.) A July 17 article in *The Morning Democrat* recounted how an old resident named Jesus Vesques, totally blind for three years, "walked from [his house] to the road as nimble as a clear-sighted man" after being treated by Francis. The healer, Vesques said, "used no medicine; in fact did nothing but hold my hand in his own."

That same day a woman named Esmerelda Sanchez showed *The Morning Democrat* reporter where Francis had spent the last five nights. The room in the adobe dwelling was small, barely wide enough to accommodate a bed; a *retablo* of the face of Jesus Christ hung on the wall. Francis's belongings were neatly stacked in a corner. The reporter was puzzled by the sight of a long wooden staff, sharpened at both ends, bound with wire and strips of animal skin, which Mrs. Sanchez said the healer swung over his head every day as he paced up and down the yard.

Mrs. Sanchez proudly displayed a pair of Francis's socks. In front of the reporter, with little embarrassment or self-consciousness, she pressed the socks to her jaw and neck.

"I have a soreness there from an old seizure that bothers me at times."

"And doing that helps?"

"That's what he told me. He says he can transfer his power to an object like socks or bandanas or handkerchiefs. He says it's no different from laying his hands on you."

***

Later that day, in another part of the Isleta Pueblo, Silvio Martin told *The Morning Democrat* reporter that Francis had cured his mother of paralysis in both arms that had afflicted her for sixteen years.

"He simply touched her hands," Silvio said, "and today she is working out in the fields."

"Where can I find your mother," the reporter asked.

Silvio led him to a garden at the edge of the village. Several women were digging a shallow trench between two rows of bean plants. Silvio pointed out his mother, a heavyset woman wearing a straw hat with an ample brim to protect her face from the sun.

"Are you Juliana Sedillo," the reporter asked.

"I am."

"Is it true that yesterday you were unable to raise your arms above your waist?"

"That's true."

"And that now you can?"

"That's true."

"How did this come to happen?"

Juliana's face flushed with the happy memory. "It was the healer, señor, *el Sanador*. The man from the desert. He touched me and said something over me, and the use of my arms came back to me. I owe it all to him." (*The Albuquerque Morning Democrat*, July 17, 1895)

***

Andres Romero, a respected Isletan elder, vouched for the integrity of both Jesus Vesques and Juliana Sedillo. He stood with the reporter in the shadow of a scaly-barked sycamore. The time was midmorning, and the sun was already hot. Behind the tree soared the twin belfries of the St. Augustine church.

"I tell you, señor, the work of this man is something wonderful."

Romero was short and compact, with the fine-boned features and dignified mien of a man of substance and power. Despite the heat, he wore a dark suit and a clean white shirt buttoned at the throat.

"There is something in his touch that seems to heal the sick."

"I have heard that he is also fasting," the reporter said.

"Yes," Andres said. "He intends to fast for forty days and nights."

***

The next day the reporter renewed his search for Francis Schlatter. The people he asked said he could be in any of the little villages along the Rio Grande: Peralta, Los Padillas, Los Lunas, Armijo, Tome, Pajarito.

"We don't know, señor," an old man with a bent spine, one shoulder tilted at an odd angle, declared. "He starts out in the morning and he seems to go off in a straight line. Then he gets distracted and wanders off someplace else."

That afternoon the reporter finally caught up with Francis in Pajarito at the house of an Isleta tribal official. Francis was sitting on a stool next to an open window that looked out over a bare-earth courtyard, packed with people waiting to see him.

The tribal official introduced the reporter to Francis. The reporter observed him carefully. Francis was "solidly built," he wrote in the July 17 edition of *The Morning Democrat*: "Broad shoulders, thick chest, sturdy wrists, big hands with prominent knuckles. Like an athlete with trained muscles," he added. "Long flowing brown hair, carefully groomed, curling at the shoulders, parted in the middle, combed smoothly over the ears. A knotty brown beard that falls in tangled folds to his chest. The corners of his mouth are high-lighted with hairless white patches. His sky-blue eyes are lit with a kindly light. Firm, delicate mouth faintly visible between his mustache and beard."

The reporter saw a startling likeness between the man sitting on the stool and the print of the face of Jesus Christ hanging on the wall above his head. "Every line and touch found in the picture are found in this man," he wrote.

Francis wore a blue calico shirt with a white line running vertically down the front; a denim jumper fell to his hips. Salt-and-pepper-colored socks rose up past his ankles; he wore no shoes. The reporter thought he radiated a serenity and gentleness that had a soothing effect on all who came into his presence.

***

A short, slim, fine-boned man in a tan summer suit, wearing a derby hat with a dimpled crown, sat down in the chair between Francis and the reporter. A fist-sized goiter protruded from the side of his jaw. Francis squeezed the man's elfin hands in his big ones. For the next few minutes he hummed a wordless incantation, his blue eyes fluttering in their sockets like butterflies. Francis commenced to shudder. He rocked and swayed on the stool. The goiter bulging from the man's neck seemed to quiver and throb, but it didn't shrink or disappear. After a minute or two the little man stood up and bowed to Francis in a courtly manner. He slipped from the room, out into the street.

The reporter caught up with him. "Señor," he called. "I'm from *The Morning Democrat*. How do you feel? Can you talk to me?"

The man turned. The right side of his mouth slumped toward his jaw. The goiter knotted at his neck glowed like a ripe peach.

"Do you believe in the Healer?"

"Of course."

"Why?"

"He makes me feel better all over. My joints, my insides, my feet. He may not have made the goiter go away, but I feel better in other parts."

"Is he a fraud? Is he a faker?"

"You insult me, señor," the man replied. "You do both me and the people here and *el Sanador* himself a grave injustice by asking that question. He is not a faker. He has been sent by God to bring relief to poor people everywhere in the world." (*The Albuquerque Morning Democrat*, July 17, 1895)

***

Back in the house, a hot, dry breeze curled through the open window. Francis sat on the stool tending to people. A bevy of buggies, wagons, and buckboards was tied up to the posts and hitching rails in the courtyard at the back of the house. "I shall be forty years of age on my next birthday," Francis told the reporter. "I was born in Alsace-Lorraine when it was a French possession, and consequently I consider myself a Frenchman and not a German. Before I left there, about twenty years ago, the territory had passed into German control. I landed in America at New York harbor.

"I am a shoemaker by trade. Until about two years ago, I worked at a shop in Denver at 1848 Downing Street. One day after finishing my work, I was sitting at my bench when a voice inside my head told me to write a letter to a friend living on Long Island in New York state. The voice told me that my friend's right arm had been paralyzed in an accident and that if I wrote to him, he would be healed. I doubted my own powers back then, so I didn't write. A second time the voice came to me telling me the same thing, and I doubted no longer. I wrote, and after my letter had reached my friend, I received a reply saying he had been healed."

"Did the voice come to you in a dream?"

"No. I was sitting at my bench, thinking of nothing in particular. For the next few months I kept at work making and mending shoes and healing other people by letter. Then one day the voice told me I needed to go out into the world and heal as many of the sick as I could find. In order to do that, I had to suffer. I had to go without food and water. I had to walk alone in the wilderness without shoes or a hat."

The reporter's pencil skittered across the pages of his notebook.

"Prior to that I had fasted," Francis said, "but not much. I had to train myself to get used to it."

"And you still fast?" the reporter said.

"Yes, whenever my master tells me to. I'm in the middle of a fast right now. I haven't touched food for ten days. I hope this time to fast for forty days. Food is not necessary for him who has the proper faith in my Master."

"From whence do you get your healing power?"

"From my Master. It lies alone in faith. Not faith in me, but faith in one's self and my Master. I am only a poor shoemaker. I simply do as I am told."

"Do you heal by the Christian Science method?"

"I know nothing of Christian Science," Francis retorted. "I do only what my Master tells me." (*The Albuquerque Morning Democrat*, July 17, 1895)

***

Francis might have been a little evasive. While living in Denver in 1892 and 1893, he belonged to a New Thought group that met regularly to discuss the spiritual life. It's highly doubtful he had not heard of the Christian Science faith.

Founded by Mary Baker Eddy in the 1860s, Christian Science propounded the belief that the physical matter we see around us in our waking hours is no more real than the images we see in our dreams. Eddy believed the system she came to call Christian Science was wholly based on the spiritual nature of God and man as revealed in the Bible. Corporeal sickness was a mental condition, an invention of humans that manifested itself in negative physical symptoms. Simply put, disease could be construed as the consequence of what Eddy termed the "mortal mind" and had nothing to do with God. Only that which emanated directly from God was valid or worthy—everything else was negligible.

Eddy believed that to be spiritually minded was the same as being scientifically minded—to think correctly, to express or reflect God's nature, to show intellience, capacity, practical ability while embodying and conveying qualities such as purity, truthfulness, and loving-kindness.

Eddy taught her adherents that anyone among them could become a healer. She had first studied the technique of healing, the theraputic laying on of hands, with Phineas Quimby. Quimby felt it was the patient's faith in the remedy that brought about the cure as much as any intrinsic virtue in the remedy itself. No medicine was necessary; a positive attitude was all that was needed to cure the patient.

Quimby also practiced "absent treatment," the curing of people at a distance by writing letters. To do this, both healer and patient had to acknowledge their inner Christ—the luminous, incorporeal, spiritual counterpart to Jesus the physical man.

Eddy came to understand a different definition of Christ—that which is in the consciousness of God—and this she believed was "man." If one realized this, she taught, then healing could occur.

***

According to the anonymous *Morning Democrat* reporter, wherever he went in those early days on the Isleta Pueblo, Francis was accompanied by scores of people who tried to get him to go to their homes and work his healing power on sick family members. Although the Father continued to dictate his movements, it was hard for Francis to say no to these requests. At this early stage, he was eager to help everyone. Weather permitting, he preferred to doctor outdoors, but because of the desert heat, he frequently had to settle for being inside.

The July 17 article about Francis that appeared on the front page of *The Albuquerque Morning Democrat* said that upon taking the healer's hands, many people felt a jolt pass through their bodies similar to a current of electricity. "Now and then a shudder seemed to pass over [Schlatter], his body swaying with emotion," the reporter wrote; he added that Francis usually pressed the patient's hands in a rhythmic fashion. He rolled his blue eyes toward the ceiling, all the while—like a cicada in the heat of summer—mumbling a wordless whisper that only the patient could hear.

Immediately after being treated, some patients departed saying "they were relieved of pain, [while] others vacated with a look of pain still upon their faces." Francis told those who said they felt no change for the better to come back for additional treatments.

***

The July 17 article caused a furor; on the streets of Albuquerque and the Isleta Pueblo, at every gathering, it was the topic of conversation. The newspaper printed an extra issue, which sold out by noon. Subscribers telephoned the editorial office or dropped by looking for spare copies to send to out-of-town friends.

The next day, July 18, a story about the healer appeared in *The Morning Democrat* that hinted at another facet of his power. South of Albuquerque, in the vicinity of the village of Los Padillas, a group of people observed Francis carrying a wool blanket. As always, his presence attracted a crowd. *The Morning Democrat* reporter described how he snapped the blanket with a flourish and let it flutter to the ground. Then he turned to the crowd and commenced attending to them one by one. While he was distracted, a man tried to pull the blanket off the ground, but, as if staked to the dirt, it wouldn't budge. The man asked another fellow to help him, and together they tried to prise the blanket off the ground, but it wouldn't stir. To the jeers of the crowd they stood there, baffled. A while later Francis, taking a break from his labors, picked up the blanket and walked away.

***

How to get Francis to come to Albuquerque? The question was

on everyone's mind. *The Morning Democrat* had scored a big hit with its two articles, earning the plaudits of its readers, whose curiosity about the singular man intensified to a mania. Having the healer in Albuquerque would be a major coup for the community.

***

Albuquerque was a bustling town with a cosmopolitan veneer, a mix of Indian, Hispanic, and Anglo. Founded in 1706 by the Spanish in honor of the Duke of Alburquerque [sic], Viceroy of New Spain, the original settlement centered around an area of winding streets and adobe dwellings and leafy plazas known simply as Old Town. Old Town was occupied by U.S. troops in 1846, at the beginning of the Mexican-American War. It remained a military outpost until 1870. In the early 1880s the railroad arrived at the red-brick depot in the new section north of Old Town laid out in the rigid, right-angle grid favored by Anglo developers.

***

Word of the healer's northward march from the Isleta Pueblo to Albuquerque rippled like waves across the surface of a shallow pond. He came on foot, insisting it was best for him to walk, accompanied by hundreds of well-wishers riding horses and burros or driving buggies and wagons who tried to entice him to climb onboard and ride with them. But Francis knew something about the importance of entrances, and he came into Albuquerque Old Town on foot, likely on the afternoon of July 19, 1895, barefoot and bareheaded, his splay, calloused feet kicking up puffs of grainy dust. He went immediately to a clapboard house at the corner of Third and Romero streets owned by a devout New Thought adherent named Mrs. Werner. Alerted by the cries of her neighbors, Mrs. Werner stepped out on the porch to receive him, a plump dumpling of a woman, wearing a gingham dress, her smooth gray hair tied in a bun at the back of her head. Francis slowed his pace as he approached her front gate and pressed his broad, flat palms together in a silent greeting. Mrs. Werner shook his hand; his sculpted lips parted in a shy, disarming smile that exposed the toothless gap in his upper jaw. In the glare of the afternoon sun his eyes looked steady and cool, twin pools of cerulean blue from which glimmered a kindly light.

"Welcome, welcome," she effused. "You must be thirsty after your long walk. I have a cool drink of water for you."

***

At about that same time, a man named Harry Hauenstein sat on a train rolling south from Denver, along the Front Range of the Rocky Mountains. With him was his friend E. L. Fox, a former alderman from the Colorado capital, a properous grain and coal merchant. Before losing his eyesight three years ago, Hauenstein had worked for the Denver Fire Department. Since then he had traveled widely in search of a cure—to doctors in Denver, Chicago, and New York—but to no avail. Francis Schlatter was his last hope.

One evening in late July, Ed Fox opened a Denver newspaper and saw a headline "Miraculous healings in Albuquerque by the remarkable French-American Francis Schlatter." Fox thought he recognized the name; evidently, this Schlatter possessed a special curing power. Maybe he was worth a visit. Fox suffered a hearing deficiency as well as a recurring kidney problem. He walked to Hauenstein's house a few blocks away in the north end of Denver and read him the article. Fox recommended that the two go to Albuquerque as soon as possible. Hauenstein agreed. Two days later they boarded a train and headed south.

The Denver and Rio Grande chair car was comfortably appointed. As the train rolled south through the towns of Pueblo, Walsenburg, and Trinidad, Fox immersed himself in a book by Helen Wilmans entitled *The Blossom of the Century* (1893). Hauenstein folded his hands in his lap, closed his sightless eyes, and lapsed into a comfortable sleep.

Based on faulty information that Francis Schlatter had left Albuquerque to return to the Isleta Pueblo, the two Denver men arrived at the tiny depot on the pueblo outskirts at 2:50 the following morning. They sat outside on the platform where a breath of wind stirred the heart-shaped leaves of a towering cottonwood—Fox with his suitcase under his head, his wire-frame spectacles clutched in his left hand, his chest rising and falling in a flutter of snores. Hauenstein sat erect on a bench backed by the depot's brick wall, legs crossed, hands clasped. It was difficult to detect his sightless condition from the strong, steady manner in which his clear brown eyes reflected the glow from the kerosene lamp the station master had left out for them. The air was dry and warm. Coyotes yipped in the bosque bordering the Rio Grande.

At daybreak the two men rented a carriage and started out to find the healer. They were told he had spent the night in the village of Peralta. They were on their way in that direction when a teenager carrying a bundle of firewood advised them that Francis was still in Albuquerque. "They won't let him leave," the boy said. "They think he's Jesus Christ and that he belongs with them and nobody else. You'd best head up that way."

***

Not everything was rosy for Francis during his tenure in Old Town. For every sympathetic person, there were those who were skeptical. A July 20 headline in *The Albuquerque Daily Citizen,* the conservative competitor of *The Morning Democrat,* trumpeted "HEALING HUMBUG!" followed by "Blaspheming Imposter Holds Out in Old Town." The day before, a *Daily Citizen* correspondent had found the mysterious "Francisco Schlader" (sic) at Mrs. Werner's house and interviewed him as he was treating a ten-year-old boy. The scene was "farcical," the reporter claimed. "Schlader (sic) held with steady nerve the boy's hands in his, and sent all the volts of a powerful magnetism through the little human figure, but he remained uncured and was dismissed as he had come."

The reporter introduced himself to Francis. "In what religious denomination were you brought up," he asked brusquely.

"I was raised in the Roman Catholic Church," Francis replied.

"You have been then a good Catholic?"

"No, I cannot say that. But I have been called by the Master."

"What Master do you mean?"

"The Father, whose instrument I am."

"Have you the sanction of the Catholic clergy in your work?" the reporter wondered.

"It is for them to come to me, not for me to go to them. I am of the Father."

"When were you called to your mission?"

"March twenty-fifth, eighteen ninety-three."

"How was the call made, by voice or in what manner?"

"That belongs to the Master. Only He knows."

"What cures have you accomplished so far?"

"My work speaks for itself."

"You appear to have a corner on the miracle business."

"Of myself, I can do nothing. All lies with Him."

***

Present that evening in Mrs. Werner's house was an Old Town curate, the Reverend Father Mandalari, a fussy, officious fellow with plump cheeks, red-rimmed eyes, and a sly, lipless mouth. "I know nothing of this man," he said to *The Daily Citizen* reporter, "and it is needless for me to say that the church does not sanction or approve of such proceedings."

Before heading downtown to file his copy, the reporter heard from Mrs. Werner that Francis had taken no food for thirteen days.

***

Every afternoon around two o'clock it grew hot and stuffy in Mrs.

99

Werner's parlor. Despite the heat, the house and yard were crowded with people of every social and racial distinction, seeking an audience with the healer. A few, certainly a minority, suffered no infirmities but showed up simply to bask in his presence. Old people, their faces ashy and drawn, sat in chairs under the covered front porch, roiling the air with straw fans. Most poignant of all were the sickly, colicky, red-faced infants, gripped with hacking coughs, their skin splotched with livid rashes, attended to by their anxious mothers.

The line of people seeking help ran through the house, out the front door, across the porch, and down through the yard to Romero Street. It seemed as if everyone in town passed by the house at least once a day to check on what was happening, to wave to friends, to stop and chat. Mrs. Werner's had become the most important gathering place in Albuquerque. Francis sat for hours in front of an open window at the back of the parlor, attending to the sick and lame. Next to him, during the hottest time of the day, stood a kindly matron with strong, fleshy arms, who stirred the air around his head and shoulders with a straw fan.

***

Ed Fox and Harry Hauenstein finally caught up with Francis at Mrs. Werner's. Francis greeted them warmly. Alhough Fox's kidneys were hurting him, he deferred treatment so Francis could have more time with Harry. Francis shuddered visibly as he sat down by the window, took Harry's hands in his, and rolled his eyes up toward the ceiling. A few minutes later he touched the blind man on the forearm and whispered something that Fox leaned in to hear: "You will need more treatments. Any cure, partial or complete, is going to take time."

Harry was well aware of this. "Thank you," he said in a crusty voice. His sightless eyes were slick with tears.

***

Later that day, at the office of *The Albuquerque Morning Democrat*, Ed Fox told some editors that "my friend Mr. Hauenstein does not see, yet he declares he has never felt so well or been so hopeful since he lost his sight three years ago. The severe pains which heretofore racked his head and neck are gone. The healer told him he would have to take additional treatments, so we are going back to him, and back to him again, until the job is done. As this is only his first treatment, Mr. Hauenstein has the sublimest confidence that he will recover the use of his eyes."

***

Something happened to Francis in the village of Tome before he went to Albuquerque that in all future accounts of his activities in New Mexico would be told and retold. According to a correspondent from *The Albuquerque Morning Democrat* (July 21, 1895) who witnessed it, the crowd in the little village spilled out to the edges of the modest plaza. Francis stood in a tight space in the center, his weathered face turned up to the sun, treating each patient in turn. A man with crippling rheumatism, cured on the spot by Francis's touch, tried to give him money. Francis shook his head and said no. But the man kept shoving bills into Francis's pocket, which Francis promptly gave back.

"I have no need for money," he said.

Overcome with gratitude, the man came at him again. This time Francis took the money and looked around for the scruffiest person he could find and handed the bills to him.

"I have no use for money," he repeated.

***

Meanwhile, up in Denver, spurred by the reports coming out of Albuquerque, reporters for *The Rocky Mountain News* fanned out all over the city to find out what they could about the curious figure who was causing such a stir down in New Mexico. The results, appearing in *The News* on July 21, 1895, made the connection between Francis Schlatter's mysterious disappearance from Denver in July 1893 and his equally mysterious reappearance in Albuquerque two years later.

It seems that after he vanished in the summer of 1893, he was hunted high and low by friends, associates, and the police. He was described as five feet nine or ten inches tall, with broad shoulders and a barrel chest—a man of more than ordinary good looks with a smooth, fleshy face highlighted with a full beard and a clear, restful gaze.

The article also stated that Francis had come to the United States from eastern France by way of England twelve years earlier. He lived for a while on Long Island in New York State before moving to Denver in 1892, where he rented a downstairs shop from a Mrs. I. J. Ingersoll at 1848 Downing Street.

The people the reporters interviewed described Schlatter as industrious and hardworking; he always paid his bills on time. He lived a regulated, orderly, conventional life save one oddity—he kept company with a curious assortment of New Thought spiritualists. These spiritualists—followers of the edicts of Mary Baker Eddy and popular author Helen Wilmans—met in each other's homes to discuss religion, faith healing, and the immortality of the human soul. They all agreed that Francis, by the depth of his feelings and the keen edge of his sensibility, possessed a special understanding of these subjects.

Francis quickly became a favorite among the spiritualists, who found Denver's high-altitude climate congenial to their lofty speculations. The July 21 *Rocky Mountain News* article concluded that "to those who had labored and studied with him in Denver [word of his healing in Albuquerque] seemed like the fulfillment of the promises of the still small voice that he had often said separated him from ordinary mortals and told him to be patient; that the day would come for him to preach, to heal and to reveal."

Before leaving Denver, Francis had told Mrs. Ingersoll that he had a revelation that he would go to the Chicago World's Fair sometime between July 1 and July 25, 1893, where he would meet up with Wilmans, with whom he had corresponded. Francis gave Mrs. Ingersoll a copy of Wilmans's book, *The Blossom of the Century*, a dissertation on the science of mental healing in hopes, as he said in *The News* article, "that she would thus be put in the right way and save herself and those dependent on her."

* * *

No correspondence between Helen Wilmans and Francis Schlatter seems to have survived; how much influence she had over his thoughts and feelings is difficult to ascertain. She was born in 1831 and died in 1907. Her books about the power of the spirit, the mind over the body, and material reality were popular sellers in the 1890s. Many of her thoughts echo and amplify what she understood of the Christian Science beliefs espoused by Mary Baker Eddy. She certainly shared Mrs. Eddy's dictum that "all disease is of the brain. A belief in disease is the brain's own under-estimate of its power." (*Blossom*, 36)

Some of Wilmans's impressions subtly underscore the apocalyptic tone of the prevailing mind-set of the fin de siècle. The pages of her book tingle with the advent of something inexplicably promising. It's coming, the subtext of her musings seems to say; a major change in human consciousness is on the way. Anything can happen, and when it does and people recognize it for what it really is, it's going to have a salutary and uplifting effect. "But now the greatest truth that has ever dawned on the race is here," Wilmans rhapsodized at one point, "the absolute truth that all is Life; and there is no disease, no death and no old age; and that this truth simply awaits the universal recognition in order that its vitalizing influence shall be expressed in one unbroken current through all the members of the race." (*Blossom*, 146-147).

Francis claims to have been influenced by Wilmans's writings and to have followed her teachings to the letter. But one quote—"No one who leans on a power outside of himself can be anything but weak" (*Blossom*, 103)—seems to refute that. As is abundantly evident, Francis relied at the outset almost exclusively on the authority of the Father; even now, more than two years later, the Father continued to tell him what to do. The point reinforces the primary purpose of Francis's life, the grim, lonely path he was obliged to follow. Wilmans might have influenced thousands of readers, among them Francis Schlatter, but true to his "faith," he remained steadfastly committed to working out his destiny on his own terms.

***

One afternoon as he stood on Mrs. Werner's front porch, Francis announced that all who wished to do so could form a line and pass by and shake his hand. Within minutes a line looped off the porch all the way into the street—a long, lazy, serpentine coil, anchored at one end by a solitary man standing barefoot on a smooth, wood-plank surface. Near him stood yet another anonymous *Morning Democrat* reporter, taking it all down. A few minutes later a quartet of Zuni Indians shuffled by, bearing a wounded comrade, his eyes swollen and enflamed from the flash of a mine explosion. Within a few feet of Francis, the five men suddenly fell to their knees. Francis took each man by the arm and raised him up. "I want none to kneel to me," he said.

He ran his hand over the injured man's eyes. Witnesses declared they saw the swelling around the sockets go down, the inflamation become less irritated. Francis cautioned that it would take several more treatments to restore the man's sight. (*The Albuquerque Morning Democrat*, July 23, 1895)

***

That evening, as the light between the live oaks in Mrs. Werner's front yard turned a deep yellow, a rumor rippled through the crowd still milling about that the police might arrest Francis for posing as a healer. An Old Town grandee named Perfecto Armijo took exception to this. Perfecto was dressed in a black suit and white shirt tabbed at the collar with a gold stud. His smooth-toed boots were stitched with colorful thread. He wore a hand-tooled leather belt, cinched at the waist with a silver buckle.

"Impossible," he declared to *The Morning Democrat* reporter with an emphatic shake of the head. "Anyone, police or not, who would lay hands on this man would be torn to pieces. I know these people. I know how deeply they are wrought up over this matter. I know what they would do."

***

Perfecto Armijo's mother-in-law, Conception Garcia, had a paralyzed arm. She was determined to have a session with the man she called "*el Gran Hombre.*" The family, including Perfecto, tried to talk her out of it. "None of us had any confidence in him," he confessed to the reporter. "We considered him a crazy humbug who traveled around the country, deceiving the ignorant classes."

Dutifully, the day before, Perfecto had brought the family carriage around to take his mother-in-law to Mrs. Werner's. Garcia worked her way through the crowd and into the house, to the chair where the healer sat. Perfecto, skeptical as ever, remained outside. Presently, Garcia reappeared, waving the bad arm over her head.

Perfecto shrugged as he told the story to the reporter. "That's all I know about the man, but that's enough to change my opinion of him. A fact like that, coming right home to me, in my own house, doesn't admit of any argument, or leave room for any doubt." (*The Albuquerque Morning Democrat*, July 23, 1895)

***

The Morning Democrat reporters took a lot of heat from Schlatter's critics. On July 25, 1895, the newspaper was accused by its arch-rival, *The Albuquerque Daily Citizen*, of "sensationalism and of trying to suggest that the people of New Mexico were more gullible and ignorant than those of other regions."

In its defense, printed the same day, *The Morning Democrat* declared in an editorial that "the Democrat never has offered, and does not now propose to offer, an explanation of these things. Its duty ceases when it presents the facts as it finds them." (July 25, 1895).

***

On a lighter note, the majority of Schlatterites conceded that the healer's feet ought to be properly shod; receiving people barefoot or sheathed in socks was not correct form for a man of his fame and accomplishments. According to a *Morning Democrat* article (July 26, 1895), an Old Town elder named Gregorio Ribera prevailed upon Francis to wear shoes, if any could be found for him. Ribera searched everywhere in the city for a big enough pair and, failing to find them, ordered an Old Town cobbler named Tom Dye to make them. Dye went to Mrs. Werner's to measure Francis for a fitting. His stockinged feet were more than thirteen inches long.

***

At about this time, Francis left Mrs. Werner's and moved in with Captain Raphael Tafoya in his house at the foot of Third Street, in the Barelas precinct of Old Town. The split was amicable; Mrs. Werner needed her house back to accommodate her daughter and family who were coming for an extended stay. Francis thanked her effusively. Wearing his new shoes cobbled by Tom Dye, solid lace-up black brogans, he shuffled through the fine, particulate, yellow dust of the Old Town streets to Captain Tafoya's abode, carrying his own luggage.

***

On July 26, Walter C. Hadley, a prominent banker, hosted a dinner party in his palatial home on Copper Avenue in New Town so Francis could meet and be scrutinized by the Albuquerque business and social elite. A carriage came to fetch him at Captain Tafoya's; clad in a dark suit coat with shiny brass buttons, baggy pantaloons, and his stiff new shoes, Francis spent several hours at the Hadley home. Hundreds of people followed the carriage through the streets as it conveyed the healer from the captain's modest dwelling in Old Town to the fancy houses of the nouveaux riches in the newer section of Albuquerque. The people who had followed Francis's carriage forgot they were on private property and swarmed across the front and back lawns of the Hadley estate in an effort to gain access to the house. The servants had to lock everything to keep the house from being overrun by people the Hadleys didn't know.

Inside the house, with the evening glow sealed off by tight-fitting windows and doors, with the gas jets hissing and sputtering, Mrs. Hadley served a light supper. About forty people showed up for the soiree, business types for the most part—bankers, merchants, railroad officials, City Council members, the chief of police, plus two or three reporters. Mr. Hadley, an adventurous type despite his portly frame and pronounced lisp, sat for a treatment with Francis and discovered for himself the remarkable magnetic power the healer possessed. "As he held my hand in his," he said to a *Morning Democrat* reporter, who wrote an account of the evening for the July 27 issue, "I felt the electric surge pass through my body as lively as if I had grasped the coil of an electric battery. It seemed to me as if the upper portion of my arm was melting into a puddle of flesh. I could feel the current shoot down my back like hot arrows."

"This much I will say for him," police chief Emmitt Anderson told the reporter, "he is not an imposter. He is just what he represents himself to be, and nothing more. He's not highly educated, but he's certainly not ignorant either. He seems to occupy the middle ground. At all times he conducts himself consistently with his teachings."

Cinco Montoya, one of the councilmen present, cut to the quick when he added, "The man has done more to advertise the fair city of Albuquerque to the rest of the world than anything which has occurred here in years."

***

A few days later a writer for *The Morning Democrat* reported what he called a "boomerang effect" taking place among some of Francis's patients. "Many persons who were treated by him and who were willing to testify that they felt better," he wrote in the July 30 edition, "are now reporting a return of their ailments."

An Albuquerque physician who requested anonymity told the reporter that "many of this man's cures have undoubtedly been the result of two things: first, his apparent electric power, and second the imagination of the patient. It is a well-known fact among physicians that cures are frequently due to the imagination, as it is a well-known fact that disease is often the result of imagination. The effects of imagination have about worn off, as have the effects of the Healer's magnetic touch."

***

The sarcasm continued to drip from the pages of *The Albuquerque Daily Citizen*. In the August 6 edition a snide paragraph noted that the "nos. 3 and 1 passenger trains from the north last night brought to the city half a dozen or more cripples and demented people with their relatives and friends, all poor, to see 'The Healer.'"

***

A ripple more akin to a shudder passed through the Albuquerque populace on August 10 when it was first reported in *The Morning Democrat* that Francis Schlatter had declared that he was Jesus Christ.

Among the recent callers at Captain Tafoya's home in Old Town was the Reverend Charles L. Bovard, pastor of the United Methodist Church, who was determined to test the veracity of several statements made by the healer regarding the origins of his spirituality. Bovard was

haughty and corpulent, with a high, sloping forehead and a shiny mane of silver hair. He bowed to his host, who returned the bow in his best Spanish manner. Bovard then bowed formally to Francis, who sat in a cane-backed chair in a corner of the room. With an ominous rustle of the skirts of his ecclesiastical gown, the good reverend drew near.

"Are you the man who claims to be Jesus Christ come back to earth," he asked.

Francis returned the reverend's imperious gaze with a steady, impassive stare. "I am," he replied. "Since you have asked me, sir, I say plainly, I am."

Bovard asked Francis a few more questions. Nothing seemed to rattle the healer. He fit into the slipcase of his skin like a fist into a hand-crafted glove. To each inquiry he returned a measured response. Unable to intimidate him, Bovard turned to go. Out in the front yard, he told *The Morning Democrat* reporter, "The man is insane. And you can quote me on that. If harmlessly, then pitiably."

***

It was a slow night after the reverend left. A dozen people traipsed through the living room of the house. Francis dealt with them speedily. *The Morning Democrat* reporter waited for his chance. The following exchange was reported in the August 10 edition of the paper.

"With your permission, Mr. Schlatter," he said when the last patient had left the room, "picking up from where the Reverend Bovard left off, is it true that you claim to be the Christ?"

Francis leaned forward in his chair, combing his beard with the tips of his fingers. "I am not here to give information, but I will always answer a direct question," he replied.

"Do you claim to be the Christ who died on Calvary?"
"Yes."
"Do you believe in the teachings of the Bible?"
"Of course. It is Holy Scripture."

"But the Bible says Christ was a Hebrew. You are not a Hebrew."

"No, but this is my third life on this earth."

"Why do you call upon the Master, as you call him, for aid in your work?"

"I have not yet reached perfection. When my forty-day fast is over—I have yet six days more—I will get stronger, and someday I will reach perfection."

Francis's reply was puzzling. First, he had never admitted to anyone that he had lived on earth in a previous lifetime. Second, he had never spoken of the possibility of living in "perfection"—of being so in tune with the Master's wishes that everything he did or said was a flawless reflection of His Desire and Will. Protestations to the contrary, all was not well in Francis's world. Not that he struggled with any uncertainty, but there were some unresolved issues. At times he seemed touched by an excess of hubris that struck an off-key note for such a modest man. There were also times when he seemed to speak in circles, revealing things that upon reflection, didn't reveal much at all. *The Morning Democrat* reporter alluded to this in the August 10 article when he said, "Every day he [Schlatter] grows to be more and more of a riddle."

***

On another matter, both Captain Tafoya and Mrs. Werner swore that in the time he had been a guest in their respective homes, the healer had touched no food. No one could understand this. Where does he find the strength, people whispered to one another. How can he live at such an intense pitch and not eat properly?

***

Accompanied by Ed Fox, Harry Hauenstein returned by train to Denver. Over a period of five days, he had been subjected to twenty-seven treatments by the healer. To a *Rocky Mountain News* reporter who met them at the Denver depot on August 7, he said, "After the first treatment he [Schlatter] told me I would see differently. Everything up to that point had been of one color. I couldn't tell light from darkness. We were sitting in the room of a house in Old Town. Behind us was a half window. When he let loose of my hands, everything in front of me was still dark. As I turned around, it seemed a little lighter. That was Saturday. The next Tuesday he said to me, 'the Father tells me that you will regain your eyesight, but it will be slow.'

"The last day he gave me five treatments, one after the other, over a period lasting from ten thirty in the morning till twelve fifteen that afternoon. I was sitting in a chair next to him. At the end of each treatment he said, 'Thanks be to the Father.' The feeling up my arms and all over my chest and down to the waist was just like a rubber suspender giving way then coming back again. I can't describe the feeling. At the close I could distinguish objects between me and the light. That was six days ago. Ever since then I have been regaining my sight—everything looks brighter. I can see that there is something when I swing my hands before my face. I believe firmly that I will regain my sight."

***

The long, jolting train ride back up the Front Range from New Mexico had aggravated Ed Fox's kidneys. To dull the pain, he'd taken his entire supply of laudanum. Now, in the murky half-light of the billowy, steam-filled depot in downtown Denver, his eyes glowed with damp fervor. "We've got to get the healer to come back to Denver," he said to *The Rocky Mountain News* reporter. "He belongs in Denver. I've already talked to him about it, and he agrees. He could do wonders for our city. I intend to see to it personally myself."

***

When the reporter from *The Albuquerque Morning Democrat* entered Captain Tafoya's home the evening of August 11, 1895, he was surprised to find Francis Schlatter half asleep in a chair in an empty room at the back of the house. The healer had put in a busy day. The reporter was startled by how fatigued he looked. The prolonged fast was taking its toll.

"Your paper this morning claimed that I am now in my third period on earth," Francis said in a weak voice. "That is not correct. It is only my second appearance. I would be grateful if you would correct this with your editors."

A correction was duly included in the August 12 edition of the paper, along with a transcription of the following exchange between Francis and the reporter.

"When is your fast up?" the reporter asked.

"Next Thursday."

"August fifteenth."

"I am not certain of the date."

"We hear that you plan to leave Albuquerque. Is that true?"

"Yes."

"When do you plan to leave?"

"On the evening train of the twenty-first."

"Where will you go?"

"Denver."

"How will you get there?"

"Mr. Fox will send me a ticket."

"Where will you live when you get there?"

"At Mr. Fox's house."

"How long do you plan to stay in Denver?"

"Three months, possibly."

"Where will you go then?"

"Only the Father knows. Probably I will disappear, and no one will know where I am."

"Will you ever come back to Albuquerque?"

"Yes, most likely, but not as I now am."

Another riddle. What did Francis mean? Would he return to Albuquerque in another guise? As another person? Or was he just being coy?

The man could be maddeningly evasive.

***

On August 13, 1895, Francis was thirty-eight days into his fast, with two days to go. The hard work and long hours and lack of nourishment had taken their toll—he looked gaunt, wasted, and worn out. His normally rotund chest had shrunk in size; his soft blue eyes looked pasty and dull; a rumor circulated that yesterday he had experienced a fainting spell.

The next afternoon, a Wednesday, at five p.m. sharp, he was to eat his first regular meal in forty days (960 hours). Medical authorities presumed he would partake of very little, although that might not be the case. Francis hinted that his hunger was so keen he might be tempted to consume a heavy repast. Friends and associates were concerned that, in his present weakened condition, too much food could make him sick, or worse.

***

That same day (August 13) a package for him was hand-delivered to Captain Tafoya's residence, accompanied by a note:
> Dear Sir—We herewith beg to present you with a suit of clothes, a shirt, and a tie, which please accept with our compliments. Trusting that both you and your Master will be pleased with the same,
> we remain very truly yours, . . . Grunsfeld Bros.

After consulting with the Father, Francis accepted the gift and wrote a note to the donors, thanking them warmly.

***

The August 14 edition of *The Albuquerque Daily Citizen* contained a curmudgeonly letter by a Mr. William D. Clayton, calling Francis "a fraud of the very first water." Clayton was fed up with Francis's habit of telling everyone they would feel better in three hours without even knowing whether they were feeling bad in the first place. Clayton also objected to the fact that Francis healed for free and that the majority of his patients came from the bottom of the social ladder. "All the poor who are not able to pay doctors' bills go to see him," Clayton grumped. "He ought to be in an insane asylum."

* * *

The next day Francis broke his forty-day fast. A reporter from *The Morning Democrat* was there to witness it, along with a Denver writer, James McCarty, who wrote under the pen name "Fitz Mac." The scene was the pine-paneled dining room of the J. A. Sommers residence in New Town. A crew of first-rate cooks, led by Mrs. Sommers, prepared a bounteous feast, which they brought on steaming platters to a table festooned with colorful flowers, hand-picked that morning by Mrs. Sommers. "The fast is broken," the reporter wrote in the opening line of his front-page article in the August 16, 1895, edition of *The Morning Democrat*, "and Francis Schlader [sic] still lives."

He filled in details of the momentous occasion: "Yesterday evening as the first stroke of the clock sounded for five p.m., Francis Schlader [sic] stood up and after slowly repeating the Lord's prayer, blessed himself and sat down to eat his first food for forty days and nights."

"Fitz Mac," in an article entitled "The 'Christ Man' of Denver" that appeared in the November issue of *The Great Divide Magazine*, described the opening moments in a spate of gushy prose: "The brief and only half audible prayer he offered, standing at the table with eyes uplifted before sitting down, was absolutely the noblest dramatic effect I have ever beheld—simplicity, solemnity and grandeur."

The Morning Democrat reporter went on to say: "A gentleman present requested the 'Healer' to allow him to feel his pulse before he ate, and this request was assented to. His pulse was 100 at two minutes past five o'clock.

"The meal occupied one and a quarter hours, and was eaten slowly and with relish. Eleven fried eggs, nine slices of salt pork, eleven ladles full of rich gravy, seven pieces of cheese about four inches long and one inch broad, two tablespoons full of chile con carna [sic], three helpings of pickled apples, eight slices of rye bread, three pieces of roast chicken, one cup of coffee, one slice of cake and four glasses of port wine, slowly but surely disappeared."

At 5:30 Francis's pulse registered 80 beats per minute. At 6:00 his pulse was 92. At 6:15 it dropped slightly to 90. At 6:30, at the close of the feast, it had risen to 96.

When he had finished, Francis daubed his lips with a fancy napkin. He crossed his arms over the rounded mound of his full stomach and reminisced about his days on the road. People were astounded; no one who had seen the amount of food he had just packed away could believe it. Surely, he was in danger of keeling over. But Francis looked fine. His voice was steady and clear. His eyes glowed a deep sky blue. Still, he was weary, and he stumbled over a word or two. Finally, he excused himself and retired to an upstairs bedroom reserved for him.

***

The day following, all of Albuquerque was agog that Francis had survived such a gluttonous feast. He sought to dispel rumors of any unpleasant aftereffects by telling *The Morning Democrat* reporter the next evening, "I am first rate. During my long fast everyone remarked how cold and lifeless my hands felt, but you see how warm they are now. I feel remarkably well."

He told the reporter he intended to take a few days off from healing. "I need to rest," he said, "so I will not be treating anyone until next Monday. I will then be better able to heal than ever before."

***

That evening, sitting in the parlor of the Sommers's house, he answered twenty-five letters concerning various medical matters. The letters were short and to the point:

> My Dear Madam:
> Take this handkerchief and place it upon the afflicted area. Recite the Lord's prayer as fervently as you can. If you believe, God will believe in you and make you well. You must have faith. It is all about faith.
>
> Sincerely . . . Francis Schlatter

***

The August 18 issue of *The Albuquerque Daily Citizen* contained a long letter written by A. L. Mahaffey, M.D., entitled "The Healer. A Medical Opinion on His Peculiar Insanity."

> Now this man has delusional insanity, delusions of grandeur and personal exaltation. He is a monomaniac. The insane asylums are full of such patients—many not so insane as he is—gods, Napoleons, kings, queens, etc., who reason correctly, if one concedes the truth of their false premises, until their brains are so deranged by the progress of the disease that their reasoning is insane as well as their premises.
>
> He thinks that if they believe in the Father and His works then they believe in him, and if they believe in him they believe in the Father, which is the same thing.
>
> He does not know enough to distinguish between the sick and the well, but heals all indiscriminately, faith or no faith. I presume if he would see

a man with one leg or one eye, he has understanding enough to know he ought to have another, and would proceed to heal him immediately.

He is not an imposter nor a deceiver. No one need be deceived by him unless they want to. He is honest and sincere and believes in himself. But he is not a free agent. He is not responsible for his actions.

Delusions of grandeur may be only a nuisance or annoyance, but may, at any time, become sources of danger. Suppose he becomes possessed with the idea that he ought to remove any person or persons?

He would do so with as much deliberation as he shakes hands with you, and verily believe he was performing the will of God. Or suppose he should command others to do so, who have the utmost blind faith in him?

Dr. Mahaffey pinpointed a crucial element in the Francis Schlatter conundrum. What if the voice inside his head had been malevolent and directed him to do homicidal deeds? Would Francis have responded accordingly? Instead of trying to help people, would he have harmed them? How fortunate that the Christ-like example he followed was motivated by benevolent feelings and not malicious urges.

***

Late-nineteenth-century America was a period of tremendous political, social, and religious upheaval. Anarchism, "propaganda by deed"—the urban terrorism of its day—fueled by virulent hostility between workers and factory owners, was rampant in the major cities. By the mid-1890s, clashes between the two groups were numerous and bloody. Frightened employers clamored for federal troops to quell the fury of angry demonstrators. The industrial baron George Pullman, among others, adamantly refused to negotiate with his workers at the Pullman Company; in retaliation, the American Railway Union, led by the charismatic Eugene V. Debs, called for an all-out strike in 1894, which led to a virtual nationwide shutdown of freight and passenger service.

***

News of Francis's impending departure for Colorado cast a pall over his followers. On August 20, 1895—Francis's last full day in Albuquerque—an unusually large crowd thronged the streets of Old Town. *A Morning Democrat* reporter tried to talk to him, but Francis sent word that he did not feel up to talking with anyone. He did no healing that day. It was late afternoon when the reporter was permitted to see him. He found Francis in his room sprawled on a cot, looking spent and wasted.

When asked the cause of his discomfort, Francis said, "The Father is preparing me for my trip to Denver, and He has some good reasons for making me sick."

When the reporter asked him what those reasons could possibly be, Francis wouldn't say. He had firmly decided to leave for Denver the next day. Ed Fox had sent him a ticket. Francis was packed and ready to go.

"Why Denver?" the reporter wondered in an exchange that appeared in *The Morning Democrat* on August 21, the same day he was scheduled to depart.

"Because there are more people," Francis replied. "I am finally ready to cure crowds of people. I feel as if I have come into the fullness of my power. I am here to do God's bidding."

The reporter asked what he'd had to eat that day.

"A plate of cornmeal mush and some milk. I expect to eat the same again for supper."

***

Scores of people called at the Sommers's house that final day, but few were admitted. A reporter overheard a group of downtown store owners express deep concern that Francis was about to leave them. "The man is a gold mine," one merchant said.

"Single-handedly he'll turn the economy of Denver around and pull it out of its doldrums," said another. "Their gain is our loss."

***

The day he was to leave Albuquerque, Francis woke around eight a.m. A half hour later he sat down to breakfast, hustled up by Mrs. Sommers—three boiled eggs, four slices of toast, two cups of coffee.

Afterward, he retired to his room to rest. Other than a glass of crushed ice, he ate nothing else the rest of the day.

At ten a.m. a crowd assembled outside, hoping to catch a glimpse of him. Francis felt weak, but he sent word that if people would stay in the yard and not press too close, he would come out on the porch.

The people agreed with cries and murmurs of delight. With a wave of the hand and a raspy *"buenos dias"*—wearing the new suit and tie Grunfeld Brothers had sent him—Francis sat in a wicker chair in the shade of the porch for about thirty minutes, staring down at his shoes and fanning himself. A few people, overcome by the sight of him and realizing this might be the last time they would ever see him, tried to scale the porch to reach him but were held back by police.

Others tossed handkerchiefs, bandanas, watches, and necklaces onto the porch for him to touch and beatify. Francis remained seated, oblivious to the crowd. Finally, with a feeble wag of the hand and a whispered *"adios"*—his voice sounding ominously weak—he retired to his room.

***

The Morning Democrat reporter found him in that room around four p.m. Francis's eyes were closed and he was breathing heavily. His complexion looked pasty. His fingers, entwined on his chest, twitched and quivered. He said virtually nothing about the upcoming Denver trip. He seemed confident that everything would be all right.

"Tell the people," he said to the reporter, who compiled the article for the August 22 edition, "that my new address in Denver will be sixteen twenty-five Witter Street. Also, all people who have proved their faith in the Father either by writing a letter or trying to see me in person, will be cured of whatever it is that troubles them."

He lay back against the pillow. "I don't know what is the matter," he said. "It has been a long time since I have felt this weak."

***

At eight that evening a fully enclosed carriage, draped like a Black Mariah and driven by a black man named Oaky Clifford, drew up in front of J. C. Sommers's house. Francis said his goodbyes to Mr. and Mrs. Sommers. Then, with Captain Tafoya and two burly policemen paving the way, he plowed through the crush of people in the front yard. Even after the door to the carriage was shut, Clifford, fearful of injuring someone, guided the horses slowly along the dust-filled street. Well-wishers, their cheeks wet with tears, thrust their hands through the open windows. Francis shook as many as he could reach.

Inside the carriage, in addition to Francis and Captain Tafoya (the policemen sat up on the driver's bench with Clifford), were Mrs. Werner and *The Morning Democrat* reporter. The reporter felt especially honored to have been chosen to accompany Francis on his final ride to the Union Pacific depot in New Town. They traveled through the crooked streets of Old Town so as many people as possible could obtain a last glimpse of Francis.

At the station, hundreds of people surrounded the carriage as it crunched to the curb in front of the ticket office. Flanked by the policemen, with Captain Tafoya in the lead, Francis climbed the steps to the office, where he signed the necessary forms and pocketed the ticket Ed Fox had sent him from Denver. Five minutes later he stepped onto the platform to cries of protest and alarm; some of the Indian and Hispanic women in the crowd let out wild, keening wails. People surged forward, eager to touch him one last time. Women reached out with trembling fingers to stroke his hair and shirtsleeves. Men doffed their hats.

The Pullman car was riding in place at the spot where Francis was to board. He shuffled to the door, clutching a canvas bag with his clothes and personal effects. A porter in a black hat and crisp white tunic took his bag and disappeared inside. Francis swept his bearish arms around Mrs. Werner's shoulders and clutched her to his chest. He shook hands with Captain Tafoya and waved to Oaky Clifford. He thanked the policemen and wrung the reporter's hand with heartfelt feeling. Inside the Pullman car, at his window seat, Francis lowered the wide glass pane and leaned out and touched the fingers of as many hands as he could reach before the train, with a shrill toot and a screech of its solid steel wheels, rolled out along the tracks.

***

Midnight. Offices of *The Albuquerque Morning Democrat*.

While his editor and compositor stood waiting for him to finish his copy, the reporter's arms and legs trembled as he reached the bottom of the last page. He knew what he was about to say was filled with personal feeling. He knew his editor would probably cut it for that reason, but he couldn't help himself—Francis Schlatter was far and away the most astonishing human being he had ever known.

"Last night," he wrote in pencil with a quivering hand, "the curtain dropped on a drama which will forever claim a place in the history of the Territory of New Mexico."

***

The Albuquerque (NM Terr.) *Morning Democrat*,
August 23, 1895.

Special to *The Democrat*

Denver, August 22—Francis Schlader [sic], the "Healer," who left Albuquerque at 8:45 o'clock Wednesday night, did not arrive in this city [Denver] as expected this evening. At 5 o'clock when the train was due an immense crowd awaited at the depot, all desirous of getting a glimpse of this wonderful man, but they were doomed to disappointment. He was delayed along the road for some reason unknown.

Passengers who arrived tonight say that at all points along the road the train was compelled to pull into the depots very slowly owing to the throngs of people who crowded the tracks to obtain a glimpse of the "Healer."

At Bernalillo, Cerillos, Lamy, Las Vegas and in fact every place at which the train stopped, people prayed for him to come forth and treat them. They were informed that he could not be seen but at many of the places he came out and made a few remarks, saying that the Father would cure them of their ills for this proof of their faith.

He will arrive in Denver at 6:15 o'clock tomorrow morning.

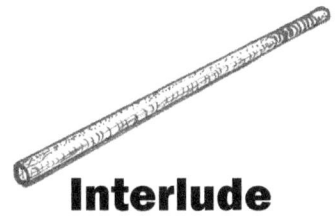

Interlude

The arrival of the railroad from Cheyenne, Wyoming, down to Denver, Colorado, on June 15, 1870—a modest distance of 106 miles—provided the first viable commercial link between the fledgling High Plains town and the outside world. To ensure this connection, local Denver moneymen had to twist themselves into more contortions than a pretzel to satisfy the demands of the rapacious owners of the Union Pacific Railroad, who constructed the first coast-to-coast rail system in 1869. Denver sold its soul early in the boisterous Gilded Age sweepstakes that transformed the nation in the decades following the Civil War. But without a link to this all-important transcontinental artery, the town might have languished on the prairie, another sleepy burg that came awake for a few hours on Saturday afternoons when locals brought their livestock and produce to sell in the public square.

The appearance of the railroad—first the Central Pacific spur down from Cheyenne, followed by the Kansas Pacific tracks straight west out of Topeka in 1872—connected Denver with the vast transportation network that was exfoliating at a dazzling pace all over the continent. The figures speak for themselves: Denver's population in 1870 was 5,000; twenty years later it had soared to 106,000.

The influx of new money from back East enabled the booming community to fund a host of basic amenities: mail service, graded roads, water mains, fire hydrants, telephone lines, pumping stations, a horse-drawn streetcar system. Wholesalers and merchandisers, the foundation of the local economy, followed in the wake of this initial outlay of speculative wealth. Small manufacturing plants and retail outlets sprang up on every street. Workers poured into the city. The streets rang with the sounds of construction. At the same time, the air became fouled with soot and smoke. The stench of refuse, open latrines, and dead animals seeped into the cloistered shelter of the fanciest parlor. Despite these distractions, by 1890 Denver had become the banking and commercial hub of the High Plains and central Rocky Mountains. It was also a supply depot, communications center, and tourist mecca.

Invalids flocked to the city, attracted by its inflated reputation as a health resort, especially for pulmonary afflictions such as tuberculosis. Hundreds of makeshift sanitariums, many little more than tent colonies staffed by ill-trained doctors and nurses, ringed the outskirts. Local folklore included stories of miraculous cures delivered to sick people by itinerant healers who drifted down from the mountains or up off the plains leading pack mules burdened with bottles of home-brewed elixir. It was the era before scientific examination eliminated intuitive guesswork from the quirky art of medical prognosis. Reportedly—and the city fathers did little to counteract this notion—Denver's climate was so healthful that after a few days, those who had come to be cured threw their crutches away and returned home, happy and healed. The great showman P. T. Barnum declared of the infirm who flocked to Denver that "two thirds came to die, and they couldn't do it."

The truth is that some found a cure while others expired, penniless and bereft, after spending their last dime on some quack nostrum hawked on the streets or the bad advice of a bogus healer. Denver knew all about health mavens by the time Francis Schlatter arrived from back East in 1892. The place was like a magnet for them. "No city on earth is so overrun by fortune-telling fakirs as Denver," wrote Herbert V. George in *The Road* (March 3, 1896). The sweep of the plains, the stirring profile of the mountains, the invigorating air that blew off the snow-capped summits—the town was located at the nexus of a dramatic overlap of geological forms, alpine heights soaring through the crust of sedimentary layers, igneous minerals fusing with the petrified remnants of huge ferny plants. At night, in the moonlight—with coyotes screeling, the stars wheeling in mysterious orbits, the clouds clotting over the foothills in suggestive shapes—the humblest stones seemed to sing a song of prosperity and renewal.

***

In the 1890s, few cities in the United States exhibited such a marked contrast between the haves and have-nots as Denver. Behind the lavish homes and plush hotels lurked a muddy, dirty, dangerous town. Juveniles in rival gangs roamed the streets. Police in stiff blue uniforms and conical helmets with stubby visors toted guns and lead-lined billy clubs. Immigrants fresh off the trains from back East camped in the side streets, under cover of makeshift lean-tos made of cowhide and plywood sheets.

In the 1880s the founders of Denver's early fortunes had built opulent homes, primarily in the Capitol Hill area. Skilled workmen and exotic materials were shipped in from all over the world. The houses reflected a variety of architectural styles: colonial, Queen Anne, Italinate, Roman, Greek, Byzantine. Manicured gardens sheltered stately groves of imported trees and topiary sculptures. Cupolas, turrets, mansard roofs, dormer windows, carriage houses, porte cocheres, and servants' quarters bristled from the massive domiciles that rose on the city's east side, tributes to the success of the early economic barons—William Byers, Jerome Chaffee, Charles Kountze, David Moffat, John Evans—who built them.

A few blocks away, the squalid underclass lived in shacks and hovels covered with canvas and loose boards. Smoke from hundreds of cooking fires soured the air. Half-naked children ran around barefoot. Men and women reeled drunkenly through the garbage-strewn streets.

Open sewers leaked a raft of fetid odors. Dead animals rotted under the blaze of the High Plains sun.

Despite the filth and poverty, the town worked hard to present a prosperous and progressive image to the world. Throughout the 1880s, ugly and unstable public and private buildings, cobbled together from local materials during Denver's pioneer era, were replaced with elegant and durable structures. Only the finest elements were used to construct and decorate Denver's public and domestic edifices—granite, terra-cotta, pressed brick, marble, onyx, native sandstone, gold, silver, bronze, nickel, black-iron work, mahogany, teak, the list was endless. No material was too lavish or expensive.

The theory was simple: the more beautiful the architecture, the more outsiders and potential investors would be tempted to pump money into the local economy. The plan seemed to work. "The streets are full of activity," wrote English writer Emily Faithful in *Three Trips to America* (1884). "There are fine houses and fast horses; carriages are to be seen with heraldic crests familiar to Europeans but somewhat out of place in this land of equality. . . . Considerable extravagance is also to be seen—gorgeous clothes and pretentious entertainments; but at the same time there is energy and liberality—schools have been built, an excellent university opened and, if Denver has its faults, she also has the virtues of a wealthy Western city."

Horace Tabor, the Leadville mining millionaire, set the standard for architectural grandiosity. The five-story office complex he built at 16th and Larimer in 1879 became the city's premier commercial property. In 1881 Tabor outdid himself with construction of the Tabor Grand Opera House. Located at 16th and Curtis in the heart of downtown Denver, the opera house cost $750,000 to build, a staggering sum for those profligate times. The interior was paneled with Japanese cherry and Honduran mahogany. The walls were slabbed with massive cubes of Italian marble. The floors were covered with miles of Belgian carpet. Cathedral domes attracted generous doses of sunlight during the day. At night, flickering gas lamps lit the stalls and private boxes. The drapes and curtains were made of French brocaded silk, costing $150 a yard.

By 1895 Denver had acquired a worldwide reputation for the quality of its major hotels: the Windsor, Albany, Oxford, and Brown Palace. The Brown Palace opened in 1892; built of Arizona sandstone, it quickly became the city's major entertainment establishment. The walls of the cafes, drawing rooms, and restaurants were lined with gold-flecked Mexican onyx. The eight-story atrium was domed with a pastel, stained-glass ceiling. Amusements included bars, card and game rooms, billiard tables, bowling alleys, Turkish baths. Services included a crematorium in the basement, should the unthinkable happen and a body needed to be disposed of as soon as possible. Fresh cream for the dining tables came from the hotel's own herd of pampered cows. A secret tunnel connected the hotel to a brothel and gambling parlor across the street.

***

The Festival of Mountain and Plain was launched in the fall of 1895 by the local Chamber of Commerce to counteract the doldrums of the 1893 economic depression. In look and feel, minus the erotic innuendos, the festival resembled the New Orleans Mardi Gras. Civic leaders, as well as their wives and daughters, masqueraded as kings, queens, and princesses; fully caparisoned in elaborate masks and sumptuous robes, they rode atop huge floats festooned with balloons and fake sunflowers carved out of stiff cardboard.

The opening event was a street parade called the Pageant of Progress, led by a contingent of Ute Indians on horseback dressed in full regalia—feathers, face paint, warbonnets, beaded buckskin tunics and leggings—carrying curved staffs and lances bedecked with eagle feathers and otter fur. The floats that followed featured covered wagons with girls and boys in period costumes from Colorado's pioneer era. Famed western entertainer Buffalo Bill Cody trotted by on a magnificent white horse. Miners with picks and shovels staged competitive drilling contests. There were noisy brass-band playoffs. The fire department rattled past in its water wagons, dousing the exuberant crowd with blasts from its hoses.

***

Behind the scrim of hilarity and good times, life remained difficult for the majority of indigent Denverites. During the boom years of the 1870s and 1880s, the city fathers sent out circulars all over the country, advertising the opportunities Colorado offered. The work in the new factories, smelters, and railroad yards was long and hard; the average workload for men was sixty hours a week, for a wage of eight to ten dollars. Women worked nearly as long for four to six dollars a week. Laden with dust and grit, the smoke from the industrial plants, sealed off by a layer of cool mountain air, hung like a pall over the city—the infamous thermal inversion that plagues Denver to this day.

The city was checkerboarded with immigrant settlements—Germans, Hispanics, Irish, Italians, Poles, Hungarians, Asians, Native Americans, African Americans, Jews. Animosities between rival factions frequently erupted into violence.

***

Denver's rough-and-tumble legacy included whiskey establishments and gambling joints, plus a boisterous red-light district rivaling that of New Orleans and San Francisco. The lavish wickedness of the tenderloin district elicited a curious pride among the city fathers, who looked the other way in 1892 when an enterprising publisher brought out *The Denver Red Book*, which listed and even rated the charms of the city's major fleshpots. (The book was conveniently pocket-sized for the gentleman to tuck discretely into his vest pocket for quick consultation.)

Acceptance of rowdy or controversial behavior was part of the prevailing ethos of tolerance and openness that marked the spirit of the city. In the 1880s a self-righteous City Council decreed that every "public woman" should be forced to wear a yellow ribbon on her arm. In a spontaneous act of solidarity, Denver women of every social background, from sleazy tarts to wealthy dowagers, swept into the

streets wearing yellow gowns and gold slippers and carrying saffron parasols. The ordinance was quickly repealed.

***

What to do with the poor and out of work whose numbers seemed to increase exponentially as the 1893 depression dug its tentacles deeper into the social and economic fabric of Colorado? As the hard times worsened, populist sentiment among the idle members of the working class intensified. Denver's money elite feared the angry protests against Wall Street and the robber barons by the discontented would scare off potential investors from back East. What better way to cool their ardor than to round them up and send them packing?

The Denver Chamber of Commerce came up with a plan to provide the have-nots with a one-way ticket out of town. The railroad fare to Kansas City was six dollars—too expensive for most of the men, camped out on the sandy bottoms of the South Platte River eating rabbits (if they were lucky) and prairie dogs. In the spring of 1894, a dreamy idealist and former Civil War general from Ohio named Jacob Coxey organized a mass march on Washington, D.C. Coxey felt it was time for the people to take their grievances directly to the politicians. He envisioned thousands of unemployed workers striding through the streets of the nation's capital, badgering Congress and the president to appropriate money to build a network of free roads so ordinary people could travel around the country without having to risk their lives trying to swing onboard a moving train. A public works project of this magnitude, Coxey believed, funded by the federal government and backed by the executive branch, not only would curb unemployment but would also subvert the power of the railroads and help pull the economy out of its disastrous slump.

The railroad was reluctant to transport thousands of unemployed workers gratis from Denver to the Atlantic seaboard. Why should it make it easy for these malcontents to reach the nation's capital so they could badger the federal government on behalf of their bizarre ideas?

The Denver Coxeyites hit on another plan. The winter of 1894 had been a particularly wet one. By April, meltwater from the snows high on the slopes to the west was flowing freely from the Rocky Mountains into the South Platte River. Why couldn't the hundreds of men living along the river on the outskirts of Denver transport themselves by homemade rafts from the Colorado capital all the way back East? On paper, the plan seemed feasible. Riding the crest of the high water streaming off the Front Range, they would cross the Great Plains on the Platte River, which runs the length of Nebraska. At the confluence of the Platte and Missouri rivers south of Omaha, they would turn downstream for Kansas City; from there, still riding the tawny current of the Missouri River, they could float across the state bearing the same name to St. Louis and the Mississippi River. From the Mississippi, they could make their way up the Ohio River to Pittsburgh, where it was but a short hop over the Pennsylvania and Maryland hills to Washington.

The Colorado branch of Coxey's quixotic dreamers got busy building the boats and rafts that would carry them downstream to the promised land. That spring, rain drenched the Denver region; water in the tributaries tumbling from the mountains was steady and deep. On June 6, 1894, a bright spring day, Coxey's lubbers, to the huzzas of their comrades standing on the banks, launched 100 boats into the gritty current of the South Platte River. The boats were constructed from flimsy sheets of wood nailed together with plank boards, limbs and logs lashed across their thwarts; they were flatboats for the most part, with few keels or stabilizing centerboards, steered by primitive tillers and paddles. The first day was a fiasco. Within a few hours at least half of the craft had disintegrated, spilling men into the river, many of whom drowned. Those who survived swam to shore. Packs and bundles and suitcases sank into the water. The current was so strong it swept hundreds of people, flailing wildly, downstream.

Denver city officials, delighted to have the dissenters out of town, were less keen about having them return. No sooner was the first wave of rickety boats rollicking downstream than the police sealed off the campgrounds in the South Platte sand flats. Those who managed to avoid drowning when their boats broke apart were unable to return to their shanties. In some cases, the swift current propelled them so far downstream they couldn't make it back to Denver. Instead, without water or food, they started walking east over the arid, shortgrass prairie. A few put their hobo skills to work and hopped an east-bound freight to Omaha or Kansas City, where they were pounced upon by railroad security and thrown in jail. Federal troops were sent out to round up the rest. By the summer of 1894—about the time Francis Schlatter was trudging across Texas—the initial enthusiasm of the western branch of Jacob Coxey's ragtag army had spent itself. Thousands of vagrants roamed the countryside, and there seemed no end in sight to the misery and suffering.

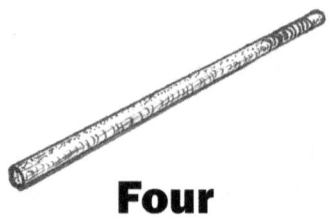

Four

The Healer in Denver

I t's the darkest time of the night in Denver, Colorado, the hours between three and four in the morning. The moon, glimmering over the mountains to the west, leaks a tarnished light down onto the wide, empty streets that fan out over the prairie in every direction. A few people are abroad, mostly men lurching between beer and whiskey joints; a few uniformed and helmeted constables whose job it is to maintain the peace; a few prostitutes looking to turn a final trick before calling it a day; a few reporters for the local newspapers filing their copy for the morning editions, due to hit the streets at six a.m.

Francis Schlatter lies awake in a back bedroom of the Ed Fox residence at 1625 Witter Street, in the northern section of the city. He has awakened from a refreshing sleep, not because it's time for him to get up but because the voice inside his head has begun to grumble and stir. Francis has been in Denver for nearly a month, resting, recuperating, marshaling his strength. Today, he is scheduled to begin a grueling bout of hands-on therapy to the sick and indigent of Colorado's capital city.

Albuquerque was demanding, but at no time did he think he would be unable to give his all to everyone who needed it. Each person he touched and prayed over seemed to prepare him for the next. The effect was cumulative; the more people he treated, the more confident he became. Someday, he hoped to be able to heal entire populations—not just those he touched in person but those whose handkerchiefs he blessed or to whom he wrote letters or whose names he said out loud. He looked forward to the day when he would be able to sweep a crowd with his long, athletic arms and, as if dispensing an electric charge—something Christ-inspired, something intimately linked to God's ineffable power—cure everyone in sight.

Denver posed a special challenge. With a population over 100,000, it was one of the fastest-growing cities in the nation. The Panic of 1893 had hit hard, and as the 1890s continued, the population had fallen off. But that wouldn't last forever. Francis knew that, the city fathers knew that, political mentors like Ed Fox knew that. Denver was destined for big things. Every day a steam engine pulling a line of dilapidated cars packed with immigrants chugged into the downtown Union Station. In the month he had been there, Francis had seen the influx of people from all over the world—Mexico and Canada, Europe and Asia. Despite the flaccid economy, the gold and silver mines tucked away in the Rocky Mountains to the west would eventually reopen. The coal seams glimmering in the foothills would soon be mined and their contents loaded onto open cars and sent back East to fuel the booming factories in Pennsylvania and Ohio. This recovery, in turn, would attract a host of new settlers.

Another major attraction, although he was too modest to admit it—too ingenuous even to be aware of it—was Francis himself. Word of his healing gift had spread all over the nation. The close watch the

Albuquerque and Denver newspapers kept on his activities had been taken up by major journals on both coasts. By mid-September 1895 Francis was something of a celebrity—there seemed no limit to the multitudes he could rehabilitate with the power of his touch. Denver's population was twenty-fold that of Albuquerque. In New Mexico, Francis had dealt with patients in the hundreds; in Denver, that number would escalate into the thousands. That morning as he lay in bed, Francis was beset with a fretful anxiety that the spiritual and physical strength he had so assiduously built up over the past two years might flounder and pall, his healing touch dry up and disappear. In the moody depths of the early morning darkness he could hear people queuing up along the wooden fence marking the boundary of Fox's property. The people were quiet and respectful. They spoke in hushed voices. They sounded steady and calm. They had arrived early to ensure that they would have an opportunity to encounter Francis Schlatter in the flesh. Their eagerness was understandable; for many, teetering between life and death, the remarkable man from Alsace-Lorraine with his astounding curative gifts was their last hope.

***

September 16, 1895. Tuesday. At exactly nine a.m., Francis Schlatter stepped out the back door of the Fox residence. He ambled across the grassy yard with a grave, steady gait, his arms dropping straight from his shoulders, his knuckles pointing forward—a curious, simian-like walk—to a waist-high fence running along the south side of the house that cordoned off the property from the street. Hundreds of people on the other side formed a ragged line that stretched into the street and down the block. The weather was mild; Francis appeared without a coat or hat. Three weeks' seclusion, plenty of rest and regular meals courtesy of Mary Fox, Ed Fox's wife, had bulked up his weight. His complexion was rosy and pink, his eyes playful and bright. His deep, chesnut-colored hair swept down to his muscular shoulders in smooth tresses.

Nothing on this scale or magnitude in the way of the laying on of hands for healing purposes had ever occurred in Denver. The sight of Francis Schlatter standing in the yard of a modest house in a modest neighborhood brought a respectful hush to the people lined up to receive his blessing. Men tipped their hats as he took his place under the shade of a leafy sycamore at the end of a long, wooden gangway. Few men felt bold enough to look him directly in the eye; most, fearful of his power, averted their gaze. Some women curtsied; others broke into tears. He said nothing directly to any of them. A fluid buzzing whirled between his lips as he took their fingers and pressed their palms. The muscles of his smooth white face, especially around his prominent cheekbones, pulsed and quivered as he leaned into his work.

A rich diversity characterized the makeup of the people he reached out to heal. Bankers and businessmen in three-piece suits and high starched collars, carrying briefcases and umbrellas, waited alongside bricklayers and pipe fitters. Silk-clad society ladies wearing fancy hats with delicate veils stood in line with the wives and children of Italian gardeners.

From nine in the morning to four-thirty in the afternoon, Francis received literally hundreds of patients at a rate of three a minute who filed past his station in a slow, shuffling, orderly fashion. Even though his lips moved constantly in silent prayer, he spoke few audible words. His method was the same as it had been in New Mexico; he grasped the patient's hands with both of his and held them firmly for a few seconds before letting them go.

At noon he disappeared into the house for lunch, which lasted thirty minutes. During his absence the people in line sat on the ground or on camp stools they had brought or stood on weary legs, waiting for him to reappear. Soon the kitchen door at the back of the cottage swung open and Francis came out, shambling across the leaf-strewn yard to his post at the head of the gangway. Without fanfare or comment, he took the hands of the first person waiting for him and began mumbling a prayer. The line started up; on the people came, funneling from a shapeless crowd out in the street to the width of a single person upon entering the gangway. On they came, some seeking attention for specific maladies, other simply to gaze for a precious moment into the healer's serene blue eyes.

Because of his press credentials, a correspondent for *The Rocky Mountain News* was able to stand directly behind the healer in Fox's yard, where he could look into the faces of the people. "Every nationality was represented in the throng," he wrote in a piece printed in the paper on September 17.

> The blind, the lame and the deaf were there, and scores of people afflicted with rheumatism appeared during the afternoon. Many came to see, and after satisfying their curiosity, they retired wondering what manner of man it was that thus gave his strength and his time without money and without price, for the benefit of his fellow beings.
>
> Some persons of both sexes seemed strangely infatuated with the healer. They stood for hours in the yard, as close as they could get, looking steadily into his face, and even after [he] retired from his arduous task, many lingered as if standing on sacred ground.

The sun had settled behind the barrier of the Rocky Mountains that first day when the people finally began to disperse, but not before leaving a huge pile of handkerchiefs the healer would take into his hands and bless that evening. Ed Fox, standing close to Francis, estimated the total number of handkerchiefs at about a thousand. It was Francis's wish that every person applying for treatment would leave a handkerchief that could later be placed against the afflicted area in the privacy of his or her home. Fox worked out a system whereby the distribution of handkerchiefs would take place twice a day, at ten o'clock a.m. and four-thirty p.m. A large wicker clothes basket would be left outside overnight so people could drop off handkerchiefs for the healer to bless.

***

That first afternoon a diminutive lady in a gray silk dress was lifted out of a fancy brougham fringed with black velvet tassels by a tall, distinguished, well-dressed man and carried across the yard to where Francis stood. Her chalky face, gravely voice, and hollow eyes indicated a terminal condition. Men and women near the healer bowed their heads as Francis took her hands and squeezed them and whispered a prayer that hummed through the air like the whirr of a bumblebee. She couldn't stand, and as Francis attended to her, she lay limp in the arms of the man who had carried her from the carriage. Francis stayed with her for several minutes, eyes closed, face tilted skyward, massaging her dainty, fine-boned fingers. Then he stepped back and nodded and whispered in a husky voice that only those gathered close by, including *The Rocky Mountain News* reporter, could hear: "That's enough for now."

Her escort bore her back to the carriage and tucked her into the enclosed cushioned seat.

The reporter looked at the healer. "Can you save her?" he murmured.

Francis looked genuinely perplexed. His pale forehead was furrowed with uncertainty. "When He sends it, I have it," he replied. "When He does not send it, I do not have it. It all depends upon what He sends. God is the giver of all things. Not everyone I treat is going to recover. Somebody has to pay the price for those who do."

***

At one point that first morning the reporter left his place behind the fence, where he'd been standing behind Francis, Ed Fox, and several others, to mix with the crowd and speak to some of the people Francis had treated. D. K. Tammany, a well-known Denver impresario, a fleshy man with a choleric face, his eyes banded by bright gold spectacles, held up his right arm to the reporter. "I have suffered from a stiffness in my right wrist for six years," he declared. "It was impossible for me to bend my wrist or move my thumb. See what I can do now."

He wiggled the thumb and wrist without any display of pain or discomfort. A giddy smile creased his plump cheeks.

W. C. Dillon of 1738 Champa Street had suffered from inflamatory rheumatism for several years. He told the reporter he had arrived at the Fox property at four that morning to get in line early so he would be sure to see the healer by noon. Dillon was a short, compact, red-bearded fellow, dressed in a dark suit and lime-green vest threaded with a shiny brass chain.

"Most of the pain is already gone," he announced. "When Mr. Schlatter first took my hand I could not close my fingers. Within a minute my grasp was as strong as his. Before seeing him I could barely move a joint. Now all my joints are flexible."

"How do you think he is able to do this?"

Dillon's face grew solemn. "I am not a particularly religious man. I attend church with my family. I pray as often as I can. I have seen several doctors about this matter, but they haven't been able to help me. And now, today, this man cures me with the power of his touch. It has to be a miracle. It has to come from God. Schlatter is obviously a conduit between this world and the next. He is gifted in a manner that cannot be adequately explained."

***

On that first long day of healing in Denver, in addition to those waiting in line to be treated, people on foot, on horseback, in carriages, walking or riding along Witter Street stopped to watch the healer. These were not the lame, the halt, or the infirm; their health was robust. They came alone, worshipfully, or in small groups. They were curious. They were lured to this spot by what they had heard about the healer. They watched for a while, some for several hours, amazed by the spectacle, transfixed. The people in the streets saw a line of well-behaved worshippers quietly making their way along a wooden chute toward a man with long, curly-brown hair who leaned against the fence and, with one hand or both hands, reached out to grasp the hands of the patients who paused in front of him. The crowd was respectful and subdued. A faint hubbub rose from the swollen ranks: the snort of thirsty horses, the squall of fussy children, peals of high-pitched adolescent laughter. Women, especially those closest to the healer, let go now and then with long, wailing cries. A big dog with sleek black hair belonging to Ed Fox, confused by all the fuss, the hordes milling about, barked incessantly in the backyard until Mary Fox dragged it into the house.

By midday, the wicker basket next to the fence was heaped high with bandanas and handkerchiefs and silk scarves. Several times that first day the postman knocked on the front door of the Fox house to deliver stacks of letters postmarked "The Healer, Denver" from people all over the country.

The long day finally came to a close around four thirty that afternoon when a weary Francis Schlatter, without a word or a signal, turned on his heel and shuffled through the dry, uncut yellow grass of the backyard and disappeared inside the Fox abode. Mary had prepared a warm supper for him, which he sat down to hungrily, scraping his plate clean. He thanked her and carried his dish and glass to the sink before she could remove them. *The Rocky Mountain News* reporter had been invited to speak with him, and as soon as Francis finished his meal, the two fell into conversation.

"It's day and night work," Francis declared. "The mail this morning amounted to 65 letters, and the afternoon delivery has not yet arrived. I try to answer every letter. The Father gives me strength."

With Francis gone from his post and no one to police the place, people crawled over the fence and crowded into the backyard. Like spectators at a freak show, they pressed their faces against the windows of the modest house for a glimpse of the healer, until Ed Fox stamped outside and told the trespassers in a firm voice to back off or he would call the police. The crowd finally melted away into the shadows of the sycamores and linden trees shading the backyard.

Francis and the reporter were sitting at the kitchen table when another wicker basket piled with handkerchiefs was brought inside. Francis dipped in, picking up several at a time, and began kneading and squeezing them with his long fingers.

The reporter took out his pencil and notebook. "Do you notice any difference between the ailments of the people who seek your help," he asked.

"Not really. I could, of course, but I don't have time to trouble myself about that. It all boils down to this: the greater the faith, the quicker they get well. Some have more disease, some have less. The disease didn't come in a day, and it can't be healed in a day."

"Despite the long day today, outside, attending to all those people, you seem so cheerful. How is that?"

"I am always happy. I'm just as happy in a jail as I would be in a palace. I have no need of money. It only causes trouble. When the father wants me to have anything, I get it. I do His Will."

He paused, as if searching deep inside himself for what he wanted to say.

"It's all healing now. I have no use for creeds or castes or religious beliefs; such matters do not figure with me. I minister to all alike. My mission is to cure the afflicted when the Father directs me. I never preach. I never have. I never try to convert anybody to anything. I am here to relieve them of their ailments. I am here to make them feel better."

"What is it exactly that you say when you pray over people?"

"I say the Lord's Prayer. It is enough. You may say whatever you like, but the Lord's Prayer is enough for me." (*The Rocky Mountain News*, September 17, 1895).

***

The second day of Francis's healing stint in Denver dawned hot and dry. He emerged from the Fox house dressed in a long-sleeved shirt, baggy trousers belted at the waist with a leather strap, and heavy black shoes laced with rawhide strings. Although the day promised to be blistering, he wore no hat; by midmorning the sun was ferocious. Several people in the crowd fainted before noon; a beefy wholesale beer distributor was coaxed back to consciousness by the healer himself, who left his post behind the fence to go to the stricken man and chaff his wrists and the backs of his hands. Rumor buzzed through the ranks that the man had faked his swoon to receive priority treatment from the healer. Within the hour several others were afflicted with fainting spells, but Francis stayed behind the fence, attending to those who remained in line.

As the day progressed and the sun grew more sweltering, the crowd became more demonstrative; there was some pushing and shoving, but for the most part people were well behaved. "Right this way to the healer's house," a trio of young, flirtatious women barked from the front porch of a house three doors down from the Fox domicile. Every few minutes the Highlands tramcar stopped at the corner, letting off a fresh load of people.

On the whole, the crowd was hushed and reverent. There was little levity or high jinks—the carnival energy stayed in the street. Closer to the spot where the healer presided, the mood was serious and grim. People shuffled up the boardwalk at the solemn pace of pallbearers. Women curtsied. Men and boys doffed their hats as if they were about to receive the sacrament. Upon being touched by Francis, many women wept openly. The simplicity and earnestness of his manner were profoundly affecting.

That second day *The Rocky Mountain News* reporter estimated that an ordinary encounter with the healer lasted little more than ten seconds. A shudder like a seismic wave rippled through Francis's features as he took the hand of each new patient and rolled his eyes skyward. The reporter thought the amount of energy he expended on each person had to be exhausting. People who had questions about the procedure or what they were required to do as they came into his presence were usually referred to Ed Fox or one of the assistants who stood at the healer's right side. Sometimes Francis answered a question; he always tried to answer any question reporters put to him, even while he was treating someone.

At one point *The Rocky Mountain News* reporter asked him about faith, and was it a criteron for being healed, and how he could ask it of children who had no idea what it meant.

Francis replied, "Little children are all faith. It might be unconscious, but it was absolute. It is only as they grow older and learn the ways of the world that they lose it."

"Do you ever read the Bible?"

"When I get the chance."

"Then it's not necessary?"

"Oh yes, certainly, but if one can't find the time, what do you do? I always try and read a little on Sunday morning. I try and make time for that. But when I stand outside all day helping people, then write letters at night, I am left with little or no time to read the Bible."

In the September 18 edition of *The Rocky Mountain News*, Francis was described as having finished his second day of work "in a sunny temper and seemed not to be fatigued in the least."

***

The people had taken to him enthusiastically, but what about local church and medical authorities?

An article entitled "Miracle Claims Derided" (*The Rocky Mountain News*, September 24, 1895) described a meeting of regional Methodist ministers in the study of the local Trinity Church at which no business was transacted; instead, the entire time was devoted to a discussion of the validity of the healer's activities.

It was carefully noted at the top of the article that none of the ministers present at the meeting had observed the healer in action. The general consensus was that there was no conclusive proof that any cure had been "properly effected" by the healer.

A lengthy discussion ensued regarding the history of "miracles" in the early founding of the Christian church. All the learned men in attendance that night agreed that God had worked by means of miracles to establish His Church at the moment of its inception in a hostile world. But the day of miracles was over, and with the supreme miracle of regeneration (Christ's resurrection), the need for any further deeds of a supernatural nature had ended. Put simply, miracles were no longer performed because they were no longer needed to help advance the church. The church was now in a position "to do its own talking," and as a consequence such miracles were "useless."

The elders unanimously pronounced Francis Schlatter a "lunatic" and a "quack," capable of doing great harm. What was the point of people coming for miles to see him, spending their money, and exposing themselves to the hot sun, especially once they woke up to the fact that his so-called cures did more harm than good?

The ministers argued that, unlike Christ, Francis Schlatter did not heal instantaneously—a dismissive reference to the fact that Francis frequently told patients they would be feeling better by such and such a time; in fact, his methods, said the ministers, were directly opposed to those of Jesus Christ. In a fine bit of hairsplitting, they declared that because Francis did not heal by his own powers but rather by the power transmitted through him by the Almighty, he must be a fraud; if he were really blessed with divine power, his cures would take effect immediately, just as Jesus's had.

***

A well-known Denver physician, an expert on diseases of the brain—who asked to remain anonymous—declared in conversation with *The Rocky Mountain News* reporter that appeared in the paper on September 24, that a "mental impression" was responsible for the majority of Francis's cures:

> A mental impression is the same thing as the faith cure and the faith cure is hypnotism. It is the influence of the mind over the body. For example,

a man suffering from a toothache feels frightened. Instantly, his pain is gone and remains away until the excitement of the fright goes away and the pain returns.

A boxer getting smashed in the face doesn't really feel the pain until after the bout is over and he has won or lost. Until that point, his body is consumed by hypnotic feelings that crowd out all other emotions.

Organic disease cannot be cured by hypnotism, but the symptoms can. Half the success of ordinary physicians is due to the mental impression their patients form of them. Schlatter does not know that he possesses hypnotic powers, and as a result he believes it comes from above. In his own unconscious way, he does good.

***

An anonymous article in a local publication entitled *The Road* (December 7, 1895) offered an explanation of the physical process by which healers like Francis were thought to perform their miracles:

> Now as every atom in our body has a vibration of its own, and each and every organ a vibration of its own and then all are vibrating in harmony, the result must be perfect health. But let the vibrations of some of the organs get out of harmony with the rest of the body, then pain is felt and disease is the result.
>
> Now let an old soul, which has had many embodiments, has had all the power and glory to be had from earthly possessions, and whose atomic vibrations are away up in the millions per second—a soul like Schlatter, for instance, who has no earthly

desire but to tell and act the truth—let him place his hands upon the sick person and if the atomic vibrations between them concur exactly there will be a case of instant cure, because harmony will have been restored to the diseased organ by the harmonious vibrations of the corresponding organ in the healer.

***

Not all impressions of Francis among the religious and medical elite were unfavorable. At the end of the first week of his Denver tenure, correspondents from local newspapers fanned out around the city to solicit as wide a spectrum of opinions as they could gather. The results were surprisingly favorable—an indication, perhaps, of the city of Denver's vaunted liberality and openness to paranormal matters.

★ The Reverend Thomas Uzzell, head of the Denver City Mission, declared that Francis Schlatter "possesses as much power as the apostles of old" (*Colorado Springs Weekly Gazette*, September 19, 1895).

★ The Honorable James B. Belford weighed in on the matter of Schlatter's authenticity in the September 29 issue of *The Rocky Mountain News:* "I believe we have in our midst today a man whose credentials are as good as those possessed by Jesus of Nazareth. . . . Another thing in his favor is that he holds himself above the reach of all monetary influences. In addition, he recognizes no distinction of race, color, or condition."

★ In *The Rocky Mountain News,* October 7, 1895, the Reverend Edward Southworth observed: "His presence in the city has already proved a benediction to public audiences. I never saw so many people together in the street keep so good order. He inspires a quiet reverence."

★ On the negative side, Baptist minister Robert D. Graham denounced Francis as a "blatant infidel" for suggesting that his powers came from supernatural sources (*The Rocky Mountain News,* November 12, 1895).

★ The Reverend G. L. Morrill, in a speech at Calvary Baptist Church, praised the healer in broad strokes while complaining that "Christ's earthly ministry was characterized by the two agencies of preaching and miracles. . . . [His] healing power was available to all who were helpless, humble and trustful. It was instant and did not ask a man to wear a handkerchief fourteen hours a day for four months before his sore throat would leave him, and was rational in that it did not ask the patient to stultify his reason by pretending that his blindness was a mere mental state with no basis in fact. Modern healers have had many ancestors and will have many successors—but the Divine Healer [Jesus] stands alone." (*The Rocky Mountain News,* September 23, 1895).

***

The Reverend Myron W. Reed commanded a loyal following among Denver's rank and file. Although he had never met Reed, Francis knew of him and admired his life and work. "I have read Mr. Reed's sermons for years," he declared, "and I have been in sympathy with him. If the world had more men like Mr. Reed in it, the world would be a better place."

Reed was born in Vermont in 1836. He was a schoolteacher, a lawyer, and an officer in the Union Army before becoming a minister in 1866. He lived in Indiana before coming to Denver in 1884 to head the First Congregational Church, where he became a dynamic spokesman for the Social Gospel Movement, which stressed that organized religion had an obligation to combat economic injustice. "The more helpless anything is, the more rights it has," Reed was fond of saying.

Reed championed many causes: women's suffrage, the eight-hour work day, a better deal for Native Americans. "Whatever the Indian of today is we made him," he said, "and he wears our shoddy blanket and eats our government steer. We have raised Americans to kill him while he is loading his pony to go. It is a shameful, dastardly thing."

In defense of homeless vagrants, Reed said: "The tramp is a product of our kind of civilization. He is a warning to us that our social system has failed."

As to what Denver should do about the problem of a few rich people thriving in the midst of a mass of poverty, Reed's answer was, "Why not try socialism here in Denver?"

***

Francis spent his Sunday evenings in Denver attending services at various churches. One evening, accompanied by a contingent of enthusiasts who invariably followed him wherever he went, Francis—escorted by Mr. and Mrs. Fox and a friend named Clarence Clark—entered the Broadway Theatre downtown to hear Reverend Reed. A *Rocky Mountain News* reporter went with them. "I used to be interested in politics," Francis told the reporter, "but no more. I was a populist back then, red hot. I know now that the evils of the world cannot be cured by politics, and I am out of politics entirely."

Francis was entranced by Reed's oratorical gifts. Reed was blessed with a smooth, fluid baritone that lapped into the deepest corners of the capacious Broadway Theatre. Afterward, backstage, Francis waited for the opportunity to meet him. The two men approached one another hesitantly. Ed Fox made the introduction. Reed later confessed to feeling a kind of "battery sensation" when the healer shook his hand, an "electric impulse" that ran up his arm to his shoulder and across his chest. He was deeply impressed by the simplicity and dignity of Francis's presence.

"[People] must understand," Reed said to the adoring crowd that gathered to watch the two heroes shake hands, "that money, power or rank are not the chief end of man; that he [Schlatter] is in the world simply to be good and to do good."

Reed called attention to the scriptural authority for Francis's use of handkerchiefs in his healing, citing the nineteenth chapter of Acts, verses 11 and 12:

"And God wrought special miracles by the hands of Paul, so that from his body were brought unto the sick handkerchiefs or aprons, and the diseases departed from them, and the evil spirits went out of them."

"This is the only time that the term 'handkerchief' is mentioned in the Bible," Reed added.

Reed, a handsome man with a leonine head of wavy white hair, a formidable mustache thatching his upper lip, was effusive in his praise for Francis. "When I see him," he said, nodding at the stolid, self-effacing cobbler standing next to him, "I seem to see a vision of the actual Christ, receiving the multitude by the Sea of Galilee."

Francis, hands folded, head down, basked in the glow of these flattering remarks.

Reed went on to declare unabashedly that he was impressed with Francis Schlatter for several reasons, but especially because of the manner in which he defined the term "self-sacrifice." "I believe, if I can quote this correctly, that he said something to the effect that 'self-sacrifice is an act for which you want nothing and for which you don't necessarily get anything in return.'"

Reed broke out in a wide smile and raised his hands toward the ceiling. "The man is a genius," he declared. "I'm still trying to figure out that one."(*The Rocky Mountain News*, September 23, 1895).

***

A well-known story of Francis's gift of "second sight" was related by a *Denver Post* junior reporter named Joseph Emerson Smith. Smith was only fifteen when he was assigned to cover Francis during his stay in Denver. In a five-part retrospective series published in 1941 by *The Denver Catholic Register*, Smith reminisced about those heady days in the fall of 1895, and what he had witnessed. Perhaps more than any other reporter from any publication, he was able to observe Francis nearly every day from September 17, when he first started healing, until his mysterious disappearance from the Denver area two months later.

"And let me say here," Smith declared in the first of the interviews that appeared in *The Register* on August 21, 1941—nearly fifty years after his encounter with the healer—"not a newspaperman who arrived cynically bent to scoff at credulity and 'mob hysteria' wrote anything but respectfully, with a touch of wonder, of the strange happenings that were played up on the first pages of the press from the Atlantic to the Pacific."

One of the "strange happenings" Smith witnessed was a disfiguring tumor under the right eye of a Mrs. M.C. Holmes from Havelock, Nebraska, that dwindled to practically nothing in a matter of minutes shortly after she had been treated by the healer. Another was watching a man named J. P. Handy from Ellsworth, Kansas—crippled with rheumatism, his joints and extremeties crimped with pain—put down his crutches and walk off with his wife after being attended to by Schlatter.

But most uncanny of all, and one of the most oft-repeated stories in the Schlatter canon, was his encounter with a mysterious man with a secret, unsavory past.

"I shall never forget the morning when we saw something that made us ask whether he were a mind reader," Smith recounted to *The Denver Catholic Register* in 1941. "A well-built man in good clothes came in his turn before Schlatter, who put out his hands as customary, but quickly, as though they had been in contact with flame, drew them back.

"'I cannot treat you,' he said in a low voice, and with a motion of his head directed the man to pass on.

"'Why?'

"'Shall I tell you?'

"'Sure. What's the matter with me that you can't give me relief where I need it?'

"This tone was so sharp we plainly heard it over the rustling of the [people in] the line and the calling of their wares by the hawkers of refreshment.

"The healer looked him directly in the eyes.

"'Do you want me to tell you right here, before all these people?'

"Yes, and you're off your nut, old fellow, if you say you know anything about me. You've never seen me before.'

"Schlatter, never relaxing that probing stare, was silent.

"'Well, come on! What's eating you?'"

"The voice was not only impudent, but truculent. Charles E. Clark, Union Pacific engineer from Salt Lake City, was third behind the fellow and, as he told us afterwards, was about ready to yank him out of line, when the healer replied: 'I cannot treat you. Go! You are a murderer.'

"Those who heard shrank back. The man's head dropped. A tremor shook him and the muscles in his cheek twitched and quivered. He turned, with a quick, mincing step reached the corner of the street, where he vanished from sight. The line moved up before the patient figure with golden [sic] hair, curling over his shoulders and reflecting the sunshine like an aura, with hands extended in tender pity while his bearded lips moved in prayer."

***

Francis was quick to deny that the phenomenon known as "electrical psychology" had anything to do with his ability to heal. "Magnetic healing," as it was also known, was popularized in the 1840s by a Universalist minister from Boston named John Bovee Dods, who referred to the practice as "the highest and most sublime science in the whole realm of nature."

Dods believed electricity was the connecting link between mind and matter; proper utilization of that link was the key to restoring the physical body to health. A fluid known as "nervo-vital blood" circulates through the human system, Dods believed; the flush and vigor of this fluid is one of the primary ingredients of good health. Any imbalance or dissolution of the fluid can bring on a bout of sickness.

Said Dods: "There is but one grand cause of disease, which is the electricity of the system thrown out of balance."

The causes of this anomaly were not important, as the effect was invariably the same. Dods treated the patient by taking his hand and pressing on the nerves. "Close your eyes," he said, and while the eyes were closed he brushed the lids with his fingertips. Thus properly mesmerized, the patient was ready to have his or her nervo-vital fluid reserves restored.

"Now let a person whose brain is fully charged with nervo-vital fluid come in contact with one whose brain is greatly wanting in its due measure of this fluid," Dods declared, "and let the person possessing the full brain gently and unchangeably hold his mind upon the other, and by the action of the WILL, the fluid will pass from the full brain to the other, until the equilibrium between the fluids in the two brains is attained." (*Nature Cures: The History of Alternative Medicine in America,* 114).

***

By mid-October the weather had cooled down pleasantly. Some of the curiosity about Francis had worn off; fewer gawkers stood around, arguing as to whether he was the real thing. People appeared to have adjusted to his presence.

Every day of the week, Sundays excepted, Francis took his place at the head of the gangway. The length of the daily line remained about the same, reaching out into the street and down the block. Several concessionaires set up a half-dozen tents in the street and dispensed coffee, doughnuts, soup, sandwiches, popcorn, lemonade, ice cream, candied apples, and other refreshments.

Denver Post reporter Joseph Emerson Smith expanded upon the scene in the August 7, 1941, issue of *The Denver Catholic Register*:

Enterprising hawkers concocted in large whiskey barrels mixtures of water, lemons, and sugar, in which blocks of ice floated tantilizingly, sparkling in the sun, to satisfy the thirst of the thousands standing in the street. Bare-legged urchins passing up and down the line, dipping with tin cups out of the large tin buckets the cooling lemonade, did a rushing business. . . .

A two-wheeled popcorn and peanut stand, its whistle merrily blowing, was wheeled up almost directly opposite . . . the crowd, and boys with baskets filled with gay colored paper-wrapped balls followed the lemon vendors. Toward noon a delivery wagon, loaded with hundreds of box-lunches consisting of different kinds of sandwiches, an apple and an orange, or a piece of pie, drew up and proceeded to sell out in quick order.

People waiting their turn to see the healer brought stools, chairs, and benches to sit on, leaving them afterward for others to use. A warped and wobbly settee turned up one morning at the edge of the street, crowded with old people who clung to it like rats to the spar of a sinking ship. People seriously in need of seeing Schlatter arrived around two or three in the morning, wrapped in blankets and warm overcoats. Fires, fueled by dead twigs and dry leaves, tended by teenage boys, popped and crackled in the streets. The authorities worried about the fires getting out of hand. They worried about thieves taking advantage of the people who wandered about after nightfall. They worried about shysters working the crowds with false information regarding the health and welfare of the healer. At least one tent remained open all night where people could get a cup of coffee, a sandwich, and a bowl of soup. Uniformed police patrolled Witter Street in pairs, flipping their billies. A Black Mariah pulled by a pair of dappled horses stood parked against the curb across from Fox's house, ready to haul troublemakers downtown if necessary.

***

During the morning hours until noon, when he broke for lunch, Francis attended to people in the line. From one to four in the afternoon he often left his post to go into the street and treat those in carriages who were too sick to be brought to the fence. Occasionally, he recognized an acquaintance from his early Denver days. He smiled and nodded and shook hands. At moments like these he looked like a ward politician, canvassing the crowd, getting out the vote. It was a way of working the line, reducing the volume, being friendly at the same time he indulged in a little extracurricular healing. He didn't say much. His hands did all the talking. Some people stepped back as he approached; others held their ground and shut their eyes as if fearful of being bowled over by a big wind. A stir rose from the ranks, a shiver of anticipation, a collective intake of breath. People called out his name—"Francis! Francis!"— in supplicating voices.

When the weather turned cool, he took to appearing at nine in the morning like clockwork wearing a corduroy suit, the trousers a darker shade than the coat, the coat a dull tawny color, cut in a double-breasted style and buttoned at the throat.

***

On October 28 an anonymous letter from a Denver man appeared in *The Rocky Mountain News:*

> That Mr. Schlatter has caused a great commotion throughout the civilized world is not surprising.
>
> In this day of rapacity and greed the advent of one soul who has lost himself in the Christ-like desire to do good is sufficient to cause vibrations that will envelop the globe. That hundreds have been healed by him and thousands greatly benefited is known to be true. But the greatest good he has accomplished is that he has started people to

thinking. He has awakened more thought upon the right subject than all the sermons ever preached within the corporate limits of the city of Denver.

***

The Rocky Mountain News reported on October 30 that the police had arrested three men for selling handkerchiefs allegedly blessed by the healer for a dollar apiece. Not only in Denver but in other major cities, the men had sold "schlatterized" handkerchiefs through the U.S. mail. Many of the handkerchiefs contained a likeness of him on one side. The gang members were apprehended in their shop on 15th Street and put in jail. Francis was told to show up at a hearing in federal court as a witness.

A curious crowd assembled at the downtown courthouse in hopes of seeing Francis, but he failed to appear. He told Ed Fox that appearing in court would detract from his healing, so Fox pleaded his absence in a letter to the judge, who granted Francis a delay until November 14.

***

Francis affected people differently. Those standing in line waiting to see him uttered good comments and bad. One day a woman of mature years with a curvaceous figure in a high-waisted dress said Schlatter had a "perfectly divine look." Another woman with a pinched, dyspeptic face said he looked "cheap and nasty." A medical student at Denver University remarked that his liver looked as if it were out of order: "His digestion doesn't look good. He's getting fat." (*The Colorado Sun*, October 29, 1895).

This last was apparent to everyone. Three weeks without much exercise and eating heartily of Mary Fox's good cooking had fattened him up, not just around the waist but in the flesh under his chin and the thickness of his chest and shoulders.

Francis overheard these remarks, whether they were delivered in a whisper or in a regular voice. His uncanny ability to read what people were saying, not just their lips as they said it but their minds as they were thinking it, was part of the paranormal dimension of his consciousness.

***

As the days slipped by, the reporters became more curious about Francis's cures, whether they were real, how long they might last.

"It would require a week of persistent inquiry to locate and question a person or persons who had been successfully treated by Mr. Schlatter," a reporter wrote in *The Rocky Mountain News* (October 30, 1895), "especially in cases where the cure was sufficiently demonstrated to stand the test of a careful examination."

"The most difficult task," the reporter continued, "is to verify cases of reported cures. Whenever a person alleged to have been cured is located and a statement obtained of his condition before and after treatment, something always seems to be missing. And that something usually deals with a time factor. Yes, the patient feels better, but he or she has been instructed to come back for another treatment before a cure can be properly effected. Or, he or she won't really feel the positive effects of the treatment for several hours or several days or even several weeks; meanwhile, the person in question slips away into the streets, never to be seen again."

How to keep track of all this, the reporter wondered. To verify anything, each patient had to be properly identified and followed wherever he or she went. But how could this be done when the healer had contact with as many as 2,000 people a day?

A number of physicians testified that patients treated by the healer with some success rarely went back to their regular doctors. However, after several weeks, if the healer's cures began to wear off, the patients did return to their doctors.

"There's an army of invalids in every community who never get well," one reporter declared (*The Rocky Mountain News*, November 8, 1895). "If they should meet with such a contingency, their avocation would be lost. Such people have so little in life. Their time must be filled in some way, and a sick habit fills it, and appears to have a wonderful fascination for them after it has been established."

***

Francis's relationship with the press was fairly good. He read The Denver Post and The Rocky Mountain News every day, and if he saw something he didn't like, he complained to the reporter. For all his vaunted indifference to things of this world, he took exception to what he perceived as misrepresentations of his character in the daily news. One day in late October a correspondent for *The Denver Post* wrote that Francis knew how to play the crowd, especially the ladies, flattering them with "calculating" looks that practically "made them swoon." Francis took exception to this. He told Ed Fox not to let the correspondent stand among the small, select group of "insiders" in the yard behind the fence.

***

Francis's vanity was continually kindled by the constant adulation heaped upon him. Not even the chaste cobbler, who had subjected himself to terrible deprivation during his periods of withdrawal, could withstand the blandishments of the adoring women who made up more than half his audience.

One day a slim, attractive, well-coiffed, middle-aged lady, standing in line on the boardwalk, passed up several handkerchiefs for Francis to bless. She was four or five places back in the line; the hour was drawing close to four-thirty, Francis's quitting time, which he always promptly observed. He glanced at the house, where Mary Fox stood on the back porch stirring something in a bowl. All day Ed Fox and

Clarence Clark and several others had maintained their positions to Francis's right, answering questions from querulous patients, calming them, getting them emotionally ready for their encounter with the healer.

"Do you think I'll be treated today," the comely woman wondered. "I know he ceases his activities promptly at four-thirty. I have come eighteen-hundred miles and been here for two full days already without having seen Mr. Schlatter. Won't you intercede for me?"

"I'm sorry," Ed Fox said with a frosty smile. "I don't think I can help you."

"Oh, please ask him to stay a little while longer, won't you?"

Fox stepped close to Francis and whispered in his ear. The woman looked at the healer provocatively. Francis pulled a gold-lidded timepiece from his corduroy coat. The line continued to inch forward. The closer the woman drew to Francis, the more eager and expectant she became. As she stood next in line to be treated, she slipped off a gray suede glove and flexed her bare fingers. Finished with the man in front of her, Francis leaned over the fence and took her hand in his and without really looking at her began moving his lips in prayer. A shudder passed over his smooth white face. The sight and feel of his calloused fingers entwined with her pale, smooth ones sent a visible jolt through the woman's ample bust, up her neck, to the nib of her quivering chin. Her eyes rolled skyward; she appeared on the verge of fainting. Francis caught her slim wrist with his other hand and steadied her. With a determined effort she recovered, and, flashing a radiant smile, she stepped past him.

A reporter who witnessed the whole thing from his post directly behind the healer caught up with the woman as she made her way dazedly out to the street.

"Madame, a thousand pardons," he gushed. "I'm from *The Colorado Sun*. Could I ask you a few questions?"

The expression in the woman's eyes was bleary and unfocused. She covered her mouth demurely with her hand.

"Is it true that you came a long distance to see the healer?"

"Yes. I came all the way from Grand Rapids, Michigan."

"And you heard of him way back there, did you?"

"Oh, everyone knows of him there."

"But how did you learn of him? Was it through the papers?"

"Why through the Denver papers, of course," she replied. "My son lives in Denver, and he sent me the papers. My husband is deceased, and I live alone. I came out all this way by train and coach on my own. I'm grateful I didn't have to wait long. My legs are so weak I can hardly stand." (October 29, 1895).

***

People hung around the Fox house day and night. The police were lenient and let them stay as long as they weren't disorderly. Many were teenage boys, high school misfits, kids in off the farm or from the back alleys downtown, with no money to spend. Their kick was to stand in line as long as it took for Francis to grasp their hands and mutter a prayer. They liked the shock that ran through their bodies like a bolt of electricity.

The boys picked up litter at the end of the day left by people queued up to see Schlatter and tossed it into the fires they built at night out of limbs and twigs and scrap wood. So far, they hadn't touched Ed Fox's plank fence or the boardwalk or the picket fences that enclosed the property of other houses in the neighborhood.

A few of the boys worked in the commissary tents that stayed open all night, serving coffee and soup. Others just loafed about, afraid they might miss something, keeping a keen watch on the house and any movement inside. Several reporters relied on them to sound the alarm if the healer decided to do something different, like go to church on Sunday or walk downtown to a restaurant to eat a couple of dozen oysters, washed down with a stein of beer.

The youngsters' ingenuity was remarkable. An article in the November 8 issue of *The Rocky Mountain News* told how an enterprising lad had announced to a long line of waiting people that for a nickel apiece he would furnish them with hot bricks to warm their fingers and toes or to shove under their coats to heat their chests. Where he obtained the bricks was a mystery. The day was cold, and he sold every one.

***

On cold days Francis wore a black, rubberized hunter's coat, lined with sheep's wool, that fell to his knees. Gloves were out of the question. Even on rainy or sleety days he went hatless.

He never caught cold. His nose never ran. His throat never got sore.

"He is probably the ruggedest man I have ever known," Ed Fox said.

***

For a period of about a week in early November, Francis was photographed by a man from Raton, New Mexico, named W. A. White. White went back and forth on either side of the fence, his head and shoulders draped with a dark cloth, capturing images from every angle with a clumsy 8" x 10" camera equipped with a tripod and glass plates. The flash from the powder in the dry pan lit the healer's face with a quick green glow. White's assistants developed the plates in an improvised lab in a rented office in downtown Denver. The photos were then reproduced and printed on slips of paper and hawked by boys through the streets for a dime apiece.

***

One morning, as Francis stood at his post next to the boardwalk, a scabrous-looking woman with a beaked nose and droopy ears, blurted out in a shrill voice, "Can I wash the handkerchief without endangering its healing power?"

Francis stared at her, appalled by her rudeness.

When the woman repeated the question, Francis looked irritated. "No, it won't hurt it," he gruffly replied.

The next day, in *The Colorado Sun*, this item appeared: "It is difficult to give in printed character the broken words of this uneducated man. One might call it a German accent, but it is not a distinct German accent. Schlatter mingles a smattering of slang phrases, western expressions, eastern idioms, gutteral ejaculations, French glissades, with a pronunciation that defies all attempts at imitation." (October 29, 1895).

***

The October 31 issue of the national magazine *Leslie's Weekly* featured an article by John C. Martin entitled "The Western Messiah." In it, Martin quoted Francis as saying for the first time that "his stay in Denver is limited by the Father to the 16th of November, when he will be called to the East."

The Rocky Mountain News reporter questioned Francis about this.

"So where do you think you will go?"

"Chicago."

"Why there?"

Somewhat vexed, Francis replied, "Why Denver? Why Albuquerque? Why anywhere? Because the Father wants me to."

***

Francis received an estimated 1,000 letters a day from all over the country, as well as from Mexico and Canada.

"He stays up until one or two every night answering letters," Fox said to a *Rocky Mountain News* reporter. "It's exhausting work."

Fox and Francis sat at the kitchen table. Mrs. Fox had just served Francis toast, flavored with butter and jam. Fox didn't eat anything; neither did the reporter. "The man has superhuman energy," Fox declared. "He shows no sign of fatigue."

"I have a strong grip," Francis said, flexing his fingers "If I bear down I can make the strongest man cry out. That's why when I take a woman's hand, I take it by the tips of her fingers and shake it gently."

Mary Fox gave him a long, searching look. The man was a marvel. Strong, steady, solid . . . so wrapped up in himself he did not appear to be of this world. When he spoke, his voice seemed to come from a place deep in the woods or high on a hill.

***

Sitting outside in the backyard on a mild evening was virtually impossible for the Fox family and their distinguished guest. Invariably, their privacy would be interrupted by some tortured soul who crept toward them hat in hand, full of apologies, begging Francis in a plaintive voice to absolve him of his ills. Every evening, if they wanted to talk, the family, including Clarence Clark—a slim, studious, middle-aged man with a slight stoop—had to sequester themselves in the cottage. The yards and streets of that portion of the neighborhood were crowded with people day and night, standing around, talking, gossiping. Others lay in the street or along the curb, folded in blankets and heavy coats. Still others huddled around fires, smoking cheap cigars. A drop or two of whiskey was known to have been consumed, but there was no rowdiness; everybody remained on their best behavior. Anything any individual might do to displease or embarrass the healer was regarded as a serious offense. Francis seemed to have a soothing effect on everybody. All ranks of society, from the swells to the hoi polloi, took comfort in the fact that he had chosen Denver as the place to give vent to his miraculous powers.

***

During the final week of Francis's tenure, the newspapermen

hung around the house until ten or eleven, when they finally said goodnight. They rode their bicycles to their downtown offices, where they wrote the stories that appeared the next morning in their respective papers. The reporters attracted the attention of the kids in the street, who sidled up to them: "Hey mister, is he really leaving town next week? You seem to have his ear; is there anything you can say or do to keep him in Denver?"

"I'm afraid not. I'm sorry."

Now and then the reporters were jostled and grabbed at by less respectful people, usually older men and women who felt they were owed something for the many long hours and days they had spent in the healer's presence. The street boys, tough little guys barely in their teens, took notice and offered their services: "Hey, Mr. Paperman, those folks crowding you too close? We can give you a little protection. Try us sometime."

***

Friday, November 8, 1895. After supper Francis sat at the kitchen table for a long time, listening to the concerns and complaints of Clarence Clark and Ed and Mary Fox.

Francis had just returned from treating a wealthy invalid in the Capitol Hill district. At the mention of the great crowds expected the final week, his eyes flashed and he clenched his fists.

"I can only wonder, Francis, what would happen if the power went bad and you decided to hurt people instead of help them," Clarence said.

"I have thought of that, too," Francis replied. "But no worry. It will never go bad. The Father won't let it."

"He's right," said Fox. "Watch him sometime when he's treating a baby. They are so gentled by his touch they fall alseep when he holds them."

Mary Fox sat hemming a skirt. A smile creased her attractive face. How much influence did she exert over Francis? Was she the brains behind the group that planned to take the healer to Chicago and beyond? She read the Bible regularly, but so did a lot of people. She seemed eager to touch Francis whenever she could, but that wasn't unusual—everyone who saw him wanted to touch him.

***

On November 9 came the official announcement. An article in *The Denver Post* revealed that Francis Schlatter planned to stop healing in the Colorado capital on Friday the 15th at four o'clock in the afternoon.

That same day the *Post* offered its readers a picture taken by W. A. White of Francis in the act of healing. The demand quickly exceeded the supply. Ten thousand additional copies were printed and distributed within the hour. Another 10,000 copies were made available at the *Post*'s business office at 1019 Sixteenth Street. Hawkers then took them into the streets. By nightfall the healer's face was literally plastered all over downtown Denver—on brick and wood-frame walls, around telephone and telegraph poles, pinned to jackets and coats, pasted to bicycle frames and the sides of streetcars, blown between dusty buildings by the brisk wind that swirled through the streets.

***

Saturday, November 9, 1895—from *The Denver Post*: "'This man Schlatter has done more for the merchants of Denver than any one man I can remember,' said the day clerk, Mr. Ilus P. Covington, at the Oxford Hotel. 'Twenty-seven people arrived at the hotel last nite to be accommodated, and all day long I have been sending packages of merchandise to their rooms that they have incidentally purchased during their visit. The bell boy is happy, the elevator guard is delighted, and I am exultant. Every day for the past week has been exactly like to-day. If Schlatter does no religious or medical good for his visitors, he certainly is a mercantile success.'"

***

Knowing his time in Denver was limited, Francis tried to become more talkative. The morning hours were not good; he said little before noon, either to his patients or to the assistants who stood with him behind the fence. By early to mid-afternoon he began to warm up. He answered questions as he was treating people without sounding distracted or confused. To a query as to whether a quick treatment was as efficacious as a long one, he replied, "Oh, yes. All that is really necessary is for me to touch them. In cases where the people are too weak to stand in line, their friends should send in handkerchiefs. The handkerchief is just as good as a treatment."

Later, walking with *The Denver Post* correspondent, out of earshot of any patients left waiting in line, the correspondent asked, "Is it for positive that you intend to stop public healing in Denver next Friday?"

Francis slowed his pace. Mary Fox stood on the back porch waiting to greet him. Ed Fox and Clarence Clark maintained their posts at the fence trying to assuage the ruffled feelings of people who had stood in line for ten or twelve hours that day to see the healer, only to be left hanging at the last minute. These people would be issued tickets that would enable them to start at the head of the line first thing tomorrow morning.

"It's certain that I intend to stop next week," he said, staring deep into the reporter's eyes. "No more letters after that. I intend to concentrate primarily on handkerchiefs. Here . . . come and see what I have to do."

He smiled and nodded to Mary Fox and touched her on the wrist as he passed through the kitchen door. She blushed and lowered her eyes.

Francis led the reporter into a furnished bedroom off the kitchen. A huge pile of letters, numbering several thousand, was heaped on the bed in a messy pile.

"They pour in at a rate of hundreds and hundreds a day. If I

were to try and answer each one, there would be a year's work ahead of me. All I can hope to do is handle the handkerchiefs and return them by mail or leave them by the fence for the local people to pick up."

***

The following day Francis appeared ambiguous regarding the exact date of his departure. He whispered to *The Rocky Mountain News* reporter that he might linger in Denver for a week or two past the November 15 deadline.

"Who will help arrange his departure for him," the reporter asked Ed Fox during the lunch break. "Who makes the connections?"

"Oh, there are people," Fox replied cautiously.

"Who?"

Fox appeared reluctant to say anything. "Well . . . let's just say there's a whole network out there."

"Of?"

"People who believe in him."

"That he may be the new messiah?"

"No. Not that. Never that. But that he is the embodiment of Christ's healing power reincarnated in human form on this earth."

"That sounds pretty impressive."

"Indeed, it is. Francis is at the forefront of a groundswell of spiritual feeling that's sweeping the country," Fox said. "If he wants to, he can turn everything around all by himself."

***

One evening they sat around the kitchen table in the grainy light of a kerosene lamp that dangled from a hook in the low ceiling.

Chicago was Schlatter's next probable destination. In 1895 it boasted a population of nearly a million. New Thought spiritualists, including author Helen Wilmans, had made great inroads upon the citizenry, especially the educated middle class. The positive orientation of New Thought adherents, the belief that the right mental attitude could determine success or failure in life, was part of the city's prevailing ethos. According to Ed Fox, the groundwork for a triumphant visit by Francis was being carefully put into place. Granted, Chicago was a brawling, pork-packing, rough-and-tumble town, full of people hell-bent on squeezing money from the myriad opportunities that flourished there. At the same time, there was this other side—spiritual, evanescent, transcendental—that coalesced around a fervent yearning by ordinary people for religious fulfillment. Material success versus spiritual apotheosis—American culture seemed hopelessly riven by these conflicting impulses. Clarence Clark and Ed and Mary Fox believed wholeheartedly that Francis was one of the few people who possessed the power to heal the rift. Denver was a test to see how Francis could handle big crowds. If he succeeded here, he could move on to major venues: Chicago, New York, Philadelphia.

After reaching Chicago, Francis would remain in seclusion for several weeks before entering a new, rigorous, and challenging phase of his work. Ed Fox told the healer it appeared that their Chicago cohorts had rented a hall for him once he arrived. Francis scowled. "They make a mistake if they try and do that," he said. "I have not been consulted in the matter, and it is not at all probable that I will consent to go to any hall. I cannot say at this point where I shall stop in the city, or how long I will stay, or where I will go when I leave Chicago. The Father will decide."

***

His final week in Denver, the healer ate sparingly. At lunch, he consumed only a single piece of bread smeared with butter and a glass of wine. He cut down on his food intake in the evening. He seemed more focused. An aura of energy shimmered off his face and shoulders. Someone remarked that his eyes were like openings into a fathomless pool. Simply looking into their depths could trigger a wild and wailing outburst by those waiting in line. Francis did little to incite or encourage this response. He never flailed his arms or raised his voice or balled his fingers into a fist. All he had to do was stand there. His presence was like the buildup of summer lightning as it rumbled around a stationary cloud. The storm never burst. It didn't have to; the distant rumbling was more than enough.

"I am nothing," he whispered to the others that night as he excused himself to go to bed. "The Father is everything. Have faith in the Father, and all will be well."

***

One misty autumn morning Ed Fox brought his friend Harry Hauenstein, with whom he had traveled to New Mexico that summer, to see the healer. Harry arrived early on the arm of his teenage son. Fox steered him to the front of the line.

Francis emerged from the house at precisely nine a.m. Harry was third in line, behind a wizened couple from Emporia, Kansas, afflicted with a crippling palsy that made their hands quiver like aspen leaves. Harry's eyesight had not improved in the three months since Schlatter had last received him in Albuquerque. He waited patiently as Francis prayed over the couple, then listened tremblingly as their footsteps shuffled off the boardwalk. "We're next," his son whispered. Harry heard Ed Fox remind Francis that he had treated Harry earlier in New Mexico. "Yes," Harry heard Francis reply. "Mr. Hauenstein. I remember."

The healer fumbled for his hand. A buzzing sensation shivered up Harry's arm, through his shoulder. Francis passed two fingers in front of Harry's straining eyes. Harry thought he saw something, a pale white smudge that barely registered on the dull patina. "It's getting close," Francis murmured. His voice was raw, a worried whisper. "It's getting very close. Have faith. Be patient. Come see me again."

On the way home, clinging to the elbow of his teenage son—a beautiful young boy with thick tawny hair and shining green eyes—Harry's face grew hot with tears.

***

On November 10 the Union Pacific Railroad from Omaha brought 250 men, women, and children flooding into the Denver depot. Thirty minutes later a Fort Worth train disgorged 75 more.

People got off the Omaha train looking, said a reporter for *The Rocky Mountain News,* "like the wounded after a battle"—swathed in bandages, hobbling on crutches, rolling along in wheelchairs, blind people clinging to the sighted, epileptics stepping gingerly as if over a glass-strewn floor, paralyzed people dragging useless legs, useless arms clamped against their sides. Many were incapacitated, borne on litters or carried on shoulders like bags of grain; others could walk but were visibly afflicted with wens, tumors, and goiters that knuckled off their sickly flesh. They were husbands, wives, and children of Union Pacific employees, glad to be in Denver, glad to be off the train after a long, dusty, exhausting journey of 600 miles across the Great Plains.

"Omaha is worked up wonderfully over the cures reported by persons who have come to Denver to meet this Schlatter," said a railroad official from eastern Nebraska to a *Rocky Mountain News* correspondent as he exited the car that had transported him and his family. "I never saw such an excitement as is now in that city. Everybody is talking of the healer, and people who return after being treated talk for days before their enthusiasm is exhausted. We know that Schlatter can cure, for he has cured Superintendent [Edward] Sutherland and many other railroad men. After we see the healer, we have been directed to return to Omaha as soon as possible to make room so that others may come."

The man responsible for the flood of people from Omaha was Union Pacific regional superintendent Edward Sutherland, who three days earlier, in the Omaha press and by word of mouth, had issued a directive that any employee of the Union Pacific seeking medical attention for a malady could ride to Denver for treatment from the healer at the company's expense.

The news crackled around Omaha. Passes were issued as fast

as called for, without hesitation or bureaucratic obstruction. Petitioners included conductors, engineers, brakemen, shop men, clerks, and members of section gangs. The first contingent, consisting of nearly 150 people, left Omaha at seven p.m. on November 9 on the Pacific Express; another 100 "pilgrims" were scheduled to board the train in outlying towns such as Fremont, Columbus, Grand Island, Kearney, and Cheyenne.

Superintendent Sutherland showed up at the depot a half hour early to bid farewell to his employees and their family members who were undertaking the journey. A correspondent for *The Omaha World Herald* described the scene at the depot as "near bedlam as families with suitcases, trunks, valises, picnic baskets, blankets, and pillows boarded the cars to the cheers and well-wishes of scores of friends and kinfolk who followed them down to the depot to see them off." (November 10, 1895).

Sutherland—an obese fellow with reddish-brown muttonchops and a blue diamond stickpin spangling his silk cravat—paraded up and down the platform, regaling whoever would listen with stories of his encounter with the healer several weeks earlier. Sutherland had been injured in the wreck of his private car in 1892. In addition to suffering hearing impairment, he had undergone four operations to correct structural and nerve damage to his spine. The town of Omaha (population 50,000) had placed little credence in the stories of Francis's fantastic healing until Sutherland returned from Denver.

"Obviously, the man believes in Francis Schlatter's extraordinary gifts," said the *World Herald* article, "otherwise, why would he send his wife out west to be treated if he didn't? She was accompanied by several lady friends. She arrived from Omaha in a special car early yesterday morning. Sources in the Colorado capital tell us that, owing to the fact that she is almost an invalid, she was given a position near the head of the line and was obliged to wait only a few minutes before being ushered into Schlatter's presence."

"No general superintendent of a major railway has ever extended such an opportunity to his employees," a reporter wrote in

The Rocky Mountain News (November 11, 1895). "Mr. Sutherland is obviously quite impressed with Schlatter's ability to cure. But of course railroad men all over the nation have been acquainted for some time with the healer's ability to draw a crowd. Trains in and out of Denver for the past few weeks have been packed with paying customers. The railway companies have taken in thousands of dollars on account of travel attracted by Schlatter, and lines extending as far as New York and San Francisco have been the gainers by the presence of the healer in Colorado."

The Omaha World Herald reporter added: "Sources tell us that Mr. Schlatter has been particularly sensitive to the needs of railroad employees, that he bears a special affection and regard for them. In return, the majority of the railway fraternity are ready to swear by Schlatter, and the number is by no means confined to men of ordinary salaries."

That evening at the Omaha station, a crowd gathered around Sutherland as he stood on the platform, gesturing with his cigar. "The sensation of touching the hand of Francis Schlatter is something like an electric current being turned on," he expostulated.

> When he took my hand that fateful day in Denver, it was as if the current had passed through my fingers, up my arm, and across my chest. My ears began to hum, and then as if a plug had been removed, I could hear as well as ever after so many years of partial deafness. My back is much better now. Formerly, I was unable to scoot a chair across the floor without suffering terrible pain. In addition to attending to my needs, the wonderful man blessed a handkerchief for me, which I brought back to Omaha. My precious little boy suffers from catarrh. My wife applied it to his nose and face, and now he is entirely cured. I know this sounds like a fairy tale, but it is the truth. (*The Pagosa Springs News*, November 15, 1895).

There were no skeptics in this crowd; everyone onboard the train firmly believed they would return to Omaha the following Tuesday evening relieved of all their miseries. As the steam engine at the head of the train let go with a deafening toot, several women onboard became so excited they broke out in tears, while many of the men bade farewell to their friends and relatives with trembling voices.

A hush fell over the depot as the train pulled out of the station at precisely seven p.m. The sound of cheers fell away. Sutherland stood at the end of the platform, waving his hand and beaming. "You might have thought it was a funeral cortege," *The World Herald* writer declared, "rather than a contingent of invalids on their way to being alleviated of their physical misfortunes. Good health is even more important than spiritual well-being. God will take care of us later when it comes our time to cross the bar; in the meantime, who attends to our vulnerable bodies in this lifetime? The occasion of the departure was too solemn and portentous for those in the cars and their friends on the platform to celebrate in a conventional manner."

***

Newspapers in the 1890s were full of advice about how to rid the body of illness and disease. Some papers ran a regular medical column in which writers tried to talk sense to their readers, educating them as to the causes of various ailments and recommending solutions.

From *The Omaha World Herald* (October 24, 1895):

> Pain is a sign of disease. You want to get rid of it. There are two ways. Either to cure the disease, or relieve the pain. The first way is the better. The curing eliminates the disease and the pain. The relieving only helps the pain. It will come back again. The disease stays right where it is and eats away at your health. You may not feel it while the pain is gone, but it is there just the same.

From *The Omaha World Herald* (October 24, 1895).

Pain in the back is kidney trouble. It can be cured with Dr. Hobbs's Sparagus Kidney Pills. The Asparagus, from which they are made, has such a healing, soothing, curative action on the kidneys, it is such a gentle and healthful tonic, that it cures nearly every case of kidney trouble in which it is used. Hobb's Sparagus Kidney Pills will cure rheumatism. They do it by helping the kidneys in their work of purifying the blood. They do it so thoroughly that it is very seldom the rheumatism ever comes back.

***

An advertisement in *The Omaha World Herald* (November 13, 1895) for Dr. C. W. Pangle's Herbal Medicines ("The only physician who can tell what ails a person without asking a question") featured a pen-and-ink drawing of the face of a man who looked remarkably like Francis Schlatter—gleaming eyes, high forehead, bushy eyebrows, luxuriant beard.

This wasn't the only place where Francis's name and image were appropriated free of charge or without proper attribution. An advertisement for the Nebraska Clothing Company in *The Omaha World Herald* (November 16, 1895) began with the headline "SCHLATTER NOWHERE," followed by the subhead "An Offer That Outrivals Miracles"—an obvious reference to the healer's remarkable talents—followed by a description of an all-wool, dark-gray men's business suit on sale for $6.75.

***

A reporter for *The Rocky Mountain News* was on hand the morning of November 10 when the Union Pacific Express from Omaha hissed and clattered into Denver's Union Station. The first person the reporter saw was a rubber-booted farmer from Fremont, Nebraska, who debarked from the train clutching the bent and broken form of a woman whom he carried to the street like a bag of loose golf clubs and placed within the covered interior of a hansom cab.

"How did it go on the train," the reporter asked.

"Fine."

"Did you get some sleep?"

"A little."

"How long do you think you'll be in Denver?"

"Just as long as it takes to get done," the man replied. "Sorry, sonny," he added. "Can't stop to talk now. Got to get ahead of these other folks so I can get a good place in line."

Some of the new arrivals looked as if they were too ill to travel. Herman Waring from the Omaha railcar shops suffered from epileptic seizures. He told the reporter he used to have as many as eight or ten a day, but after seeing Francis two weeks ago that number was down to two or three. "I'm hoping to get it down to zero on this trip."

***

The Denver depot had functioned as a kind of holding tank for patients ever since Francis started healing in the city. Day and night the hard wooden benches were occupied by sick and injured people. Families frequently camped out on the cold stone floor, where they were pestered by shysters and con men who buzzed around them like flies. "Need this? Need that? What can we getcha?" Sanitary facilities inside the depot were minimal. There were food kiosks, but such was the deluge of new faces that vendors frequently ran out of supplies. Some lodging was available in cheap rooming houses, located on 17th Street due east of the station. From there, the patients had to make their way to north Denver, either on foot or on the electric cars. Along the way they ran into a gauntlet of confidence men wanting to sell them something or assist them in some way.

***

Unless you were a celebrity or rich and could arrange through a middleman for the healer to see you right away, you had to wait. And waiting, especially as the weather turned cold, especially for the afflicted, could be taxing. Certain enterprising Denverites acted as brokers; for a fee, they could get you into the line within a few hundred feet of where the healer stood. For a bigger fee, they offered a package deal—not only could they get you into the line, but they would personally escort you and your family from the depot to Witter Street in north Denver. The deal included streetcar fare, several meals, cheap lodging with virtually no privacy in a room crammed with a dozen cots, plus—if you were lucky—a privy down the hall or out in the backyard.

The average stay in Denver, including the time it took to make contact with the healer, was five days. That added up to fifteen meals and five nights in an expensive hotel or a not-so-expensive boardinghouse. Maybe a little shopping, if there was anything left over to spend. Then onto the train and the slow, kidney-rattling ride back to Minneapolis or Des Moines or Omaha or Kansas City—eating stale sandwiches, inhaling sooty air from the coal-burning engines that seeped through the windows, staring out at the dull, dreary plains.

***

By the time Schlatter was slated to depart, some members of Denver's population had become adept at fleecing the outsiders who crept into the city in unprecedented numbers. A few churches and private organizations did what they could to help the strangers find their way through the labyrinth of twisted paths leading to the Fox residence, but their efforts were sporadic and ineffective. People stepping off the train from whatever starting point back East were set upon by packs of wheedling, unctuous thieves. Newspaper reporters remarked upon it. Ed Fox went downtown one afternoon to see for himself; white-faced and shaking, he gave a graphic account to Francis that evening. Mary Fox could only wring her hands in frustration. Poor Francis was in a bind; short of quitting the city entirely—a perogative he was about to exercise—there was little he could do to stop it.

* * *

By noon on November 10, some of the Omaha people who had arrived by train that morning had advanced along the line at the Fox house, including the big farmer from Fremont with his emaciated wife. When they reached Francis, seeing how far gone she was he took her hand and prayed, then took her other hand and prayed some more.

The farmer's face seethed with emotion as Francis prayed over the woman and rubbed her hands. Her colorless lips were pebbled with sputum, coughed up from the depths of her watery lungs. The weather in Denver had turned uncomfortably cold. A bank of clouds brooded over the tops of the trees.

Francis spent more time with the figure huddled in the blanket than he'd spent on hundreds of others. The farmer's face twisted with anguish. Francis flicked his eyes upward, then down. He shook his head in a gesture that was barely perceptible but that people like Ed Fox and Clarence Clark had seen many times before—a gesture of renunciation and letting go.

* * *

At promptly four-thirty that afternoon, Francis turned on his heel and disappeared inside the house. Several people at the head of the line—a man wearing a silk-lined overcoat, a slatternly, dirt-poor woman in a tattered dress and sweater, her face half-eaten by cancer—broke into fits of muffled sobbing.

* * *

Everyone who knew him, especially Mary Fox, worried about his health. Day after day Francis was exposed to the same grisly, relentless procession of human suffering. How did he remain immune? All the infirmities he was exposed to, all the sickness! The airborne bacteria these people puffed into Francis's face every day for hours on end was enough to place him in jeopardy. Mary wanted him to wear a mask to cover his mouth and nose, but he wouldn't hear of it.

***

About this time a rumor circulated claiming Ed Fox was receiving fifty dollars a day from the Denver City Cable Company as a result of all the passengers the company's cars were conveying to see the healer on Witter Street.

A *Denver Post* reporter spoke to a Colonel Randolph, general manager of the cable company, who said, "We would be very glad to make a handsome present to either Mr. Fox or the healer, or both. Our company has profited thousands of dollars by the presence of Francis Schlatter in North Denver, and of course we are thankful. I spoke to Mr. Fox the other day and asked him if he would not receive something from the company, as it was evident that his yard had been trampled, some plants uprooted, and his fence partially torn down. He has been put to a great deal of trouble."

To which Fox replied: "I have undertaken to entertain the healer at my house, and am getting along all right without any outside assistance. I do not need any."

Francis's reply was predictable. "I have no use for money," he said. "I have not a cent in the world. The Father will take care of me." (*The Rocky Mountain News*, November 11, 1895).

***

In September a man from Detroit named John Dougherty wrote to Francis describing the effects of the rheumatism that inflamed his joints and limited the use of his arms and legs. Francis wrote a brief note, telling him to have faith and be patient. Two months later, in mid-November, Dougherty wrote a second time to announce that he was well on the way to recovery. "The list of drugs I used to have to take just to get through the day could fill a column in the daily paper," he said. "As a result of writing to you last September, all that has changed." (*The Rocky Mountain News*, November 11, 1895).

By some mysterious, telepathic process, recovery began the moment Dougherty thought the healer had received his letter. He had never set eyes on Francis. It didn't matter. Dougherty's doctors pronounced him cured.

***

Not everyone was as convinced of Francis's healing skills.

A reporter for *The Omaha World Herald* had never seen Francis. He had never been to Denver. All he knew about the man was what he had learned from a few disgruntled people who returned to Omaha from the Colorado capital convinced that the so-called treatment they received at the hands of the healer did not appear permanent.

"Where Are the Cures?" blared a headline in the November 14 edition of *The World Herald.* The anonymous writer had interviewed enough unhappy people to call into question whether they had been properly cured of their ailments. "It would require a week of persistent inquiry and travel about the city to find a single case of Schlatter's where the cure was sufficiently demonstrated to stand the test of a careful examination," the writer said.

He quoted an anonymous Omaha physician as saying, "Nearly all my regular patients cease coming to me for counsel and medicine for about two weeks after seeing Schlatter. Once they realize that his so-called 'cure' is not going to work, they come back as regularly as ever.

"The more the man is studied the more it becomes apparent he is a monomaniac," the physician added. "However, everyone is agreed that he is harmless, giving the public something to amuse and distract them."

***

Not just people but entire municipalities bid shamelessly for Francis's services.

A story in *The Rocky Mountain News* (November 14, 1895) reported that a well-dressed businessman from St. Louis offered Francis $5,000 in cash to come to St. Louis before going to Chicago. Short of that, the man was prepared to fork over the money to anyone who could induce the healer to go to St. Louis.

The businessman's name was Sid Hardy. One day in early November he tried to slip in toward the front of the line but was prevented from doing so by proctors Ed Fox had hired to maintain order. It took Hardy the better part of the day to work his way through the crowd. The weather was foul—gray clouds punctuated by bouts of freezing rain. By the time he arrived at the foot of the boardwalk it was past four-thirty p.m., and Francis had disappeared inside the house.

Hardy buttonholed Ed Fox, who remained outside to try and mollify the ruffled feelings of people like Hardy who had waited so long.

"Mr. Fox, my name is Sid Hardy. I represent a consortium of businessmen from St. Louis who are interested in bringing the healer to that city."

Fox stared wearily at the man. "Oh, I couldn't get him to go there or anywhere else."

Hardy was persistent. "But isn't there anyone in this town who would take the money and persuade him to go to St. Louis?"

"Reckon not, if I couldn't. And I don't think there's anybody's closer to him than me."

"What sort of a man is he anyway," Hardy asked testily. "Does he think he's too good for money? I can pretty well get close to just about any minister I want for five thousand dollars."

To which Fox replied, "But Schlatter isn't a minister, you see. He's a man who doesn't need money. He has no use for it. You can't bribe him or buy him, and I would advise you not to try."

Later, when Fox told Francis about the man, the healer said flatly: "I don't want his dollars."

***

A prominent grain merchant from Omaha named J. A. Conner traveled to Denver for the sole purpose of enticing Francis to go to Omaha before St. Louis or Chicago. Perhaps more than any other city, Omaha had been stirred by tales of the healer; the people there were eager to have him pay a visit. Conner had been instructed by his superiors to stay in Denver until he had exhausted every opportunity to persuade Francis to visit the Midwest. Connor was acting on behalf of a coterie of Omaha businessmen who knew a good thing when they saw it. Connor even offered Francis his own special railroad car to travel in if he would return to Omaha with him.

Francis wouldn't even speak to him. Ed Fox reminded Connor, gently but firmly, that Francis was not for sale.

***

Huge crowds were expected in Denver during Francis's final week. Since mid-September he had spent eight hours a day (Sundays excepted) in Ed Fox's backyard, good weather or bad, treating as many as 1,200 to 1,500 people a day. Word of his impending departure circulated quickly around the country over the newspaper wire services. People from as far away as New York and Baltimore boarded trains and headed west. For many, the healer was their last hope. The touch of his resourceful fingers was all they wanted; they believed in miracles, and what Francis Schlatter offered was all they had left to believe in. Just the sight of him had a soothing effect. He looked so cool and serene. The expression on his face never altered. He stood in the same place every day like a sentinel or a statue carved out of rock—steady, calm, unflappable. Around him, like a wheel of exploding firecrackers, people chattered and gawked and gossiped. Might he stay in Denver a few weeks more? Where would he go when he left? How long was his healing magic intended to last? Would God call him back to heaven as He had His Son, Jesus?

Shaken and distraught by their fear of being abandoned, those seeking help grew increasingly jittery as the final days of the healer's stay approached. The stress caused some to faint dead away, others to erupt into hysterical rages. For eight weeks the people of Denver had been accustomed to having the healer in their midst—a steady, reassuring presence, the point around which their fears and anxieties coalesced into a semblance of order and hope. Now the plug that held it all together was about to be pulled, and who knew what would happen next?

***

As fast as the line of people passed by the healer that final week, others fed themselves into it; like a serpent swallowing its tail, the line seemed to have no beginning or end. At one point on Monday afternoon, November 11, Clarence Clark estimated that Francis was treating 450 to 600 people an hour, an average of ten seconds per person.

So great was the crush that for the first time in two months Francis declined to bless the handkerchiefs people brought to him. *The New York Daily Tribune* (November 12, 1895) reported that he lost his temper when a man from Grand Island, Nebraska, brought a satchel packed with hundreds of handkerchiefs belonging to his friends and neighbors to be blessed by the healer. Francis waved the man out of his place in the line and turned to Ed Fox for help. "I'm sorry," Fox announced to the throng in a loud voice, "but no more handkerchiefs. Mr. Schlatter doesn't have time. I'm sorry."

***

Meanwhile, the mail continued to pour in. Monday's mail numbered 27 bundles, each bundle containing 100 to 150 letters. By Tuesday there was no space anywhere in Francis's bedroom to pile the envelopes. Mary Fox tried to stack them against a wall, but the stacks kept falling over.

***

Tuesday, November 12, 1895. Clarence Clark estimated that Francis treated 2,700 people between nine in the morning and four-thirty in the afternoon. At a rate of as many as 45 a minute, they traipsed past his post at the head of the boardwalk. As fast as one person, dazed and discombobulated, his or her body buzzing from the effects of the healer's volatile touch, tottered off the boardwalk, 10 more joined the line that wound into the street and down the block and down yet another block. The single, orderly, well-behaved line that had been the norm during the past few weeks had swollen in width to four or five people.

Ed Fox looked askance upon the growing numbers. At his request, the police presence had been beefed up; blue-suited constables bearing billy clubs mingled with the crowds in the street. Fox shuddered to think what might happen if their presence was withdrawn. "All day long the great procession moved by the quiet man, who formed the objective point of their vigil," wrote a *Rocky Mountain News* reporter. "There were those in the crowd who, aware of the historic significance of the moment, showed up merely to have a look at the man. Those hundreds of new people who came into town on the evening trains left calls at their boarding houses and hotel desks to be awakened at three and four in the morning so they could get in line early before the Healer emerged from the Fox house."

***

181

Despite standing all day tending to the masses in a variety of weather conditions, Francis looked vigorous and healthy that final week. When four-thirty rolled around and he disappeared into the house, he looked as strong and lively as he had in the morning. Ed Fox, on the other hand, appeared physically exhausted. It was his job during those last days to circulate among the crowd and select the worst sufferers and make sure Francis got to them. The work seemed to be wearing him down. The skin on his face tightened around his prominent nose and cheeks; his mouth drew up in a taut grimace. Mary tried to fatten him up by cooking his favorite dishes, but he couldn't be tempted.

***

Weighing upon Francis that final week was the case pending in the U.S. court regarding mail fraud and the fake handkerchiefs allegedly blessed by him that had been sent through the mail in return for money. The case had already been postponed once, and it looked as if it might have to be postponed again. Ed Fox asked Francis what he wanted to do about it, and Francis replied that he wanted to get it over with as soon as possible. Fox reminded Francis that he was liable to be cited for contempt of court if he left town and failed to appear; worse, the judge might issue a warrant for his arrest.

"But I haven't done anything wrong," Francis protested. "I am innocent."

"The judge needs you in court as a material witness," Fox explained. "Your testimony against these con artists can help put them behind bars where they belong."

"That's not why I came to Denver, to appear in a courtroom," Francis declared with some heat. "I am innocent. I am here to heal. I am here to help. I don't care about the law. It's the people who need me."

"That's all well and good," Fox argued, "but when you are summoned by a court to make an appearance, especially a federal court, you can't ignore it."

Francis dug in his heels. He had had enough of the legal system of his adopted country. He remembered the terrible suffering he had endured in the Hot Springs jail. Maybe it was time for him to go his own way. He was disgusted with the carnival atmosphere that had developed around the Fox house the past few days, the blatant huckstering of food and services, the rampant buying and selling of places in line. Plainclothes detectives circulated through the crowd, arresting people and dragging them off to paddy wagons. Francis was appalled. He knew what was going on. With his acute hearing, he could pick up on encounters between the police and people in the crowd. The warm, reverent, brotherly feeling of a month or two ago had degenerated into a free-for-all.

***

Tuesday evening, November 12, 1895. A fifteen-year-old boy from the streets tapped on the back door of the Fox house. Mary answered. The boy was dressed in scuffed shoes, knickers, a soiled sweater, green-plaid chauffeur's cap, and a wool coat two sizes too big for his scrawny body, with sleeves that dangled to his fingertips.

"What can I do for you?"

"Can you please tell Mr. Schlatter that Gus Kubiloff is here."

Mary swung the door wide. Francis sat at the table with Ed Fox and Clarence Clark. Francis's eyes flashed with recognition. "I know him," he said to Mary. "I will speak with him."

He joined the boy on the back porch. Fortunately, it was dark, and Mary shut the door so no light from the kitchen could leak out and reveal their faces. People were still gathered around the gangway; if they spotted Francis, they might climb the fence and stampede through the backyard.

A few minutes later, Francis slipped back through the kitchen door. He motioned to Clark. The two disappeared into Francis's bedroom.

***

Wednesday, November 13, 1895. Francis dressed in a single-breasted brown corduroy coat, buttoned all the way to the throat, corduroy trousers, no overcoat, the same clumsy black shoes he had worn every day since arriving from Albuquerque, and, of course, no hat. The sky was gloomy, with dark clouds that promised rain or a dusting of snow. At exactly nine a.m. Francis took his place at the head of the boardwalk. People, knowing he was down to his last days, were already in line, five and six deep in places. The line stretched out into Witter Street, down the block, around the corner, along the length of another block, around another corner, seemingly on and on. A veritable deluge of the sick and wounded bearing every imaginable type of malady, from hideous disfigurements to terminal afflictions. They came at him in a long, stuttery, endless line, one after the other, clutching handkerchiefs they begged the healer to bless, bobbing along the wobbly boardwalk to where he stood. It was by far the busiest day he had experienced. Clark estimated that Francis had contact with 4,000 people that day.

For the most part, the supplicants were well behaved. They held their places in the line with a certain tenacity, knowing that in two days the healer would be gone—where nobody knew, although there was rampant speculation: Omaha, St. Louis, Chicago, New York, Canada, Mexico, Europe. As a result of his success in Denver, he was liable to show up anywhere he wanted. The stranger who had appeared in Denver a scant two months before, faceless and unknown, had blossomed into an international celebrity. It was in Denver that he made his mark. The locals were proud of that fact. They knew they could claim him as their own. What they didn't relish was the idea of having to share him with the rest of the world.

The bad weather held off. Around three that afternoon, a few snowflakes dribbled down. Ed Fox was kept busy inspecting the fancy carriages that pulled up on Witter Street. It was his job to lead (sometimes to carry) affluent people from the curb to the head of the line so Francis could treat them. Few people among the rank and file objected; the sight of rich people hobbling on crutches, wheezing with exertion, knobbled with unsightly lumps, their ghostly white faces stamped with the mark of death, had a leveling effect. Underneath, they were the same. The burden of mortality ground each and every one, prince as well as pauper, to a pile of dust.

At one point a group of Methodist bishops, in town to attend a conference, visited the Fox house and viewed the crowd from the comfort of their rented carriages. A reporter tried to solicit their impressions of the healer and the scene, but when they found out he was from *The Rocky Mountain News*, they refused to talk to him.

***

The crowd lingered after Francis retired that afternoon at four-thirty, standing in groups, talking, looking, pointing, gesticulating. People who had been through the line wandered into the crowd that packed the streets, speaking enthusiastically of their personal cures. A few people, upon being treated by the healer, threw down their crutches and canes to a round of applause, although by this time that gesture had become commonplace.

***

Mary Fox greeted the healer as he tromped into the house at four-thirty. Ed Fox, along with Clarence Clark, remained outside, dealing with the difficult chore of placating those left in the line. "He'll be here tomorrow," Fox could be heard saying. "Take this number and it will assure you a place at the head of the line. Yes . . . yes. I'll be here to personally guarantee it."

Francis told Mary that, despite the record number of people he had treated, he felt as if his power had stayed strong all day; he had to admit, however, that his neck felt sore.

"Why is that," Mary asked.

"The power comes through here," Francis said, touching his

forehead. "From out there"—he pointed to the kitchen ceiling—"it comes into here"—touching his forehead again—"and passes down through my neck, into my arms and hands. I am not complete without it."

***

Out on the street, people scurried by, turning up their coat collars against the cold. Vehicles creaked and rattled, horses whinnied and neighed. An air of uncertainty gripped the city—worry, disappointment, apprehension.

Despite the influx of money-spending visitors—mainly from the Midwest—seeking the healer's restorative touch, Denver continued to wallow in the dregs of the 1893 economic slump. The downtown streets were full of vagrants. The sandy floodplain along the South Platte River remained congested with makeshift hovels. Progressive churches such as those presided over by the Reverends Myron Reed and Tom Uzzell continued to provide soup lines and limited shelters at night. Private charities, which made up the bulk of local relief agencies, limped along as best they could. Out on Witter Street there were tents serving food, but they catered mostly to people from other towns. Denver would eventually wean itself away from its economic woes; of that Ed Fox was certain. It was too advantageously placed—at the edge of the High Plains, close to the mountains with their precious minerals and ores, tied to markets on both coasts by an elaborate network of steel rails. Not only had Francis helped restore the city's finances, but he had provided something else as well. Fox struggled to put it into words for his wife and Clarence Clark the evening of that final day after Francis had excused himself and disappeared into his room to lie down. "It's hard to say, but I think what people will miss most about him is the generosity and goodness he carries with him," Fox said. "He holds everyone accountable by his behavior. He reminds them of how the world ought to be if we really wanted it to be that way."

***

The bitter dark of a mid-November night.

A few fires in the street flicked and crackled, fed by young boys who seemed to be watching out for something. Earlier, the boys had argued in vain with a policeman about having a bigger fire so they could keep warm. "Can't be done," the policeman declared. "You're lucky we're lettin' you have any fire at all. A big fire could get out of hand. The neighbors are already fed up with the crowds, the litter, the hoopla. The last thing they need is for one of their houses to catch fire. Sorry, but you'll have to make do with what'chev got."

The night was cold; around midnight it commenced to drizzle. A stream of icy air whipped down from the mountains. Most of the boys were warmly dressed, but without the benefit of a blazing fire, they were soon frigid and stiff.

Around three a.m. a hack drove up to the Fox house. The two horses in the traces blew softly, their steel hooves muffled by the dirt heaped in the street. A teenage boy jumped down from the seat next to the driver, ran swiftly to the front door of the house, and brushed the surface with his shivering knuckles. The door swung open; out came two men muffled to the ears in heavy ankle-length ulsters. One of the men was hatless; in his right hand he clutched a leather valise. It took a few seconds for the two men to reach the hack and squeeze inside. The boy scrambled up next to the driver. The driver touched the rumps of the shivering horses with the tip of his whip, and the hack disappeared down the street.

***

An hour earlier Francis Schlatter had opened his eyes in his bedroom in the Fox house. The Father's familiar voice had sounded quietly inside his head. His eyes popped open, and without hesitation he was on his feet. In less than a minute he was fully dressed in a gray corduroy suit and was shoving his arms through the sleeves of a heavy wool greatcoat. He stepped into the kitchen. The interior of the house was bitingly cold. Just then the front door nudged open, revealing the figure of Gus Kubiloff, who beckoned urgently. Clarence Clark, wearing a knitted stocking cap, the hem of an ulster falling well past his knees, crept from the shadows shrouding the corner of the kitchen. The two men exchanged looks, then they pulled up the collars of their greatcoats and stepped outside into the bitter air.

***

Three hours later, around six in the morning on November 14, Mary Fox stirred from her bed and shuffled into the kitchen. She turned on the gas in the oven and put on the teapot. Then, crossing the split-log floor of the cold kitchen, she tapped on the door to Francis's room as she had every morning for the past two months. Each morning the response had been the same; this time there was no answer. "He always answered to the gentlest tap," Mary said later that day to a reporter. "Hearing no reply, I tried again. I heard nothing and spoke to Mr. Fox, telling him that Mr. Schlatter seemed to be sound asleep. Mr. Fox then tapped on the door himself without success and quietly opened the door."

Francis Schlatter was not there. The bed in which he had slept indicated that it had been occupied for at least a portion of the night. Francis's room was small, ten feet by eight, containing two beds, a dresser, a washstand, and two chairs. A snow-white cover on one of the beds was thrown back, revealing the imprint of the healer's form in the feather mattress. Fox noticed a blank envelope pinned to the pillow. Tremblingly, he opened it.

> "Mr. Fox,
> My mission is finished. The Father takes me away.
> Goodbye.
>
> November 13 . . . Francis Schlatter"

Ed Fox was flabbergasted. He was still in a daze two hours later when he tacked a cardboard sign to the front porch of his house that said, "The healer has fled. Where, we do not know."

***

Again and again that long, difficult day, he maintained that he had no idea that the healer had been planning to bolt the premises. They had never discussed the issue. As far as Fox knew, Schlatter had intended to honor his original departure date of November 15. Mrs. Fox nodded in agreement. She stood behind her husband in the backyard as he fielded a torrent of questions from a host of irate people who had queued up for the day.

Francis's disappearance plunged the people waiting to see him into a profound depression. According to *The Rocky Mountain News* (November 15), "Hundreds wept openly, as if their only hope in life had been rudely torn away." Hundreds more reacted with fury and indignation; a deal was a deal, and Francis had clearly reneged on his part of the bargain. The Denver public understood that he intended to heal until the late afternoon of November 15. Instead, he had absconded early on the morning of the 14th. No one could explain the motives that had induced him to flee prematurely. All day people in the street outside the house argued the point. They understood how upset he was with the disgraceful behavior that ran rampant through the ranks of those awaiting his services. The greedy bartering of places in line that final week contributed to his disenchantment (some places at the head of the line sold for as much as seven dollars apiece). Evidently, Francis had decided sometime late Wednesday evening to settle the issue by running off into the night.

Others speculated that the impending court hearing on the traffic of fraudulently blessed handkerchiefs through the U.S. mail was a motivating factor. According to Fox, Francis simply did not want to take time out from treating people to sit in court and endure the tedium and rigamarole of a formal hearing.

Criticism of his activities by local ministers was another galling incentive. Ed Fox reported that the week before, after a particularly scathing denunciation appeared in *The Denver Post,* Francis had exploded. "Oh, the hounds," he cried. "They have lost the flock and scattered it. They live in mansions and preach from pulpits to tickle the people instead of helping the poor. The day of their reckoning will come."

Fox went on to say that "[Schlatter] felt that the ministers have departed from the plain teachings of the Bible, and are using the pulpit as a profession, as a means of getting along in the world." Francis's idea of a proper and worthy minister, Ed Fox added, "is one who has given up all else to benefit humanity."

Despite what many in the crowd construed as outright betrayal, Fox still believed in the man. "I regard Francis Schlatter as truly a simple, holy man," he said to a reporter from *The Rocky Mountain News,* November 14, 1895). "He is the purest and best man I ever knew. At times I have thought him divine. This has been especially when he was in the presence of little children or in the family circle. In his mind, there is absolutely no thought of wrong and when his face lights up in talking of the Father and the power he has to relieve pain and disease, there is an expression upon it which is actually angelic."

Mary Fox, standing next to her husband, nodded in agreement.

"We still have absolute reliance in his integrity," Fox added. "We believe firmly that the disappearance will be adequately explained."

***

Word of his absence crackled around town with telepathic speed. Despite the fact that he was no longer there, thousands of sick and suffering people boarded the cable cars for north Denver; conductors on the cars had the unenviable task of telling their passengers that Francis was no longer at the Fox domicile. The majority gaped in disbelief. Such a declaration amounted to a kind of heresy. How could he not be there when they had come all this way to see him?

The standard response was, "Well, it may be true, but I just want to go over there to see for myself."

Late morning, November 14, a swelling mass of people congregated around the Fox house. Downtown, the morning trains from the Midwest continued to disgorge scores of people, who then climbed aboard the cable cars. Hour after hour that dismal day, hordes of pilgrims, many showing the ravages of various diseases, others crippled and deformed, a few toting sickly children—full of hope that Francis might still be at his anoited place at the top of the gangway—made the long trip to Witter Street.

At the site, a chilly autumn wind swept a mass of litter and dead leaves, debris, discarded food, lunch bags, and cast-off clothing around the neighborhood. "The scene at the Fox house seemed to speak of desolation and disappointment," said *The Rocky Mountain News* (November 15, 1895). "The sky was dark and lowering, the wind raw, chill, and penetrating. It was a pitiful, heart-rendering spectacle."

Said *The Denver Post* (November 15, 1895): "People turned away from the depressing scene with moist eyes and trembling lips. They toiled slowly back to the cars, grief stricken, indignant, denunciatory or apologetic for the missing man according to their temperament or the depth of their faith."

The Rocky Mountain News added: "Many a man's and many a woman's last life hope was dashed away today with a single look at the disheartening scene about the Fox cottage. It was the mothers with children who took the disappointment most to heart, and they went away hugging the little ones to their breasts almost frantic in the despair of their grief."

The fences in every yard on the block were broken or knocked down. The grass in vacant lots was completely trampled. The boards of the gangway leading to where Francis had stood every day for two months, the sturdy, truncated pillar on which he had rested his elbows, took on the aspect of sacred relics. That afternoon a stranger marched up to the door of the Fox home and offered the former alderman ten dollars for any of the boards in the backyard. Fox refused. He then went outside and pulled up the boards and took them indoors, whereupon the stranger raised the offer to twenty-five dollars.

"Not for ten-thousand dollars would I sell them to you or anyone else," Fox declared through clenched teeth.

A little while later a neighbor knocked on the door. "Mr. Fox, if you don't come out here, they are going to carry away your fence."

With the help of his wife and the neighbor, Fox broke down the fence, carried the boards inside, and stacked them on the floor of the healer's abandoned bedroom.

***

That sad, unhappy day, Ed Fox and several members of the inner circle stood in Fox's yard talking among themselves. To people who approached them politely asking what had happened to the healer, Fox was brusque and uncommunicative. He couldn't understand why Francis had slipped away prematurely, like a phantom in the night. Mary Fox tried to be helpful; the anguished expressions on people's faces were more than she could bear. Francis was gone, and although she didn't know where he had gone, she had supported him in the effort. She recognized that it was important that he go to a major city to find out how much actual healing he could accomplish. Mary and her husband were convinced that Francis was at the vanguard of a new movement of thought and feeling that, as the end of the century approached, seemed to be gaining strength and momentum all over the nation. People were ready for a change. The economic hardships of the past few years had redefined their concept of who they were and how they wanted to live. They were fed up with poverty and suffering. They wanted a better life in every way—socially, economically, mentally, spiritually.

Mrs. Fox urged her husband to be more sympathetic. "I know you are distressed at his disappearance, but the Lord has done this for a purpose which is not for you or me to question."

Fox nodded and softened his tone as he spoke to the supplicants who turned up at the healer's former haunt. "All will be blessed who come here today," he declared, "whether Mr. Schlatter is here or not. That is what he said himself. Go home and have faith and you will get better."

Few people found consolation in this. The majority went away angry that they had not come a day earlier when Francis was still around. Their anger increased when they realized that not only had Francis disappeared, but he had left no trace of his whereabouts.

An article in the November 15 edition of *The Rocky Mountain News* summed up the pervasive feeling of anger and bereavement:

> The street in front of Fox's home was a mecca for cranks of all classes for the entire forenoon, and Schlatter was as warmly defended as he was vigorously denounced. It has been a remarkable fact that during the many weeks of Schlatter's ministrations the crowds have been remarkably quiet and in manner almost reverential. The fakirs who have sold books, pictures and popcorn have gone about crying their wares in subdued tones.
>
> Street gamins have curbed their natural impulses and been remarkably quiet and orderly. But yesterday all this was changed. The peddlers were passing rude gests at the expense of the healer. Gamins threw away all restraint. They guyed [ridiculed] newcomers and seemed to vie with each other in loud talk and profanity. No cripple was too deformed to escape becoming their butt, and if ever a policeman was needed at Schlatter's shrine it was yesterday, where there was no shrine or a policeman.

***

A rumor circulated on the evening of November 14 that Francis had returned to the Fox house as mysteriously as he had disappeared. A reporter from *The Denver Post* went to investigate. He found a dozen roughnecks camped along the battered boardwalk leading up to where the healer had stood every day for two months—"shadows along the sidewalk," he described them in the November 16 issue of *The Post*. To a man, the squatters were confident that Francis would soon return to the house. "Look at it this way," one of them reasoned, "the healer said he would treat us for our illnesses until Friday night November 15—tomorrow night—and we feel as though we have a claim on him till that time." They were positive that by nine o'clock the next morning, Schlatter's regular time to begin healing, he would be back at his post.

"Do you know where he is," the reporter asked.

"Oh, we know all right!"

"And where is that?"

"We're not gonna say!"

The reporter described the men as a motley bunch, mostly deadbeats and thieves, dressed in rags, their shirts and jackets stuffed with newspaper to muffle the evening cold. They refused to give him their names. "You don't need to know that," they clamored. "We're so poor we don't got any names left to give you!"

***

The night of the 15th, while the Foxes slept uneasily in their little house, souvenir hunters stole onto their property—some to rub their handkerchiefs against the post on which Francis was wont to rest his elbows while tending to his patients, others to dig up the sacred dirt from the spot where the healer had stood for the past two months.

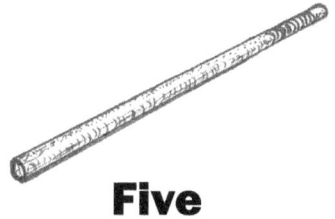

Five

Flight

Francis likely took refuge at one of the two Rooney ranches located near the town of Morrison, a few miles southwest of Denver. At least that was the rumor that buzzed around the Colorado capital in the aftermath of his abrupt departure. During his stay in Denver, Francis had successfully treated Michael Rooney, son of the land baron who owned both spreads, of a hearing defect. In return, Rooney père told Francis that if he ever needed a place to stay, he was welcome at either ranch. The editors of *The Rocky Mountain News* deemed the rumor significant enough to merit special attention, and a pair of junior reporters was dispatched to keep watch on the entry gates to both ranches. The gossip they gathered from people passing in and out indicated that Francis was somewhere on the premises, enjoying a much-needed rest after his sojourn in Denver.

One evening a tall, rangy cowpoke wearing a Stetson hat and a soiled duster turned up at the gate to one of the ranches. He flashed a badge that identified him as a federal marshal looking to serve Francis a subpoena in connection with the mail fraud deception case regarding the handkerchiefs bearing his image. The guard told the officer he had never heard of Francis Schlatter and that no one by that name currently resided within the Rooney family estate. The marshal was in a quandary; if Francis failed to show up at the U.S. courthouse in Denver, the federal government wouldn't have much of a case against the three defendants. The longer the healer stayed away, the more the case fizzled.

***

While hiding out at the Rooney ranch, Francis, with the help of his friend Clarence Clark, obtained a sturdy, white, Percheron draft horse with a thick neck and solid body named Butte. Butte was sick and lame, the result of many years' service in the Denver Fire Department, pulling heavy water wagons through the streets. Under the healer's beneficent touch, the horse quickly mended. Although Francis didn't know exactly where he was going, he sensed he would not be able to walk the distance, as he had two years earlier. Butte would be indispensable.

The healer lay low at the Rooney ranch for three days. Then, rested, reinvigorated, mounted on Butte, his few belongings wrapped in a blanket lashed to the back of the saddle, he headed off in a southeasterly direction along the edge of the Front Range to the little town of Elizabeth, nestled in the foothills. He spent the night at the home of some New Thought devotees, who welcomed him warmly.

***

Francis seems to have made a crucial decision at this point. During the flush days of healing in Denver, before things began to sour, he announced that once he had completed his work there he intended to go to Chicago. One of the biggest cities in the nation, with a population of around a million, Chicago posed a challenge to the healer that could well have given him pause. Once he was there practicing his gift, every aspect of his life, private and public, would be subject to pitiless scrutiny by the media, which in 1895 consisted of twelve newspapers—dailies and weeklies. The practice of "yellow journalism" was at its peak in the 1890s, an era when rival publishers and editors printed lurid and sensational stories designed to whet the taste of a gullible readership. What better subject to distort and slander than the personae of a naive, idealistic, deeply spiritual figure such as Francis Schlatter, who claimed in defiance of scientific fact to be able to heal people merely by touching them. Francis knew from his limited experience in Denver and Albuquerque how ruthless the media could be; on some level he must have suspected that Chicago's brash, cynical, big-city press would eat him alive.

In an article in *The New York Daily Tribune* dated November 19, 1895, Francis is said to have written a letter to W. J. Beery of Chicago saying he planned to arrive in Chicago by November 30. He had originally intended to stay with the Beery family but said in the letter that he had made different plans, although what those plans were he didn't reveal. He did say that for the first two weeks after arriving in Chicago he planned to devote himself to private healing, after which he would give "public demonstrations of his healing powers for three months."

Instead of heading east for Chicago, Francis rode south over Monument Pass marking the watershed between Denver and Colorado Springs. We know from the account of his two-year ramble around the American Southwest that he was wary of population centers and usually tried to pass through them as fast as he could. Did he decide, after his Denver experience, that he had had enough of big cities and in the future would limit his contact to people in small towns and villages? Whatever, the moment was pivotal. He fled from the major media exposure that no doubt would have brought him an international renown he simply, by temperament, wasn't suited for. Despite all the kudos he had earned as a healer, he stepped away from the bright lights of the big city to continue his healing regimen in the venues where he felt most at home—small towns and open spaces.

***

Through a day and windy night of worsening weather, Francis passed well east of Colorado Springs, following the dry, cobbled bed of Fountain Creek in a southerly fashion toward the industrial town of Pueblo (population 9,000).

On November 21, 1895, *The Pueblo Chieftain* reported that the healer had been sighted passing through a motley collection of shacks known as Little Buttes, twenty-four miles north of Pueblo. The dispatch declared he was mounted on a huge white horse, but "whether or not a Titian-haired maiden was in his wake, rumor does not say." The jocularity was intended; with half the population of Colorado out looking for him, a little humor was required to assuage the fact that no one could pin down Francis's whereabouts. The article went on to say that so intense were the rumors of his appearance that "any man with a full beard, long hair, and humble attire is now likely to be called Schlatter, anywhere from Maine to California."

The search was on. One of the greatest manhunts west of the Mississippi River had kicked into action. Up and down the Front Range, houses belonging to New Thought devotees, anyone known to be sympathetic to Francis, were placed under surveillance, as were all roads leading in and out of Denver.

***

That same day *The Santa Fe New Mexican* declared that the healer was probably hiding out in some remote spot in the mountains; otherwise, "with everyone out looking for him, he would soon be located

...[w]e expect him to reappear soon and take up healing where he left off."

These predictions proved premature. Francis wasn't hiding out. He remained on the move, heading south. On November 22 *The Chieftain* reported that he had circled east of Pueblo, far out onto the flats watered by the Arkansas River. The paper sent a squad of reporters to check, but they came back empty-handed. No one they spoke to had seen a strange man on a white horse.

Meanwhile, the weather turned foul. At the hamlet of Overton, eight miles north of Pueblo, amid a deluge of whirling snow, positive identification was made by E. W. Haggarty, the postmaster.

Haggarty knew the healer by sight as well as by reputation; he had been treated by him earlier that autumn in Denver. He spotted Francis through the swirling snowflakes and telegraphed *The Chieftain* that he was riding an "enormous white horse." Haggarty ran out into the snow and hailed the figure. "Where are you headed for," he called.

"Bound south," was the laconic reply.

Haggarty accompanied the healer on foot for about a mile south of Overton before turning back. Francis, he noticed, was dressed in a black silk shirt, leather vest, and a long brown coat that reached to his shoes. His long hair was gathered up under a hat and bound to his skull with a kerchief. He sat astride a new saddle, with a blanket and canvas tent tied to the back.

Another team of *Chieftain* reporters was sent to scour the terrain, but they came up with nothing. Francis was as elusive as a mountain lion. So where had he gone? Most likely he had reached the outskirts of Pueblo and gone into hiding somewhere. *Chieftain* reporters inquired at all the corrals and livery stables in town but turned up nothing. They also checked every hotel and lodging house, with no luck. It was baffling. Here, in the midst of their own town, smack under their noses, was one of the best-known men in the American West, and they couldn't find him. Surely, by now someone would have spotted him. In the November 23 edition of the paper, a reporter complained:

"He could not have come into Pueblo without being seen, which he was not, nor could he have moved through a single street in the city without attracting and drawing a crowd, neither of which he did."

Francis fooled everyone with a simple ploy: he circled west around the edge of town, in the direction of the mountains, instead of east, as he had done at Colorado Springs. The weather was grim, and few people were out. A man in a buggy named Charles A. Gatza, a pharmacist, spotted the healer on the street, head down, walking his horse, eyes slotted against the pelting snow. Gatza recognized him immediately. He pulled up and introduced himself. Francis pretended not to hear, but Gatza persisted; here, traipsing alone on the street, accompanied by a huge horse, was the most mysterious man in the American West. Gatza invited the chameleonic figure to join his family for dinner; surprisingly, Francis accepted. He led Butte into the stable behind Gatza's house at the west end of town and looped a bag of oats around his ears. (Gatza later described the horse as "a magnificent animal, large and white and well-proportioned.")

Francis took dinner with the family; the food, hot coffee, and a couple of glasses of home-brewed wine loosened his tongue. After departing from Denver in the dark of night, he had journeyed west toward the mountains "as he had been directed to do"—by whom, he didn't say. At a prearranged spot in the hogback formation a few miles from Morrison he found Butte (brought there, presumably, by Clarence Clark), fresh blankets, a shiny new hatchet, a small canvas tent, and a sack full of food and clothing. Later, while resting at the Rooney ranch, he had applied his healing prowess to restoring Butte to full vigor and health. Francis then rode south along the foothills to Elizabeth. Once across Monument Pass he struck a set of railroad tracks, which he followed to Overton.

Gatza tried to entice the healer to stay a few days. Francis looked at him keenly. Gatza was a small, dapper, handsome man around forty, with a trim goatee and a pince-nez that teetered at the bridge of his aquiline nose. His wife was attractive, a Spanish beauty with a curvaceous bust and lustrous brown eyes.

"I can't," Francis said. "I must go south."

The Gatzas then tried to tempt Francis into spending the night, but at around eight o'clock he insisted he had to go. A brisk wind whistled through the pitch-black streets. Mr. Gatza offered to lead him to the outskirts of town. Francis said no; secretly, he was pleased with the inclement weather—tailing him would be difficult. He took the hands of his hosts in both of his. "I feel that I will return to Pueblo," he said, "and when I do I will be more powerful than ever." (*The Pueblo Chieftain*, November 24, 1895).

It was the same old sop he had given to other people in other towns. Had his success made him cynical regarding the power of his legendary presence? Was he becoming callous and manipulative, telling people what they wanted to hear, filling them full of false hope?

***

The next day the Gatzas gave a *Chieftain* reporter a detailed description of the healer. Glossy, shoulder-length, blackish hair threaded with streaks of gray, bound close to his skull by a wool cap, navy-blue sweater, leather vest, corduroy trousers, a new hunting coat with wide lapels and baggy pockets, outsized feet encased in heel-less, size 13 shoes. Mrs. Gatza said his feet were at least six inches wide. His height she estimated at just under six feet. Weight, 180 pounds.

***

Somewhere along the way, possibly in Pueblo, Francis acquired the rod he was to carry with him for the rest of his life. The rod was made of polished brass; it was approximately three and a half feet long and weighed more than thirty pounds. A curious object, similar in size and shape to a baseball bat, only heavier and less wieldy, pierced with a hole at one end from which dangled a stout leather thong. The rod's dull brassy surface was scored with an abstract linear design.

Who presented the rod to him, where it was made, why he

thought he should have it are unknown. Pueblo, with its smelters, foundaries, and metal-working shops, seems the likely place of manufacture. There is some speculation that it was a gift of Clarence Clark. Ed Fox has also been mentioned, as have the Rooneys. Whatever, the staff's symbolic importance would not have been lost on Francis. Jesus carried a staff when he walked around Judea. Balanced in his hands, the staff would help Francis maintain his spiritual and physical equipoise. He could also use it to defend himself against predators.

***

Elia Peattie, a witty, sagacious correspondent for *The Omaha World Herald*, wrote a perceptive psychological analysis of Francis Schlatter's behavior after he left Denver. The piece appeared in the paper on November 18, 1895:

> One cannot too much admire the adroitness of Schlatter, the healer, in disappearing mysteriously. It was really the most histrionic thing he could have done, and is calculated to pique into acuter interest the curiosity of the people. A mysterious disappearance is a part of the dramatic unity of such a role as this powerful young man is playing. And it is, by the way, a role well worth the playing. People of dull imagination can see nothing but disinterestedness in his work, because he will not, forsooth, accept money for his services. But money—bah! What stuff is it compared to other things! Could money buy such elation as Schlatter feels when he sees hundreds of people awaiting his touch, believing in him, loving him, almost adoring him? Could money buy the sense of power which exalts him when he sees the crutches of the lame dropped and hears the suffering declare that their

pains have ceased? May he not well be forgiven for believing in himself?

***

On November 26, Francis took dinner at a railroad stop at the foot of Greenhorn Mountain (12,349 feet). His host was a popular local rancher named George Sears; after Francis rode off, Sears pounded his horse ten miles through a blasting storm to post a telegram to the editorial offices of *The Pueblo Chieftain*. "Francis Schlatter, the healer, took dinner at my house yesterday," he wrote. "He came quietly and undetected through your city last Thursday, and other than one family, he was not discovered by anyone; after leaving Pueblo, he rode through a storm all night. On Friday he camped in an abandoned cabin on the Greenhorn and remained there until Monday morning. I know it to have been Francis Schlatter, having seen him in Denver."

***

Around one o'clock on the afternoon of November 27, 1895—the day before Thanksgiving—Francis rode through the coal-mining town of Walsenburg (population 1,000), about fifty miles south of Pueblo. Dressed in a wool cap, corduroy trousers, leather vest, and ankle-length winter coat with sagging pockets, he was mounted on Butte, who high-stepped along the rutted street like a circus pony leading a parade.

As reported by a *Trinidad* (Colorado) *News* correspondent, just about everybody in town turned out to witness his passage. Both sides of the bustling town's main north-south thoroughfare were lined with people looking on raptly as he rode, bobbing in the saddle, in rhythm to the clop-clop-clop of Butte's heavy hooves against the hard-packed street. People watched him, transfixed. He didn't pause, and no effort was made to try and get him to do so until he had passed beyond the town limits. At that point the people awoke from their trance and pressed around him, clutching at his legs, the hem of his coat, in an effort to induce him to stay. He shook hands with as many as he could reach but declined their invitations. "I must press on," he said.

* * *

Where he went next remains a mystery. We lose track of him until he showed up in Taos, in New Mexico Territory, on the night of December 11, 1895—two weeks after he passed through Walsenburg. Most likely he turned into the Sangre de Cristo Mountains somewhere around the town of Aguilar, about fifteen miles south of Walsenburg. From there he made his way west along the narrow floodplain of the Apishapa ("Stinking Water") River, across the backside of the majestic Spanish Peaks, then south over another series of steep ridges to the valley cut by the Purgatoire ("Picketwire," in the local patois) River. The country between there and the legendary outpost town of Taos—a hundred miles as the crow flies—was exceptionally rugged. Did he travel alone, relying on the voice to guide him? Or did he procure the services of a local pathfinder to lead him around the worst obstacles he might have encountered?

Whatever, he traversed a heap of difficult country. He had to navigate the eastern slopes of the Culebra Mountains ("snake" in Spanish), a subset of the Sangre de Cristos, so-called because of their distinctive serpentine profile. From there he had to cross a maze of geologic forms: vertical ridges, extinct volcanoes, precipitous canyons, menacing lava beds, faulted rock formations, fields of sedimentary shale, seams of glistening coal—a tortuous route. He makes no mention of the weather or the difficulty of the trek, though in that wilderness at that time of year, both must have been challenging. He makes no mention of meeting anybody along the way, which might have been the case in such a sparsely settled region. The three major watercourses on the Colorado side—the Cuchara ("Spoon"), Apishapa, and Purgatoire—tumble through the foothills of the twin summits of the Spanish Peaks in a prevailing easterly direction. After leaving this watershed,

Francis appears to have deadheaded southwest through the heart of yet another ferocious wilderness, Park Plateau, cut by the Cimarron, Canadian, and Vermejo rivers, to the goldfields around Elizabethtown and Eagle Nest. He then slipped along the southern edge of the Taos Mountains, within eyeshot of the ancient Indian pueblo, into the streets of the boisterous, roughneck town.

Whoever pointed the way, the voice or a local guide, his arrival on the outskirts of Taos on Tuesday night, December 11, 1895 (according to the December 13 issue of *The Santa Fe New Mexican*), was nothing short of miraculous. He was dressed in broad-soled, heel-less shoes, brown canvas overalls, dark-blue sweater, and a dirt-stained ulster. He appeared to have lost another tooth in his upper jaw, which gave him the look of a battered pugilist. He rode a tall, chunky, whitish, fat-bodied horse that he spoke to in a steady stream of affectionate names. When asked who he was, he said he was a stranger in the service of God. When asked where he was headed, he said he hoped someday to reach the towns of Embudo, Española, and Santa Fe.

* * *

News of *el Sanador's* arrival in the Taos Valley was greeted with great enthusiasm. He was asked by many to spend a little time; much to their dismay, he said the Father had told him he must press on. He spent the night in Taos at the house of a man named Florencio Pacheco; when his host asked about his future plans, Francis was noncommittal. Pacheco had two small children, whom Francis balanced on his knee; at one point he got down on the carpet and let them crawl all over him, pulling his ears and hair.

The next morning, fortified with a bottle of wine, he mounted Butte and rode out of Taos, down into the deep, cold shadows of the Rio Grande Canyon toward the town of Embudo. Hundreds of people accompanied him, speaking in subdued voices over the creak of rusty wagons, the rasp of dry leather, the sound of horses snorting wetly in the morning light.

By late afternoon it was apparent that Francis would go first to Española, then to Santa Fe. At the depot in Lamy on the dismal rainy night of August 21, 1895, from the train bound for Denver he had exhorted the multitudes who came to greet him "to have faith, I shall come back to Santa Fe in three months." The three months were long up, and many Santa Feans, knowing he was headed in their direction, trusted that he was about to fulfill his promise. So confident were they that a contingent of excited citizens swarmed out onto the Española road to watch eagerly from a hilltop (nicknamed "Gethsemane Hill") the arrival of the legendary figure.

Early on the afternoon of December 13, Francis left Embudo and rode out of the gloomy winter depths of the Rio Grande Canyon toward San Juan Pueblo. He was expected to arrive at the village of Santa Cruz, directly north of Santa Fe, around seven that evening. All day the people in the capital buzzed with excitement as the healer drew near. Despite his evasiveness, they were positive he would settle in for a long stay. After all, Santa Fe was a special place. Taos was crude and bumptious, Colorado hovered way up there beyond the pale, Albuquerque was filled with money-grubbing people from back East. The only place where a man of his renown could possibly establish a bonafide Kingdom of Heaven had to be the estimable capital of New Mexico Territory, with its many churches, holy sites, notable architecture, and historical landmarks. Early that afternoon a welcoming delegation of important officials was dispatched northward up the Santa Cruz road as far as Pojoaque Pueblo.

The next morning the opening line of the lead article of *The Santa Fe New Mexican* asked plaintively, "Where is Schlatter the healer?" While it wasn't known for sure, it appeared he had entered the precincts of Santa Fe proper (population 5,000) at about eleven o'clock on the night of December 15 on foot, leading Butte by the bridle through the streets. He passed along San Francisco Street sometime around eleven-thirty, where he was intercepted by a pair of deputy sheriffs who offered to escort him to a hotel in the center of town. Francis told them that, as much as he'd like to, he couldn't stay. He pressed on to the west. Meanwhile, word began to circulate that he was in the area. A trio of sporting men hired a buggy and took off after the healer; they caught up with him several miles out on the road to San Ildefonso Pueblo and stayed with him until three in the morning. They were a jolly lot, squiffed but respectful; to their repeated requests that he park himself in Santa Fe for a few days, Francis replied that the Father had told him that he must keep going. He said he intended to walk alongside his big horse till daybreak, at which time he would remount "and make him get." One man offered him a drink from his flask. Francis took it. The night was nippy, the air saturated with a rheumy chill.

He spent the day of December 17 in the San Ildefonso Pueblo region. That evening he showed up in the Hispanic village of Agua Fria, where he stayed the night in the house of a man named José Cortés. The next morning a crowd of earnest petitioners from Santa Fe showed up in Agua Fria, but Francis faded down the road like a spooked coyote toward the town of Peña Blanca. Cortés informed the disappointed Santa Feans that the healer had decided to bypass the capital and head south in the direction of Bernalillo by way of Cochiti Pueblo.

On December 19 a party of people from Albuquerque found Francis in Peña Blanca. They begged him to revisit their city, the place where he had started his healing mission the summer before. Francis replied that his mission this time was in the countryside, not the cities. The Father, he declared for the umpteenth time, directed all his movements, and unfortunately neither Albuquerque nor Santa Fe was on the list.

"My steps are now to the southwest," he explained, "to the wretched and deprived who live in remote places. I have had my fill of cities for the time being. Where the Father directs me to go, I will. He may do so in a moment, or it may be years. If he says so, I will." (*The Santa Fe New Mexican*, December 20, 1895).

He kicked his heels against Butte's bulging ribs and trotted down the road.

***

Where he fled to this time, no one could really say; one rumor cited the arid country around the headwaters of the Puerco River. Everyone who knew of him seemed to have their own theory as to where he was and why. *The Santa Fe New Mexican* reported that during the final week of the year, Francis lingered in the village of La Joya in Rio Arribe County, fifty miles south of Albuquerque. He was the guest of a distinguished citizen of those parts named Don Mariano Larragoite. Don Mariano's house was virtually besieged by people seeking the healer's touch. All evening until well after midnight for several nights running, Francis tended to the sick and lame. His final day he hoped to get away by eight in the morning, but the crush of people desiring his attention was so great that he didn't depart until about noon. Don Mariano estimated that Francis must have treated around a thousand people in the short time he was there.

Don Mariano accompanied *el Sanador* on horseback as he pulled out of town astride the faithful Butte. Instead of asking him where he was going next or where he thought he might hole up for the winter, Don Mariano posed a question that troubled a lot of people in that precarious fin de siècle era: "Have you any idea how the world will come to an end?"

Francis, no doubt relieved to address a question that had nothing to do with him personally, rose to the bait like a hungry trout.

"I do not know when the end will come," he replied. "The Father knows. But it will be by fire. A scorching, cleansing, scourging flame. The unbelievers will be destroyed, and a new generation will take their place. Today, there are more Pharisees than at any other period of the world's history. They need to be eliminated."

He fixed Don Mariano with a steady, level gaze. "I will soon disappear. No one will know my whereabouts. But after a number of years, I will reappear and then I will preach again to the people. My present mission is to heal and alleviate those who believe in God." (*The Santa Fe New Mexican,* December 31, 1895.)

***

New Year's Day, 1896. According to *The Santa Fe New Mexican*, Francis Schlatter relaxed at a ranch owned by an Anglo named Whitman, a few miles east of Gallup. He spent the day lounging in a hammock, soaking up the sun, and reading the Bible—first in French, then in German, finally in English. Whitman, who spoke fluent French, was delighted with his guest. They conversed for a long time in his native tongue, which pleased Francis. That evening he drank a couple of glasses of red wine and ruminated upon his future. "I intend to go to Arizona," he said. "I may even get to Mexico and on into South America before my present mission is fulfilled."

***

January 16, 1896. *The Santa Fe New Mexican* reported that a cattleman named Soloman Block passed the healer one afternoon on a trail near the town of Cebolleta, in Cibola County, New Mexico Territory. Block recognized him; thinking he was lost, he turned his horse and caught up with Francis and warned him that the country he was about to pass through was extremely rugged. He invited Francis to stay overnight at his house in Cebolleta, but Francis said he was obliged to keep moving. Block rode along with the healer for a couple of hours, during which time he questioned him about various subjects.

> Block: Mr. Schlatter, I have seen it announced in several newspapers that you claim to be Jesus Christ. Is that so?
>
> Schlatter: Yes sir, I am Jesus Christ. The only mistake the papers have made is by claiming that this is my third appearance in the world. It is not. It is only my second appearance. I will soon disappear and return to this world in another form. What that form is exactly has not yet been determined. But when I am gone, those who have not believed in me will regret it, and they will shed bitter tears.

Block: What are your ideas as to religion?

Schlatter: All religions are good. Everyone should stick to the religion in which they are born. I belong to the Roman Catholic faith, because I believe there is more faith in that religion than in any other.

Block: What is your opinion of secret societies?

Schlatter: All the secret societies about which I know anything are good. Every man should belong to one of them and remain in it so long as the society does not attempt to interfere with his conscience.

Block: What about the future life?

Schlatter: People who go to heaven or purgatory remain there forever. Those who go to hell return to this life and have an opportunity in their new life to reform.

Block: I understand that Catholics believe that by means of masses and prayers the souls of the dead can be helped out of purgatory. Is that so?

Schlatter: When a soul is judged and sent to purgatory, it remains there for all time. When a person dies he is immediately judged according to the deeds of charity he has done in his lifetime. That is what determines his fate.

Block: I fear these mountains are too rugged and that you might die in them.

Schlatter: There is no death in me. (*The Santa Fe New Mexican,* January 30, 1896).

The two parted a short time later with a warm handshake.

***

Inquiries as to the healer's whereabouts poured in from all over the nation. *The Rocky Mountain News* on January 14, 1896, reported that Francis had told a friend in Peña Blanca that he intended to withdraw from the world for a little while, to rest and recuperate somewhere in the Mogollon Mountains in the southwestern part of the territory; in due time he would reappear in Albuquerque and Santa Fe and take up his work again.

Sometime around January 25, 1896, Francis was seen in the town of Cebolleta just as he and Butte were about to start overland across dark and difficult Putney Mesa. About the same time, a newspaper in Silver City claimed he had managed to make his way, under harrowing conditions, through the Mogollon Mountains to a mining camp in western Socorro County. From there, it was reported that he had proceeded down the Gila River and was now a hundred miles south of the San Carlos Indian Reservation in Arizona Territory. "There is much quiet concern among people everywhere of the whereabouts now and the possible plans for the future of this truly mysterious man," wrote a reporter for *The Littleton* (Colorado) *Independent* on January 30, 1896.

But they were wrong. In actuality, Francis had taken refuge at the Hermosillo Ranch outside the tiny community of Datil, in western New Mexico Territory.

***

The February 19 *Santa Fe New Mexican* reported that W. E. Martin, a politician from Socorro County, was quoted as saying that Francis Schlatter and his redoubtable white horse had taken refuge at a ranch on the outskirts of Datil, owned by a woman named Ada Morley Jarrett. In response to a letter from the newspaper asking for information regarding the healer, Jarrett replied that she was not at liberty to reply to any rumors concerning "the past, present or future" of the individual in question. Everyone knew who that was. Word was out—Schlatter was somewhere in the area. The article conjectured that "now that el Sanador has been definitely located, the natives are becoming excited again and a general exodus of the afflicted to the datils [sic] is likely to result."

It was the middle of winter. Datil was located 8,000 above sea level, and the weather was harsh and confining. The nearest town, Magdalena, was a strenuous two-day ride. Alhough some people thought they knew where the healer was hiding out, getting to that place in bitter February was a daunting task.

***

Francis apparently had not known the exact location of the Hermosillo Ranch. He found it by blazing a path down from the north across Putney Mesa, pushing Butte to the limits of his endurance, slipping and sliding along an abandoned Indian trail across a huge, trackless, undulating sea of snow-covered, cedar-dotted ridges and hills. Finding his way to the ranch was something of a miracle. Jarrett, a widow who knew Francis only by reputation from his days in Denver, had no idea he was coming. The ranch was located in a box canyon on the outskirts of Datil, at the edge of the Plains of San Augustin, a dry, fifty-mile-long lake bed that in spring provided lush pasturage for winter-hungry cattle before they were driven east to the railroad at Socorro.

Francis arrived at the ranch sometime in early February. He found the barn and led Butte inside; with a pitchfork he piled up a batch of hay for the horse. Weary after the long trek, Francis curled up in a heap of straw. He hadn't been asleep for long when a hired hand named Mr. Swingle shook him by the shoulder. Swingle had noticed a curious track in the snow outside the barn, a large, flat-heeled footprint—not the sort of imprint made by a spike-heeled cowboy boot but more like the intaglio of a Sasquatch foot, thirteen inches long by six inches wide.

Swingle escorted the healer into the house. Mrs. Jarrett nearly fainted when she saw him; knowing his reputation in Denver, she recognized him right away. "Turning and peering into the hall," she wrote, "[I] saw, framed by the dark doorway, 'The Silent Man of Denver,'—the same strange looks, the uncovered head, the long, waving hair, the gentle attitude, the peaceful face, with all those impressive characteristics that thousands saw and can never forget.... I could not move.... 'Francis Schlatter!'" I cried.

He nodded gravely. His voice was husky and soft. "The Father has directed me to a safe retreat. I must restore my spiritual powers in seclusion and prayer."

He had ridden the 700 miles between Denver and Datil in the dead of winter, much of the way through rugged, desolate country, the last stretch across dangerous Putney Mesa, where the snow lay several feet deep in places. Both he and Butte had arrived in surprisingly good condition. (*Healer*, 82).

***

For the next three months Francis remained mostly out of sight in an upstairs room of the ranch house, venturing out only when he was sure no strangers were around. A major piece of work occupied his energy during this time—the story of his two-year "wander-vogel" through the Southwest between 1893 and 1895, which he dictated to Jarrett and which she took down as swiftly as her aching hand could manage. She later published it under the title he gave it—*The Life of the Harp in the Hand of the Harper.* During his free time, and even as he was dictating to Mrs. Jarrett, Francis swung the brass rod over his head, stirring his blood, strengthening his muscles. The rod weighed well over thirty pounds, but he managed to wield it with the ease of a drum major twirling a baton. "It was a feat requiring prodigious strength," Jarrett noted, "but he did it tirelessly." (*Healer,* 9). The practice had been imposed upon him by the Father, and he had to oblige or watch his power ebb and fade.

During their extended stay together, Francis told Jarrett many stories about his childhood in Alsace-Lorraine. He used to play hooky from school and run off with the older boys, until he got caught and was reprimanded by his father. "I was as blue as a violet from my head to my heels," he said.

He had a brother twenty years older and two sisters. The older sister had recurring dreams about her little brother. "She saw me always alone," Francis said, "not the least like other young men. I was always studying, thinking, off by myself, never in the company of other young people. One night she dreamed that I started out on a long walk, and with such a sad, mournful face. Walk, walk, walk! All alone, sad and sorrowful." (*Healer*, 88).

Ada Morley Jarrett was short and slim with a delicate carriage that belied a tough, resolute, pioneer personality; an intelligent, fine-boned, middle-aged woman with a soft oval face, firm mouth, deep-set eyes, and curly blond hair cropped close to her finely molded skull. The appearance of the healer on the premises of her late husband's ranch she regarded as nothing short of a miracle—"the supreme moment of my life."

The best times, she remembered later, "were when [I was] sitting at his feet and listening to his glowing words, his joyous, detailed descriptions of his life in France, and more particularly the minutiae of that horrible [two-year] tramp and its mystic meaning to mankind." Evidently, Francis went into great detail regarding his long walk around the country, which he would not permit her to include in the memoir he dictated.

A close relationship evolved during the many days they spent together in isolation at the ranch. They stayed up late practically every evening, talking, soul mates of the deepest sort, platonic lovers, drawn to each other by the fervor of their thoughts—personal, spiritual, philosophical. "Work is all that the Father wants," Francis insisted. "There has been too much talk for two thousand years. Now it's thought and action, thought and action, thought and action!"

"Those who have not heard him talk can scarcely conceive of the intensity of his language and emotions," Jarrett commented.

"It seems that I must go away soon," Francis said at one point.

"And no one will be permitted to go with me. Then, when He brings me back! Think of it! Jesus's teachings will be fulfilled. Then no more injustice, no more oppression, no more sin. We will have peace once and forever on this earth."

As the days passed, Jarrett's appreciation of Francis became tinged with a touch of hero worship. "As the midnight hours approached it occurred to me that here was [a person] who combined the repose of the Oriental with the energy of the Occidental," she wrote, "[who] was both a Pessimist and [an] Optimist; an iconclast and [a] Reconstructionist; Indifferent and Intense; Human and Divine; who came preaching that Illuminated Christianity is to be the natural religion of the future; that the Kingdom is at hand; that he has walked for the world; that his sufferings are the fire he went through for the world." (*Healer*, 85).

Jarrett wasn't the only one with a special affection for the healer. With Butte he seemed to have an abiding rapport. At least once a day Francis visited the horse in the corral, where he would wrap an arm around Butte's neck and press his face against the warm, gritty, whitish hide. Butte responded to Francis's attentions by trying to follow him into the house. One time, clumsy as a dinosaur, he clumped after his master into the kitchen, upsetting the sugar bowl and the table on which it sat, lapping up as much of the contents as he could reach with his foamy pink tongue before Francis and Swingle lured him back outside.

At one point Francis confessed that, like a teenage boy, he was continuing to "grow." Most likely he meant spiritually rather than in the flesh, although when Jarrett applied a tape, he stood nearly six feet tall in his stocking feet—taller, he claimed, "than he had ever measured before." Francis also felt his feet were expanding and that he would soon need to cut vents in the sides of his shoes to relieve the pressure. "A life must be active, helpful and good, to count when the sifting time comes for the Kingdom," he was moved to remark. "There must be growth, and there can be none in selfishness." (*Healer*, 87)

Many a long, cold, dark evening the two spoke intensely of politics. Both agreed that humankind, possessed as it was by "greed, grind and grasp," was in a "pitiful" state of development. Francis fulminated against the capitalist system that fostered a wealthy minority over an impoverished majority. He also railed against the predominance of the gold standard in the nation's economy, which benefited the rich, over the coinage of free silver, which he felt would provide greater financial liquidity for the poor and dispossessed. "The moneyed few are the bloodsucking parasites on the common people," he insisted. *(Healer,* 91*).*

Together, but mostly from his lips, they blasted the established church. "Once the Church had all the power," Francis complained, "but what did it do? Was it true to its trust? No. It misused the trust for greed, avarice, selfishness, and personal needs. It has not cared for the Father's children, but for greed, covetousness, and the self. One and all, from the beginning, have misused power." (*Healer*, 91).

His time with Jarrett provided a rare and meaningful exchange between two profoundly kindred spirits. It had been a long time since Francis had spoken with such emotional freedom and ease. A sample of his declarations reveals not only the depth of his commitment to the populist cause but also the acute compassion he felt for the oppressed and downtrodden:

> ★ No man who wants to do right has a chance, for he is soon trampled under. If a man is too honest, they get him out of the way . . . .
>
> ★ The head of the serpent lies in London, the money capital of the world . . . .
>
> ★ The Gold Powers will win one way or another. Don't you see? They will never voluntarily let go.
>
> ★ Governments today are corrupted through and through, national, state, municipal, from north to south, from ocean to ocean. Where, then, has a reformer any chance? The world is run according to a commercial basis; and tell me what is commerce? It is piracy on the high seas of man-made traffic. [It] is legalized robbery.

★ This nation of the West is going down faster than any nation in all of history. Look at its unparalleled opportunities! It is almost an undiscovered land . . . yet see that a few men actually control the lands, foods, necessities of all other men. Think of that high-handed robbery! Do you think that is the Divine plan? This nation ought to have no poor, no hungry, no downtrodden.

★ Society is a painted shell!

★ Never forget that I was a workingman. (*Healer*, 94-97).

***

One night as the wind pounded the north side of the rambling Hermosillo house like a wet towel, Francis told Ada a story:

My mother died in her cottage home in Ebersheim at noon on Sunday, April sixteenth, eighteen seventy-one. I was fifteen years old. The children were all there, my sisters and older brother. She said something private and special to each of us, but she made me swear a deathbed oath that I would never spend any more time than I had to in a big city, mainly because of the evils and temptations that reside there. I have remembered that, and if you know anything about my life, you will understand that if I have found myself marooned in the middle of a city, I will make every effort to pass through to the other side as quickly as possible. I know in my heart that people in cities are no more inherently evil than those who live by themselves in the woods. I have lived in Paris and London and New York and Denver. People are people, no matter where you find them. But my mother extracted this pledge from me with nearly her last dying breath, and I live by it and for it. I believe it to be so. (*Healer*, 98).

In their daily discussions Ada and Francis canvassed a wide range of subjects. He was well-read and seemed to have an opinion on everything. The tenor of his remarks was part conventional man of God, part political demagogue, part social futurist in the manner of Jules Verne and H. G. Wells, two popular authors of the day.

His remarks clearly indicated that he was a supporter not just of women's suffrage but of women's rights in general. "Women," he said at one point, "need to live nearer nature, dress more naturally instead of having to truss themselves up in corsets and wear silly hats. And heels!" he complained. "If the Father wanted us to have heels, He would have put bumps on our feet."(*Healer,* 102).

No doubt the many months he had gone barefoot during his long walk around the Southwest helped formulate this opinion.

> ★ On marriage: Do you suppose the Father approves what they call monogamy today, with its prevalent hypocrisy? Is the present marriage system divine in its meaning and methods? Please don't understand me to attack marriage, or wholly disapprove of it; but look at the hypocrisy of the system generally. Up to now it has served its purpose, but the Father will teach us something far better in the [New] Kingdom. It will be Justice first. (*Healer*, 102).

> ★ On the Denver preachers and doctors who opposed his work: It would seem that they ought to have been only too happy to see one living the life they have been preaching about for centuries. The churches are the very ones that ought to recognize the real thing when they see it. But they are prejudiced. As to the doctors, of course, they are in

opposition, for [my healing] touches their pockets, where the dollar is.(*Healer*, 107).

★ On education: Teachers will take a band of young folks and go traveling. They will study nature and her methods. They will go to places in air ships. Inventors will increase and multiply when all barriers are swept to atoms.

★ On architecture (what houses will look like in the New Kingdom): They will be cooled to a comfortable temperature, heated and ventilated from pipes below, not more than one story, but that story will be forty feet or more high in order to generate pure air; they will be constructed of rare and beautiful materials, which all will share. (*Healer*,102-103).

"Each kindred subject he picked up," Ada said, "he treated and dismissed in its turn with force, precision and perspicuity. His mental nimbleness easily confounded the image of the stolid, backward, dull-witted peasant."

***

For all his sympathy for the average person's plight, Francis was naive as to what it would take to improve his condition. "But with faith in the Father," he averred, "the righteous have the most power, and they will ultimately wrench this earth from the grasp of the robbers."

All well and good, on a propaganda level at least, but such revolutionary idealism sounds specious and false today. As we have seen, Francis called for action on many fronts, although again and again he failed to specify what it would actually take to implement real change in the body politic. His social reform side was made up more of rhetorical bluster than concrete action. Other people might take to the streets or throw bombs, but not Francis. His disposition was too passive, his vision too naive. It was all about spirituality; nothing meaningful could possibly occur until people were sufficiently motivated to make it happen.

***

When they could, especially when they felt they weren't being watched by outsiders, Ada and Francis enjoyed long walks and horseback rides away from the box canyon that sheltered the house and outbuildings. Judging from the intensity and loquacity of their conversations, plus the fervor of Ada's attention and responses, a romance seems to have been in the offing; however, as with the affection he shared with Ed Fox's wife, there is no evidence that it was ever consummated.

***

By the first of April it was apparent that the time was drawing near when Francis would have to go his own way. Ada noticed that he talked and ate less but slept more, some days as long as fourteen to sixteen hours.

His body seemed to be gearing itself up for the hard trip ahead. Granted, he didn't know exactly where he was going. Mexico? South America? He told Ada the Father had indicated that he might even go to India to carry the Word there "when [his] work was completed on this side [of the world]."

Each day, more Hispanics and Indians showed up in Datil. They didn't let on that they knew anything, but it was clear from the number of sick people in their ranks that they sensed Francis was close by. Word of his whereabouts had gotten out and was circulating around the countryside. The second week of April the weather was temperate and springlike. Francis ate little and talked less. The freewheeling discussions he and Ada had engaged in on every subject imaginable dwindled to a routine exchange of pleasantries. Francis sat for hours in the living room, gazing into the fire; Ada was certain he was listening to instructions from the voice. Upstairs in his room he paced restlessly, swinging the brass rod, marshaling his strength.

Ada insisted he should take another horse to carry all the gear he had accumulated. Three hundred pounds, including his own weight, was too much for Butte, especially if the poor creature was called upon to cover a minimum of forty miles a day.

Francis disagreed. "The Father will give Butte the same strength as he gives me," he declared.

"Carrying three hundred pounds through country as rugged as the Mogollon Mountains will be terribly hard on him," she said.

"The Father will sustain him," Francis said stubbornly.

When Ada suggested that Swingle nail new iron shoes to Butte's feet, Francis agreed. Ada was relieved. (*Healer*, 112).

***

A few days before he departed, he finished dictating his memoir, *The Life of the Harp in the Hands of the Harper.* He then turned the manuscript over to Ada. "I would never have written it if the Father had not told me to," he confessed. "Take it to Denver and publish it."

And then, after a long, brooding silence, he uttered the only hurtful words he ever said to her.

"I would never have trusted this to a woman. The responsibility is too great; the trust is too sacred. But the Father says you are the right one, and He will open the door." (*Healer*, 112).

***

One day in late April, Ada walked to the post office in Datil, where she encountered inquisitive looks from the people who passed her in the street. She ran into Swingle, who knew the region as well as anyone, and asked him if he would guide Francis through the Mogollon Mountains. Swingle agreed.

"When does he want to go?" he asked.

"I don't know," Ada replied. "Soon. Probably in a couple of days. He's getting fidgety."

The next morning Francis and Ada stepped out of the house. Francis wore a rumpled vest over a blue denim shirt. He studied the pale, milky, promising early spring sky. Then he strolled over to the corral and called Butte with a familiar whistle. The big horse shambled to the fence and snuffed at Francis's palm, hoping for a treat. Francis fed him three sugar cubes and rubbed his hands caressingly over Butte's legs, back, and withers. "The Father says that Sunday, the day after tomorrow, I am to go," he called over his shoulder to Ada.

They stood in awkward silence for a lengthy moment, not daring to look at one another. "It made it none the easier because I had known it was coming," Ada wrote in her memoir. "The silence that followed was unbearable, and so I went back inside the house."

Could she have been waiting to hear something heartfelt and personal from this shy, defensive, introverted man? It's impossible to say for certain.

Norman Cleaveland, Ada's grandson, who wrote perceptively about the relationship between the two, stops short of saying that the special communication between them was ever acted upon in a physical way. Although they frequently used the language of love to express their thoughts and feelings, they did so without any commensurate sexual overtones. If any overt affection existed between them, they either never alluded to it or kept it sealed under the tight lid of conventional Victorian manners.

***

The next day, Saturday, Francis sifted through his gear, culling out what he didn't think he would need. Then he whistled for Butte and led him to a nearby spring and let him load up on water. As Butte drank, Francis drank too, cupping his hands and gulping water down his throat until he felt his stomach expand. Back at the barn, Francis fed Butte lunch, then led him into his stall. The horse looked at his master inquiringly, pawing the soiled dirt with his heavy hooves. "Even the horse felt the impending change," Ada noticed, "and I was afraid." (*Healer*, 113).

That afternoon, as they sat in the shimmering rays of the April sun, Francis read to Ada from the Bible, chapters from the Books of Daniel and Matthew. At one point he looked up at her, his face bearing that expression of ineffable otherworldliness she had come to recognize and cherish. "Preaching is a life," he declared, "not a business. When the call comes, the world must be sacrificed. Jesus was a celibate. For spiritual work there must be sacrifice of self and of the world. Teaching and preaching must be for the uplift of humanity. It is not a business but a way of helping humanity. It has always meant self-sacrifice, and always will till the Kingdom comes. The Quakers are right in that they don't pay their preachers or leaders. Father gives them the light freely, and freely they must give it back. That is the real thing. No money—no money mixed with spiritual enlightenment."

Ada thought he was sending a mixed message. "I felt that he was both anxious to leave yet hesitant to do so," she observed. "No doubt he was remembering the terrible ordeal of his two-year walk, and how he had to endure that suffering again. In contrast to the eager willingness he had demonstrated again and again back then, this time he seemed to be looking for an excuse to postpone his departure." (*Healer*, 111).

That excuse surfaced in Swingle's failure to show up on time. Few people in the Datil area knew the Mogollon Mountains better than he did. Ada assumed he would lead Francis through the mountains, maybe all the way to the Mexican border if that's where Francis wanted to go.

***

At four on Sunday afternoon, Swingle still had not shown up. By this time Francis was anxious to be off. He asked Ada to bring Butte to the back of the house. It took a few minutes to throw the saddle on his back and lash the gear into place—tent, blankets, clothes sack, food sack, hatchet, brass rod. Despite her protests regarding the extra weight Butte had to pull, Francis insisted that Ada fill the big canteen to the top. "I drink a great deal of water when I have no food," he explained.

All was ready. The late afternoon sun filtered down through the trees. "If it's all right with the Father," Ada asked, "may I accompany you for a little while?"

Francis looked off across the yard at the barn and corral with that dazed, preoccupied expression he assumed when he was seeking answers from the voice within. After a moment, eager and flushed, he looked back at her. "He says you can go."

She finished filling the heavy canteen. He draped it over his left shoulder. Then he looped the leather sleeve of the brass rod over the saddle horn.

They started out on foot together, side by side, Butte following them like a pet dog without being prompted. The long, chilly shadow of the coming night crept over the landscape. To the left, glimmering white between the tall, orange-barked pines, lay the Plains of San Augustin, fifty miles long by ten miles wide, the bed of an ancient intermontane lake, greening up with fresh grass. The two said little, content to protect their real feelings by letting them remain unspoken. Ada, her blond features reflecting a host of conflicting emotions, strode purposefully in her tiny boots and bustling skirts. Francis, hatless, wore the same ankle-length topcoat he had worn the night he slipped out of Denver. His pale, bloodless face appeared inscrutably calm. Cattle grazed in the distance, dotting the immense plain, which seemed to open like a great gaping wound as if someone had peeled back the features of the land, exposing them to the mercy of the sun. To the south, a dozen miles away, loomed the rounded humps of the Mogollon Mountains. Butte snorted expectantly.

Francis worried that in the advancing darkness Ada might have difficulty finding her way back to the ranch. It was time for them to part.

Her heart stirred with feeling. Francis swung his agile body into the saddle. Butte nickered consolingly. Ada stroked the horse's powerful neck. The healer's hand sought hers; the skin across the top of his palm felt blistered and coarse. Holding hers as firmly as he dared, Francis asked her to recite the Lord's Prayer. Ada did so in a trembling voice—the prayer, she later said, "that must have been engraved on the mighty mountainsides, on the blue vault of the sky, on interstellar space." (*Healer,* 114).

Francis stared down at her. His blue eyes looked much younger than the rest of his face, brimming with jubilation and hope in their worn and weathered sockets. He spoke his final words to her: "You will have what will seem to be certain evidence of my death brought to you. The world will laugh at you for rejecting it—but reject it! I shall not be dead. I will return to Datil. The Father has told me that Datil is the place He has selected for the New Jerusalem. Wait for me." (*Healer,* 111).

Then he told her to retrace her steps back to the ranch before the darkness obscured the path. She walked a few paces, faltered, and stopped. He looked back at her one last time, his face impassive and calm. Then he swiveled around in the saddle and gazed out at the wide, empty flatland he had to cross. Ada waved eagerly, hoping Francis would wave back, but he didn't. He kicked his heels against Butte's bulging sides. A moment later man and horse disappeared into the cool gray shadows of the gathering night.

***

A few days after his leave-taking, Ada noticed the design of a bent cross that stood out boldly on the front of the west wing of the Hermosillo ranch house. The upright curved counterclockwise, raising the crossbar slightly upward. Ada estimated that the cross was about ten feet high. It appeared to have been painted on the brick wall with some kind of whitewash. She scratched at it with her thumbnail, but it wouldn't come off. She took it as a positive sign, a kind of stigmata, as if the house, graced by the healer's presence, had responded with its own expression of holiness and devotion.

The design remained in place for several months before fading away as mysteriously as it had appeared. The local Anglos were totally baffled, scratching their heads in consternation. The Hispanics and Indians who came to view it fell to their knees.

***

> *El Paso Daily Times* April 24, 1896 (Tuesday)
> Francis Schlater [sic], the healer, is now at Pleasanton, a small village in western Sierra County. . . . He appeared at Pleasanton last Friday, having been several weeks in retreat among Mexicans in small ranch towns in Socorro County performing cures. He says he does not know where his next stopping point will be.

***

Fortunately, we know his last stopping place before he disappeared into Mexico. According to an article in *The Lordsburg* (New Mexico Territory) *Liberal* on May 17, 1896, a rancher named John McCabe reported having seen the healer at his ranch near the Mexican border, sixty miles south of Lordsburg. One warm spring day Francis rode into the ranch on his big white horse; everyone recognized him, and he was made welcome for the night. That evening he ate a hearty meal.

In addition to the healer's weight, the horse carried about 150 pounds of equipment and gear. The load was heavy for the horse, and his back and withers were puffed raw from the chafing. A ranch hand remonstrated with Francis for mistreating the animal and drew his attention to the irritated area. Francis nodded and rubbed it gently with his fingers; within minutes, all signs of discomfort had disappeared.

The brass rod dangling from the thong looped around the healer's wrist caught everyone's attention. Like Aaron's rod of biblical fame, it seemed to contain many virtues and mysteries. Francis rode up to the ranch house swinging it over his head. Rancher McCabe described it as longer and bulkier than an ordinary walking stick, forged out of brass tubing, not copper as had been rumored, and weighing around thirty-five pounds. McCabe said Schlatter whipped it around with one hand. McCabe also reported another curious practice; whenever he intended to go someplace, the healer swung the rod around his head and let it fly into the air. How it landed, in which direction it pointed, indicated the path he must follow. The rod was heavily nicked and scarred, no doubt from having been flung about many times over the past few weeks.

After leaving McCabe's ranch, Francis paused at a rancheria called Alamo Huesco, in the extreme southeastern corner of the New Mexico boot heel. There, under the shade of a palm-thatched ramada, he ran his hands over the crippled leg of a visitor from New York, who reported that he felt instantly better. He also treated a deep cut in the hand of a local rancher named Thomas Hall. He took hold of Hall's hands and held them firmly. Hall's fingers tingled, and the pain disappeared. The cut healed in five days, leaving no scar.

"I don't understand the force he possesses," Hall confessed, "but I know that it is powerful." (*The Santa Fe New Mexican,* June 8, 1896).

***

The next morning, in front of an audience of several cowboys, Francis swung the rod again. It whistled through the air, striking the rocky ground with a loud clang, the tip pointing south toward the Mexican border. Francis rode off in that direction a short time later.

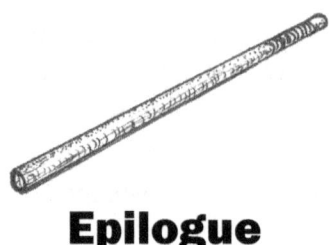

Epilogue

At first the cowboy thought the man might be sleeping. He lay under a tattered gray blanket, stretched out on a flat rock in the shade of a tall live oak. The oak grew from a patch of damp earth a few feet from the spot where a stream gurgled out of the mouth of a rock-filled gorge. The cowboy had been riding on a nearby trail when he noticed the figure lying on the rock. He reined in his horse and looked over the site. It seemed to have been occupied for some time. Dark, powdery sticks poked from the dregs of a dead campfire. A saddle sat astride one of the lower branches of the oak; ropes, bridle, a shirt, a pair of pants dangled from another branch directly over the recumbent figure.

The cowboy slid off his horse and edged closer on foot. It was then he realized that the man couldn't possibly be sleeping. He looked too rigid and stiff; his jawbone glinted in the afternoon light between scraps of sun-dried flesh. A low whistle escaped the cowboy's lips. Near the stream a pair of ravens bounced from rock to rock.

The cowboy grit his teeth and pulled back the blanket. The

man appeared to have been dead for some time; the exposed flesh of the emaciated body was baked a dark, tawny brown like a twisted stick of bread dough. The skin remaining on the bones looked leathery and dried; what had once been a mane of fine, wavy hair was now stiff and frizzled. The lids of the dull, empty eyes were nearly sealed. A long beard, crawling with vermin, covered the sunken chest. The exposed bones of the right arm, flecked with bits of flesh, lay across the shrunken waist. The left arm, similarly clotted and daubed, stretched down the dead man's side. The right leg was drawn up at a sharp angle, the bare heel of the right foot nearly touching the right buttock.

The cowboy, a Mormon who worked at a nearby ranch, tied a bandanna around his nose and mouth and began to poke around. The saddle straddling the branch of the oak bore the mark of a well-known leather crafter in Denver. A stack of clothes was close by. Three books sat on top of the stack: a Spanish-English dictionary, a gold-leafed Bible, a red leather memorandum book with blank pages. On one of the dictionary pages was written, in Spanish, "con complimentas su amiga Ada Morley Jarrett, Datil, New Mexico, 3-24-96." The signature "Francis Schlatter" was inscribed on the Bible flyleaf, along with a date, "October 27, 1895." Under it were two verses, followed by the signature "Clarence J. Clark, Denver, Colo."

In a knothole in the deep shadow cast by the oak the cowboy found needles, thread, buttons, and other sundries. A brass rod, measuring more than three feet long and weighing about thirty pounds, lay alongside the cadaver. Topped at one end by a knob, the rod resembled a baseball bat, although, as the cowboy found out when he lifted it, the rod was heavier than a bat and difficult to swing. A leather strap poking from a hole under the knob looked as if it could be looped around a wrist or saddle horn. The surface of the rod eight to ten inches below the top had been turned on a lathe to make a simple pattern of rings and curving lines. There were nick marks everywhere, presumably from the rod having been banged against a hard surface. A puzzling instrument, the cowboy thought, possibly a weapon to use against enemies, a cudgel to ward off hungry animals.

Carefully stacked a few feet from the body was a modest inventory of camp gear—slicker, tent, ground cover, blanket, rope, saddlebags, canteen, a white felt hat with a wide brim. There was no coffeepot or other cooking utensils. There was no horse. The bare, filthy toes of the man's left foot stuck up under the blanket like stiff pegs. The cowboy was baffled. Had the man walked all the way out here through the foothills of the Sierra Madre to meet his end? It didn't make sense. Nobody walked in this country unless they had to.

There were no signs of violence. As far as the cowboy could see, there were no bullet wounds or marks on the head or body. He could only conclude that the victim had likely died of dehydration or lack of food. The bottom of the big metal canteen contained a few drops of water. But, considering the stream that purled and trickled a few feet from where the body lay, death from lack of water didn't seem possible. Most likely he had starved to death.

The cowboy rode to the nearby town of Casas Grandes, where he notified the *jefe politico* (chief official). Two days later a wagon carrying several men rattled out to the site. The men loaded the cadaver and personal effects into the wagon and hauled them back to town.

An Indian told the *jefe* that several months earlier he had come across a sturdy white horse in the area where the body had been found. The horse was hobbled, off by itself, cropping grass. The Indian said he saw no sign of a body.

A few days later another Mormon cowboy came forward to say that a man rumored to be Francis Schlatter, the famous healer, had ridden into his camp forty miles west of Casas Grandes on a big white horse sometime in November 1896. Other than the formidable brass staff dangling from his right wrist, he bore no weapons; whether the staff was a weapon, the cowboy couldn't say. The few hours the stranger had stayed in the cowboy's camp, he acted aloof and preoccupied. He didn't say much, and when he did, he mumbled in a voice that could barely be heard. Although he carried no provisions or cooking utensils, he refused to eat any of the food the cowboy offered. He was fasting, he said, which he did periodically to replenish his power. When he noticed a swelling on the back of one of the cowboy's horses, he told him he could fix it.

"Are you a veterinarian," the cowboy asked.

The stranger shook his head. "I just know how to do that," he said.

He rubbed the horse's back and front legs, softly, steadily, until the swelling disappeared and the horse was fully recovered.

"How'd you do that?".

The stranger shrugged.

***

According to the version told by the first cowboy, Francis Schlatter's body was found in Piedras Verdes Canyon about ten miles from the village of Colonia Juarez, west of Casas Grandes, in the foothills of the Sierra Madre in the northwest corner of the state of Chihuahua. Some confusion persists as to the year it was found, 1896 or 1897; the date was likely May or June 1897. We know he disappeared into Mexico sometime in the late spring of 1896; he is presumed to have wandered around Chihuahua for nearly a year before he died, probably of starvation. The condition of his body indicated that he had been dead for several weeks; varmints had stripped much of the flesh from the bones. His personal effects—books, clothing, the mysterious brass rod—remained untouched. The big horse, the ever-faithful Butte, was nowhere to be found.

***

Francis Schlatter entered Mexico most likely in late May 1896. He sought refuge with several families in some caves hollowed out of an abandoned mine in the Casas Grandes region. Now, as then, Casas Grandes was best known for the ruins of a vast urban network of adobe walls and dwellings built between the eleventh and fourteenth centuries by a people known as the Paquiminians, closely related to the Anasazi of the American Southwest. Five stories high in places, featuring a complex system of acequias and aqueducts, the ruins are the most significant pre-Columbian site in northern Mexico. The Paquiminians used minerals and shells as a system of trade; they worshipped the Guacamaya (Scarlet Macaw). In the fifteenth century, at least a hundred years before the arrival of the Spanish, threats from hostile tribes, as well as strife from within, caused their civilization to decline.

According to a *Rocky Mountain News* article (July 5, 1897), Francis lived in the area of the ruins for three months, where he established a small but enthusiastic following among the locals and their families. Despite his popularity, Francis never commanded the same numbers among the lonely cliff-dwelling people of Casas Grandes as he did with those who flocked to him in Denver and Albuquerque.

After leaving the ruins, he headed into the foothills to fast and pray. Where was he going? What did he intend to do? Fatigued and disheartened, no doubt disoriented as well, could he have lost his bearings?

Accustomed to treating vast numbers of people, he must have been disappointed in the paltry few he found in the wilds of northern Mexico. Did he consider going back to the United States? What happened to his plan to go to Chicago? Did his phobia about population centers—the pledge he made to his mother—compel him to remain in the bleak and sparsely settled Chihuahuan desert? Did he think his mother had been reincarnated and was living in the region, waiting for him to show up?

Francis carried no cooking utensils; was he deliberately trying to starve himself? Somewhere in the foothills after leaving the Paquiminian ruins, he must have run out of food.

We can imagine him growing weaker and weaker. No doubt, as the days passed, it became more difficult for him to get to his feet in the morning. His tough, resilient body, on which he could always count, his astounding physical vitality began to slip away. The lack of food, the sheer physical effort—the thorns, cactus, insects, unforgiving rocks—

exacted a toll. Maybe he was bitten by a rattlesnake. Maybe Butte ran off or was stolen. Without the horse, physically depleted, unable to properly feed himself, Francis must have sensed the end was near. How many times in the past had he reached this point, only to rally and forge ahead, sustained by his unshakable faith?

What about the voice inside his head? As his strength left him, did it sink into silence and fade away?

One day he couldn't get up. He lay on a hard, smooth rock under a frayed gray blanket in the shadow of a swaying live oak. No one knows what anyone's death will be like, particularly their own. Who can imagine the unimaginable? One morning—the account here is sheer guesswork—he opened his eyes and knew he was close to dying. His body no longer responded to the dictates of his indefatigable will—the same will that had badgered and harassed him, driven him to perform one stupendous feat after another, given him the physical strength to deliver thousands of healing miracles. His limbs and joints drew up into tight, constricted knots. He thrust his left arm down his side; with a final effort, as if intending to rise, he drew his bootless right foot up until the heel nearly touched his buttock. A desperate effort to alleviate the terrible discomfort that bore down like a riveting screw into every joint of his body. Through dull, half-lidded eyes before he lost consciousness he saw two ravens bouncing toward him over the rocks.

***

When the *jefe politico* of Casas Grandes was told that the body of a gringo had been found, the body of a famous gringo, the legendary Denver Messiah, he waited a decent interval for someone to claim it. When no one came forth, he arranged for the body to be buried in the old cemetery on the outskirts of town. No one who knew Francis personally attended. A curious few likely showed up. Presumably, a Catholic priest was on hand to officiate.

The gravesite was later obliterated by units of General John J. Pershing's military expedition against Pancho Villa, which trampled the cemetery with their horses and wagons and caissons as they moved south in pursuit of the Mexican leader in the spring of 1916.

***

News of the healer's death trickled north into the United States, prompting a rash of stacked headlines in newspapers of the communities where he had once been lionized.

The Denver Daily News (June 5, 1897)
STARVED TO DEATH
Francis Schlatter's Bones Found in the State of
Chihuahua, Mexico.
Denver Saddle, Address of a Denver Man and the
Famous Copper Rod.
Mormon Cowboy Says the Healer Was Fasting When Last
Seen Near His Camp.
Identity of Body and Property as Described Corresponds with
the Denver Worker of Wonders.
Close of the Career of One of the Most Remarkable Characters
of the Nineteenth Century.

***

What effect did the healer's death have on those who knew him?

The Denver Daily News (June 7, 1897)

Mr. E. L. Fox, with whom Schlatter remained for several weeks [while healing in Denver], was found dozing in a chair at his home, 1625 Witter Street, at 11:30 o'clock last evening, and when acquainted with the death of his friend, he evinced but little surprise. Perhaps this was due to his not being in full possession of his senses at the time. Asked whether or not he had received any word from the missing man since he left here so suddenly, Mr. Fox said he had not. "The last I saw of Schlatter," said he, "was a short time before he retired that [last] night. In the morning the note of farewell was pinned on the pillow. He has written me nothing since he left, and I did not know definitely which direction he took when he left Denver. No, the news of his demise was unknown to me until you just now told me. Poor Schlatter."

When the *News* reporter left the house Mr. Fox was practically insensible to the situation, and he stood studying the porch posts for some time before he reentered the house.

***

Ed Fox did not have an easy time after Francis Schlatter disappeared from his house on November 14, 1895. People hoping to be cured by the healer took their frustrations out on him; he was jeered in the streets and roundly cursed. He received death threats, which, added to his chronic depression, played havoc with his mental health.

On March 15, 1901, *The Rocky Mountain News* reported that Fox was arrested in Louisville, Kentucky, on charges of having an illicit relationship with a woman named Amanda Leech; he had known Leech in Denver and fled with her to the Kentucky metropolis in 1899. According to the article, since that fateful day in November 1895 when Francis Schlatter disappeared from Denver, Fox's physical and mental health had deteriorated, and he took to roaming the streets of Denver in the middle of the night. His behavior became more and more erratic, prompting him to confess to his wife that he no longer belonged to this world; instead, he believed he had been singled out to perform the same divine mission of healing the sick as Schlatter had. Eventually, Fox announced to family and friends that he could no longer communicate with them; a short while later he left Denver in the company of Leech and three other women and went to Louisville, where he began prowling the streets at night. The Louisville authorities finally took him into custody and returned him to Denver, where he was placed in an asylum for treatment.

***

Not everyone believed what they heard about the healer's demise. Chief among the doubters was Ada Morley Jarrett. In a speech she made in a public hall in Denver in the summer of 1897, shortly after the news had reached the city, she expressed her disbelief in the healer's rumored death (killed by a lightning bolt, according to her informants).

"No," she declared in a firm voice before an audience of several hundred people, "there can be many bleached skeletons in the Sierra Madre Mountains, but the first one found is not necessarily that of Francis Schlatter. I admit the effects are his, but knowing his obedience to the voice, I know he would walk away from camp as he walked away from Denver, if the command was given to leave those mere worldly things and 'follow' as the 'Father' has been leading him for over four years." (*Longmont Ledger,* June 18, 1897).

Jarrett reminded the audience that in the book about his life (*The Life of the Harp in the Hands of the Harper*), which he dictated to her while staying at her ranch in Datil, Francis reaffirmed his intention to fulfill the promises given in Jesus's Sermon on the Mount to help humankind achieve peace on earth. "Certainly Francis Schlatter still lives," Jarrett concluded in as ringing a tone as she could muster. "I expressed the fear of his death the day I bade him farewell, but his reply was reassuring and convincing. 'Have faith,' he said; 'the Father will take care of me. He has called me to do His work. Of myself, I can do nothing. But I can not die.'" (*The Denver Daily News,* June 5, 1897).

Some people accepted the news, others denied it. For years a host of conflicting opinions chased each other through reams of newsprint, asserting this and claiming that. Then, on July 17, 1901, a reporter for *The Denver Times* laid it all out with compelling simplicity. "Schlatter is dead," he declared. "The 'divine' fanatic is no more. Reliable information has come that he perished miserably in a lonely Mexican desert, unattended by any of the thousands who profess themselves cured by his miraculous touch."

The article went on to say that a doctor named H. F. Gray of Los Angeles "has just returned to Denver from Casas Grandes, in the state of Sonora [sic]. While in Mexico, Dr. Gray came upon Francis Schlatter's lonely grave, located about 150 miles below the U.S. line. Dr. Gray saw all the periphernalia and wearing apparel of the healer, which are now in the possession of the jefe politico of Casas Grandes."

***

Additional confirmation of the healer's death was provided by an anthropologist named Edgar Lee Hewett, who in 1906 made a reconnaisance of the Casas Grandes ruins in northwestern Chihuahua. (Hewett later became director of the School of American Archaeology and the Museum of New Mexico.) Hewett's version of the healer's death contradicts the Mormon cowboy's account in several details. According to Hewett, his Mexican guide told him that several years earlier, when he was a little boy, he had found the body of a dead gringo lying under a big tree. The boy was going up the valley early in the morning to retrieve some cows that had wandered off when he saw a man stretched out in the shade of a tree under a blanket. At first the boy thought the man was asleep. Drawing closer, he discovered that he was dead. He ran to his village and told the *jefe politico*. The *jefe* sent a crew out to retrieve the corpse. It was several months old, they determined, a big man with long hair and maggot-ridden beard, his body twisted into an awkward posture.

The cowboy claimed not to have seen Butte. Hewett says the Mexican team sent out by the *jefe* found the big white horse not far away from the spot where Francis lay. The team also found a fine-tooled western saddle from a leather maker in Denver plus several pieces of clothing. The horse and clothing were taken to the village, where they were used as community property. Supposedly, the horse was ridden around the village by several generations of children until it died of old age.

During that first trip, Hewett spoke with the *jefe politico,* who showed him several of the artifacts: saddle, bridle, Bible with the name "Francis Schlatter" written in cursive on the flyleaf. But the most interesting item was a heavy brass rod over three feet long, scored on its cyclindrical surface with curious markings, which the *jefe* brought out from a back room and proudly displayed.

***

In 1922 Hewett returned to the Casas Grandes area, this time to retrieve as many of the Schlatter artifacts as he could find. In that interval of sixteen years, Butte had died, the saddle had worn out with use, the Bible had disappeared. Still in the *jefe politico*'s possession was the brass rod, which Hewett remembered from his previous trip; like everyone else who had seen it and hefted its weight, the object perplexed him. What was it exactly? A staff, an instrument, a weapon, a talisman of some kind?

The *jefe* needed a favor; in return for a modest contribution and a letter to the minister of education in Chihuahua City, Hewett helped the village acquire a much-needed schoolteacher. The *jefe* was grateful. Months later, a heavy package arrived at Hewett's home in Santa Fe, New Mexico. "Now as a museum man," he wrote in his autobiography *Campfire and Trail*,1941), "accustomed to collecting unusual things from the ends of the earth, I never grow indifferent to a new find. He never knows what may be coming out of an old bundle, but knows that it is likely to be something exciting. This one bowled me over. On cutting away the cords and string and burlap, there emerged the copper rod of the great healer, Francis Schlatter." (*Campfire,* 38).

Today, the rod is part of the permanent collection of the Museum of New Mexico.

**

The Denver Times (July 17, 1901)

"So ends the story of a man who achieved wonderful notoriety in the short space of two years, although absolutely unknown to the public prior to that time. As to his merits and powers, there are a thousand different opinions, but the most likely cause for his wonderful influence over human beings was an extraordinary endowment of animal magnetism."

**

The real Schlatter may have died, but the life he led inspired a host of imitators who for years cropped up all over the country. For a quarter-century following the first reports of his death in 1897, Schlatter clones were sighted in at least a dozen cities from Seattle, Washington, to New York City—people seeking, for whatever reason, to capitalize on his legacy.

Ersatz Schlatters popped up repeatedly on the streets of Denver in the years following the healer's disappearance. Nearly all were adept at pestering people for payment for their services. *The Denver Times* reported on September 20, 1901, an incident in Colorado Springs where a "Schrader" [sic] clone left the city in a huff, declaring, "This isn't the place to get healed without pay. Of course, if a person is too poor to pay, I'll heal them, though I expect everybody to contribute something. I am the original Schrader. All others who claim to be me have false hair and beard."

A headline in the January 3, 1902, edition of *The Denver Times* announced, "Man Who Looks Like Schlatter Sent to County Poor Farm."

The man was detained by police on charges of vagrancy; during his hearing, as he sat in the prisoner's dock in the courthouse, he threw back his head, turned his soft eyes heavenward, and moved his lips as if deep in prayer—similar to the manner the original Schlatter had displayed when treating a patient. Heavy-set, bearded, sporting a mane of long, flowing hair, this epigone resembled the original Schlatter closely enough to cause witnesses in the courtroom to declare that he really was the healer. He wasn't. Under further questioning he said his name was Tom Morrison and that he was a sheepherder from Montana. He added that he had no money or friends and would be perfectly content to be sent to the poorhouse, where he could sleep in a real bed and enjoy something to eat.

The August 1, 1904, edition of *The Denver Post* reported that yet another poseur had appeared on the streets, but before he could accomplish much in the way of advertising himself, he received notice from the police that "the healing game was closed." This most recent Schlatter clone, the article declared, looked like all the others: "[c]lad in a monk's cloak, tied at the waist with a rope; wearing a ragged, unkempt beard in imitation of pictures of the Divine, he paraded the streets yesterday with a look of personified sanctity, attracting attention on all sides."

"Enough," Chief of Police Michael A. Delaney was heard to say after this latest imitation was escorted to the city limits and told to make himself scarce. "No more fake healers for Denver. They have worn the graft threadbare."

***

Despite this crackdown, the Schlatter scams continued. Two men billing themselves as "Schlatter and Schrader" appeared in Los Angeles in the early 1900s and announced to local newspapers that they had established the Kingdom of the New Jerusalem on a South Sea island and intended to convert the world to their practices.

In 1909 a recluse in Hastings, Nebraska, named Charles McLean was found in a hotel, dead from "old age." At first he was thought to be the original Schlatter; then photos of McLean were found in a family vault in Boston that bore no resemblance to photos of the real healer. In an effort to close the book on further speculation, Denver's Reverend Thomas Uzzell declared that the evidence brought forth in 1897 when Schlatter was reported to have died in Mexico "fully established" the real facts of his demise; all other claims were bogus.

***

On April 4, 1916, *The Denver Times* reported that a man claiming to be the legendary healer was about to board a ship in New York and sail to Europe to help soldiers wounded in the trenches during World War I. "He does not claim that he can stop the war," *the Times* reporter said, "but states that he . . . can cure everything that cannot be reached by medicine and surgery."

This Schlatter said he was seventy-nine years old and that he had been healing since he was seven. He was, he declared, "the original Schlatter . . . all who had come after him were fakers."

His fame, the reporter said, "had already spread to the trenches, for not long ago *The Denver Times* received an inquiry about him from a soldier of the allied armies stationed 'somewhere in France.'"

***

Rumors that Francis was still alive and practicing his healing magic persisted until 1922, when it was reported that a man named Francis Schlatter, "chemist and lecturer," had died of tuberculosis in St. Louis. Word of the identity of the cadaver was given by Schlatter's so-called wife, a woman named Luverna living in Chicago. When no one stepped forth to claim the body, it was interred in a potter's field in St. Louis.

***

The story of Francis Schlatter and his heroic endeavor remains one of the great unsung sagas of the American West. Who was he, and what did he hope to prove by his selfless effort to cure others of their afflictions? Dreamer, idealist, visionary, apostle . . . he was all these and more. He genuinely felt he could help make the world a better place; how else could he have endured such terrible suffering if he didn't believe that to be true?

Figment, chimera, phantom—are we to believe what he tried to achieve? At times the story seems too far-fetched to accept—another fanciful yarn from out of the fabled American Southwest, spun from the filaments of the lively, myth-making imagination that flourishes there. And yet, from all accounts, it really did happen. Francis Schlatter truly believed in the identity he fashioned for himself—a solitary healer, buoyed and sustained by an implacable faith, gifted with a restorative touch he shared with everyone he encountered.

***

Some people come to the American West to garner a fortune, others to reinvent their identity, still others to conflate the ordinary facts of their lives with the legendary dimensions of the landscape. Francis Schlatter remains a curious figure in American history—an outsider, a provincial, a man from the margins—whose strength derives from the singularity of his personality, the profound religiosity of his spirit, his stubborn alienation from the mainstream. Plagued by his own demons, he plowed his own track—willfully, determinedly, ecstatically. In the process, says famed Colorado newspaperman Gene Fowler, he "became a part of old men's legends. For years he was reported as having been glimpsed on desert trails, mounted on a white horse, a beatific smile on his face, a hand upraised in apostolic hello—and then he would vanish as though taken to the skies above the Bad Lands, where mirages are born."

A Note on Sources

Every event recounted in this book pertaining to the life of Francis Schlatter is grounded in documentary fact. No pivotal events or major happenings have been freely imagined or blithely conceived; at the same time, the author confesses to having exercised a limited imaginative license in the enumeration of descriptive detail regarding certain incidents where there was no detail, and where, for story-telling purposes, some detail was clearly needed.

Critical to the sense of versimilitude that conveys the reality of the man and the era in which he lived are the many reports, interviews, and editorials about him that appeared in newspapers and magazines between 1893 and 1901. These references are amply notated throughout the book. Once he came to the attention of the public in the summer of 1895, first in Albuquerque then in Denver, rarely did a day pass without some mention being made of him in the print media. At the apex of his fame, the fall and winter of 1895-1896, so compelling was his story, so firm his grip upon the popular imagination of the American public, that he achieved a kind of celebrity status throughout the country.

Despite its inconsistencies and errors, the primary document regarding the life of Francis Schlatter is the memoir he dictated to Ada Morley Jarrett in the winter of 1896, while staying at her ranch near Datil, New Mexico Territory. Apparently, he told her a lot more information about his life, not just his early days in Alsace-Lorraine in eastern France but details pertaining to the grueling walk he made across the American Southwest between 1893 and 1895, which (regrettably) he did not allow her to include when she published the memoir in 1896 under the title *The Life of the Harp in the Hand of the Harper*.

The second richest trove regarding biographical detail is the wealth of newspaper and magazine references about Francis. For a period of nearly two years, from the summer of 1895 when he showed up in Albuquerque after his two-year trek, till June of 1897 when word of his death rippled through the American press, his trials, tribulations, and triumphs were eagerly absorbed by readers all over the nation.

In truth, not much information has surfaced thus far about the life of Francis Schlatter. Huge gaps exist which remain to be filled in by future researchers regarding his childhood in Alsace-Lorraine, his ten-year interlude in London (approximately 1874 to 1884), his early years in New York City before he moved to Long Island in the late 1880s. Using these limited resources, I have attempted to write an introductory biography of a complex, baffling, and remarkable human being who, since his death in 1897, seems to have fallen off the historical map. This is unfortunate, as he deserves to be better known; how many people achieve the status of a genuine legend in their lifetimes? If what I have written inspires a reader or two to delve into their own research and reconstruction of his life and times, I will feel generously compensated for the preliminary efforts I have made on his behalf.

—Conger Beasley, Jr.
St. Joseph, Missouri
2008

Bibliography

I. Books

Ackernecht, Edwin H. A Short History of Medicine. (New York: Roland Press,1955.)

Amato, Joseph A. On Foot: A History of Walking. (New York: New York University Press,2004.)

Baker, Gail, Ph.D. Denver: A Boomtown History. (Santa Barbara: HarborTown Histories,2004.)

Bloomfield, Susanne George, ed. Impertinences: Selected Writings of Elia Peattie, a Journalist in the Gilded Age. (Lincoln: University of Nebraska Press,2005.)

Brenneman, Bill. Miracle on Cherry Creek. (Denver: World Press, 1973.)

Bunyan, John. The Pilgrim's Progress. (New York: New American Library,2002.)

Burroughs, William S. The Adding Machine: Selected Essays. (New York: Arcade Publishing,1993.)

Chace, James. 1912: Wilson, Roosevelt, Taft & Debs—The Election that Changed the Country. (New York: Simon & Schuster, 2004.)

Cleaveland, Agnes Morley. No Life for a Lady. (Boston: Houghton Mifflin,1941.)

Cleaveland, Norman, ed. The Healer: The Story of Francis Schlatter. (Santa Fe: Sunstone Press,1989.)

Creel, George W. Rebel at Large: Recollections of a Crowded Fifty Years. (New York: Putnam and Sons,1947.)

Cumming, John. Runners & Walkers: A Nineteenth Century Sports Chronicle. (Chicago: Regnery Gateway,1981.)

De Kruff, Paul. Microbe Hunters. (New York: Harcourt Brace & World, 1926.)

Dorsett, Lyle W. The Queen City: A History of Denver. (Boulder: Pruett Publishing Co.,1977.)

Dresser, Horatio W. The New Thought Movement. (New York: Thomas Y. Crowell Co.,1919.)

Faithful, Emily. Three Trips to America (1884.)

Feied, Frederick. No Pie in the Sky: The Hobo as American Cultural Hero. (New York: The Citadel Press,1964.)

Fergusson, Erna. Albuquerque. (Albuquerque: Merle Armitage Editions, 1947.)

Fergusson, Erna. Our Southwest. (New York: Alfred A. Knopf,1940.)

Flexner, Simon and James Thomas. William Henry Welch and the Heroic Age of American Medicine. (New York: Viking,1941.)

Fowler, Gene. Timberline: A Story of Bonfils and Tammen. (New York: Covici Friede,1933.)

Fowler, Gene, ed. Mystic Healers & Medicine Shows. (Santa Fe: Ancient City Press,1997.)

Fremont, John C., Looking Far West: The Search for the American West in History, Myth, and Literature, ed. by Frank Bergon and Zeese Papanikolas. (New York: New American Library,1978.)

Garland, Hamlin. Main-Travelled Roads. (New York: New American Library, 1962.)

Gerber, Richard, M.D. A Practical Guide to Vibrational Medicine: Energy Healing and Spiritual Transformation. (New York: Quill,2000.)

Glasser, Ronald J. The Body is the Hero. (New York: Random House, 1976.)

Goldman, Eric F. Rendezvous with Destiny: A History of Modern American Reform. (New York: Vintage Books,1956.)

Gordon, Mary. Joan of Arc. (New York: Viking Penguin,2000.)

Graff, Henry F. Grover Cleveland. (New York: Henry Holt and Company, 2002.)

Griffith, James S. Folk Saints of the Borderlands: Victims, Bandits & Healers. (Tucson: Rio Nuevo Publishers,2003.)

Haigh, Jane. King Con: The Story of Soapy Smith. (Whitehorse, Yukon: Friday 501, no date.)

Harrell, Jr., David Edwin. All Things Are Possible: The Healing and Charismatic Revivals of Modern America. (Bloomington: Indiana University Press,1975.)

Hechtlinger, Adelaide. The Great Patent Medicine Era. (New York: Grosset & Dunlap,1970.)

Hewett, Edgar L. Campfire and Trail. (Albuquerque: University of New Mexico Press,1943.)

Hicks, Dave, ed. The Denver Westerners. (Denver: The Johnson Publishing Co.,1972.)

Hofstadter, Richard. The Age of Reform: From Bryan to F.D.R. (New York: Alfred A. Knopf,1955.)

Hogan, Frank X. The Denver Messiah. Unpublished play. Produced Engine House Theatre, Madrid, New Mexico,1989.

Josephson, Matthew. The Robber Barons: The Great American Capitalists, 1861-1901. (New York: Harcourt Brace Jovanovich,1962.)

Keleher, William. Memoirs: 1892-1969. (Santa Fe: Sunstone Press, 2008.)

Larson, Erik. The Devil in the White City: Murder, Magic, and Madness at the Fair that Changed America. (New York: Vintage Books,2003.)

Lindsay, Vachel. Adventures: Rhymes & Designs. (New York: The Eakins Press,1968.)

London, Jack. The Road, with an Introduction by King Hendricks. (Santa Barbara and Salt Lake City: Peregrine Smith,1978.)

Long, Haniel. Piñon Country. (New York: Duell Sloan & Pearce,1941.)

Lummis, Charles F. A Tramp across the Continent. (Lincoln: University of Nebraska Press,1982.)

Magill, Harry B. The Biography of Francis Schlatter "The Healer," with His Life, Works and Wanderings. (Denver: Schlatter Publishing Co., 1896.)

McNeil, William H. Plagues and People. (New York: Anchor Press, 1976.)

Meltzer, Milton. Bread And Roses: The Struggle of American Labor 1865-1915. (New York: New American Library,1967.)

Moody, William Vaughn. The Faith Healer (1910)

Morris, Richard B., editor. Encyclopedia of American History. (New York: Harper & Brothers,1953.)

Muir, John. A Thousand-Mile Walk to the Gulf. (Boston: Houghton Mifflin Co.,1981.)

Mumford, Lewis. The Brown Decades: A Study of the Arts in America, 1865-1895. (New York: Dover Publications,1971.)
Noel, Thomas J. The City and the Saloon: Denver,1858-1916. (Boulder: University Press of Colorado,1996.)
Nolan, William A. Healing: A Doctor in Search of a Miracle. (Greenwich, Connecticut: Fawcett Press,1974.)
Ramsay, E. Mary. Christian Science and Its Discoverer. (Boston: The Christian Science Publishing Society,1923.)
The Denver Red Book. (Denver, 1892.)
Stacey, Michelle. The Fasting Girl: A True Victorian Medical Mystery. (New York: Tarcher/Penguin,2003.)
Steele, Volney, M.D. Bleed, Blister, and Purge: A History of Medicine on the American Frontier. (Missoula: Mountain Press Publishing Company, 2005.)
Whorton, James C., Ph.D. Nature Cures: The History of Alternative Medicine in America. (New York: Oxford University Press,2002.)
Wilson, Colin. Rasputin and the Fall of the Romanovs. (New York: Farrar, Strauss and Company,1964.)
Young, Elizabeth. On Colfax Avenue: A Victorian Childhood. (Denver: Colorado Historical Society,2004.)
Young, Marguerite. Harp Song for a Radical: The Life and Times of Eugene Victor Debs. (New York: Alfred A. Knopf,1999.)

II. Articles

Anon. "The Divine Healer"(1895).
Bullock, Alice. "Francis Schlatter: A Fool for God." El Palacio (1975); 83 (1); 38-45.
Dawson, Thomas F. "Francis Schlatter—Denver Healer of the '90s." The Trail: A Magazine for Colorado (October 1918).
Everett, Millard T. "Strange Cures Verified by Skeptical Newsman." The Denver Catholic Register (August 21, 1941).
"Fitz Mac," "The 'Christ Man' of Denver." The Great Divide Magazine (November 1895).
French, Wesley B. "Denver's Mystery Messiah." Empire Magazine (September 30, 1951).

George, Herbert V. The Road (March 3,1896).

Hoffman, Charles. "The Depression of the Nineties." The Journal of Economic History (1956).

Leavitt, Judith Walker et al. Medicine Without Doctors: Home Health Care in American History. New York: Science History Publications (1977).

Martin, John C. "The Western Messiah." Leslie's Weekly. (October 31, 1895).

Sharpe, Tom. "Mystery Still Surrounds Eccentric Faith Healer." New Mexico Magazine (March 1993).

Szasz, Ferenc M. "Francis Schlatter: The Healer of the Southwest." Mystic Healers & Medicine Shows, ed. by Gene Fowler. Santa Fe: Ancient City Press, 1997.

Wallrich, William Jones. "Christ Man Schlatter in New Mexico." Folklore Record (1949-1950).

III. Newspapers

The Albuquerque Daily Citizen, July 19, 20, 25; August 6,14,16,18,1895.

The Albuquerque Morning Democrat, July17,18, 20, 21, 23, 24, 25, 26, 27, 30; August 10, 11,12, 13, 16, 18, 21, 22, 23, 1895.

The Brooklyn Daily Eagle, November 19; December 2,1895.

The Colby (Kansas) Free Press, August 10,1893.

The Colorado Springs Weekly Gazette, September 19,1895.

The Colorado Sun, October 4,29,1895.

The Deming (New Mexico Territory) Headlight, January 31,1896.

The Denver Catholic Register, July 24; August 7, 21, 28, 1941.

The Denver Daily News, June 5, 7, 1897.

The Denver Post, November 4, 9,15,16,1895; August 1,1904.

The Denver Times, July 17, 1895; September 20, 1901; January 3,1902; April 4,1916.

The El Paso Daily Times, April 7, April 24, 1896; May 17, 1896.

The Las Vegas (New Mexico Territory) Daily Optic, August 22, 1895.

The Littleton (Colorado) Independent, December 27, 1895; January 30; February 28,1896.

The Longmont (Colorado) Ledger, June 18, 1897.

The Lordsburg (New Mexico Territory) Liberal, May 17,1896.

The New York Daily Tribune, November 12,19, 1895.

The Omaha World Herald, October 24; November 10,13,14,16,18, 1895.
The Pagosa Springs (Colorado) News, November 15, 1895.
The Phillipsburg (Kansas) Weekly Dispatch, August 17,1893.
The Pueblo Chieftain, November 12, 21, 22, 23, 24, 27, 28, 29,1895.
The New Road, June 19, 26; July 10, 24, 1897.
The Road, March 28; September 28; October 5, 19, 26; November 16, 23, 30; December 7,1895; March 3,1896.
The Rocky Mountain News, July 21; September 17, 18, 23, 24, 29; October 4, 7, 23, 28, 30; November 8, 9,11,12, 14, 15,1895; January 14; February 14, 1896; July 5, 1897; March 15,1901.
The Santa Fe New Mexican, July 25, 26; August 1, 22, 24; November 21; December 13,14, 16, 17, 18, 19, 20, 23, 28, 31,1895; January 2, 9,18, 30; February 19; April 4, 25; May 18; June 8,1896.
The Tilden (Colorado) Republican, October 26, 1895.
The Trinidad (Colorado) News, August 22; November 12, 14, 15, 16, 20, 29,1895.

www.ingramcontent.com/pod-product-compliance
Lightning Source LLC
Chambersburg PA
CBHW022111150426
43195CB00008B/362